JN313967

聖書
に由来する
英語慣用句の辞典

小野経男 編

大修館書店

はしがき
――英語に活きる聖書慣用語句――

はじめに

　現代英語の発達に大いに貢献したものは，聖書とシェイクスピアとオックスフォード英語辞典だと言っても異論はないであろう。考古学的発見によって，聖書は紀元前の世紀までさかのぼることができるが，そのころの英語の祖先であるゲルマン語に聖書が影響を与えたとは考えられない。関心は近代以後である。

　三大影響源のうち，語句の伝承という点から見ると，聖書，なかんずく 1611 年の欽定約聖書（King James Version）が最大である。これ以前の英訳聖書がなかったわけではない。とりわけ 1382 年のウィクリフ（John Wyclif）訳聖書や 1528 年のティンダル（William Tyndale）訳聖書が欽定訳聖書にかなりの影響を与えたとされている。しかし，今日の現代英語に活きている慣用語句を考えると，欽定訳聖書の慣用語句がその源になる。言い換えると，聖書慣用語句は欽定訳聖書（以後 KJV と略す）より始まるのである。

継承してきた英訳聖書

　欽定訳聖書以後，数多くの英訳聖書が刊行された。翻訳当時者次第で言葉遣いにばらつきがあるが，次第に平易化されてきている。この平易化過程で聖書慣用語句はどのように変わってきたのであろうか。この言い方は，慣用語句というものが定式化であることから矛盾を孕んでいるが，聖書慣用語句は確かに変化してきている。現代英語に訳された数多くの英訳聖書を見ると，慣用語句の形式を留めながら，部分的に変えているものや，その比喩的意味を大胆に採用しているものもある。種々の変異形を持ちながら聖書慣用語句は現代英語に活きている。その歴史上

の変遷を辿ってみたのが本書である。

　幸運なことに，BibleGateway というオンラインで参照できるソフトが出現し，そこにリストアップされている 22 の英訳聖書を調査することができた。その略歴を説明すると，以下の通りである。(カッコ内記号は本書内で利用する省略形)

1. 21st Century King James Version 〈21KJV〉

　これは欽定訳聖書の最新版である。元の形を踏襲しているが，末梢的な，廃れたスペリングなどは現代風に改めてある。聖書慣用語句の源として本書が利用する欽定訳聖書は 1611 年版を基にしているが，廃れてしまったスペリングや語法は 21KJV を参照して 改めてあることをあらかじめ断わって置く。この版は 1994 年 Deuel Enterprises より出版されたものである。

2. American Standard Version 〈ASV〉

　これについてはオンライン上のソフトには特段の記述がないが，アメリカでの標準版である。1901 年出版。

3. Amplified Bible 〈AMP〉

　オリジナル・テクストを正確に訳すために語の意味と文脈を考慮し，キーになるヘブル語とギリシャ語に英語相当語を当てはめて，聖書の意味を明確にし，敷衍させたもので，1987 年に Lockman Foundation より出版されたものである。

4. Contemporary English Version 〈CEV〉

　オリジナル聖書の忠実な翻訳であるが，平易な現代語訳で，一般読者や外国人読者向けに American Bible Society から 1995 年出版されたものである。

5. Darby Translation 〈DT〉

　アングロ・アイリシュの聖書学者，John Nelson Darby が Plymouth Brethren と組んで 1890 年に出版したものである。

6. Douay Rheims 1899 American Edition 〈DRAE〉

　ほとんどのカトリック聖書の基になっているもので，オックスフォード大学の学者，Gregory Martin によって翻訳された。ラテン系聖書の影響を受けて，まず新約聖書が 1582 年，ついで旧約聖書が 1609 年に

Rheims で出版された。年代が近いことから欽定訳聖書に少なからず影響を与えた。この版は 1899 年にまとめて John Murphy Company から出版されたものである。

7. English Standard Version 〈ESV〉

過去 500 年間続いた英訳聖書翻訳の古典的な主流にある。その源と流れは 1526 年の William Tyndale の訳，1611 年の欽定訳〈KJV〉，1885 年の改訂訳聖書〈RV〉，1901 年のアメリカ標準訳聖書〈ASV〉，1952 年と 1971 年の英語改訂訳聖書〈RSV〉と続いてきた。この ESV は 2001 年に Good News Publishers から出されたもので，語源のヘブル語，アラム語，ギリシャ語を注意深く調べ，文字通り根源的に翻訳され，原書の的確な訳と訳者の個人的スタイルを生かしたものである。

8. Good News Translation 〈GNT〉

最初は 1976 年に American Bible Society から「共通言語の聖書」として出版された。外典もつけられている。ここに載せられたのは 1992 年のものである。

9. Holman Christian Standard Bible 〈HCS〉

現代英語を使って世界中の英語を話す人々に提供するために出版された聖書で，視覚的にアピールし，読みやすさがモットーになっている。IT 文化の下，変化の激しい現代英語に合わせて字句通りの翻訳と内容理解の翻訳のバランスを考えている。Holman Bible Publishers から 1999 年に最初の翻訳が出され，以後 2000 年，2002 年，2003 年と改訂されている。

10. King James Version 〈KJV〉

英国王ジェームス一世が 1604 年に認可して翻訳させたもので，1611 年に世に出た。ここに採録されているのは 1987 年のものである。

11. New American Standard Bible 〈NAS〉

1901 年の ASV を保持しながら現代英語の文法（特に時制）を取り入れ，過去 20 年間の意味変化に合わせてアップデートしたもので，1995 年に the Lockman Foundation から出版されたものである。

12. New Century Version 〈NCV〉

語源に忠実なのはもとより，NIV，NAS，NKJV などの翻訳経験のある学者・翻訳者を集めて，2005 年 Thomas Nelson, Inc. から出版された

ものである。

13. New International Reader's Version 〈NIRV〉

NIV を基として，より多くの人々が聖書に親しめるように，より短い単語や節を使ったり，説明的語句を添えたりして，読みやすく理解しやすいことを目指した。聖書の各章をセクションに分け，それにタイトルをつけた。ヘブル語やギリシャ語は最良の最古のコピーを参照した。1998 年に Biblica から出版されたものである。

14. New International Version 〈NIV〉

100 名以上の学者がヘブル語，アラム語，ギリシャ語の原典に忠実に現代英語に翻訳した。1967 年に Biblica がスポンサーとなり，「正確」，「美しさ」，「明瞭」，「権威」を目的として企画が進行し，1978 年に最初の出版があり，追加改訂があって 1983 年に出版されたものである。

15. New International Version-UK 〈NIVUK〉

NIV の英国版。

16. New King James Version 〈NKJV〉

オリジナルな KJV の純粋さと文体的美しさを保ち，考古学，言語学，テクスト研究の成果を取り入れて，1975 年 Thomas Nelson Publishers から出版されたものである。

17. New Living Translation 〈NLT〉

翻訳理論の最近の成果の上に立って，古代のヘブル語やギリシャ語のテクストを正確に再現したもので，語句ばかりでなく，底に流れる思想も日常英語に翻訳された。1996 年版と 2004 年版が Tyndale House Publishers から出版された。

18. The Message 〈MSG〉

オリジナル言語のリズムとイディオムを重視し，同時に意味変化を起こした語を他に代えたりして現代英語に合わせた。1993 年から毎年出版され，最新のは 2002 年版で NavPress Publishing Group から出版されたものである。

19. Today's New International Version 〈TNIV〉

NIV を継承しているが，その成果を反映させているばかりでなく，聖書語句を最新化し，1984 年に新しい世代の聖書読者に時宜を得た現代版聖書として Biblica によって提供されたものである。

20. Worldwide English New Testament 〈WE〉

　KJV のパターンに忠実にしたがっているが，一般聖書読者向けにやさしい英語で書かれた英訳聖書である。種々の版があるが，ここに採録されているのは 1971 年のもので，SOON Educational Publications から出版されたものである。

21. Wycliffe New Testament 〈WNC〉

　初期の版は 1382 年に出された。最初は聖書歴史学者によって逐語訳的だと指摘されたが，のちの版に比べて評価が高く，のちの欽定訳翻訳者はあとの版に則りながら，先の版の語句を取り入れている。いわば混交された版で Terrence P. Noble によって出版されたものである。

22. Young's Literal Translation 〈YLT〉

　文字通り逐語訳で，1898 年に Robert Young の手によったもの。ギリシャ語やヘブル語の原典の時制や語法を守ったために，スペリングなどで不手際が生じ，後に Baker Book House によって修正されて，コンピュータ版として印刷されたものである。

主に参照した英訳聖書

　すべての英訳聖書を取り上げるのは得策ではないし，スペースの問題も起こってくる。全体を眺めると，全面的に KJV の慣用句を踏襲するグループと，それと類似した語句・構文を使って表す英訳聖書群と，それと異なった語句・構文を用いて表す英訳聖書群とに大別することが出来る。このグルーピングを上手に使うと，グループの代表的な英訳聖書をあげれば済むことになり，経済的である。

　例を挙げると，マルコの福音書 2:19 は，KJV では And Jesus said unto them, Can the children of the bridechamber fast, while the bridegroom is with them? As long as they have the bridegroom with them, they cannot fast.（イエスは彼らに言われた。「花婿が自分たちといっしょにいる間，花婿につき添う友だちが断食できるでしょうか。花婿といっしょにいる時は，断食できないのです。」）とある。この中の the children of the bridechamber（花婿につき添う友だち）に注目して類似表現のグルーピングをしてみる。

The children of bridechamber (the sons of bridechamber)
　　KJV, ASV, DT, DRAE, NAS, NIV, WNT, YLT
The wedding guests (the guests at a wedding party)
　　NLT, AB, ESV, GNT, HCS, TNIV, GW, NET, ISV
The friends of a bridegroom (the guests of a groom)
　　CEV, NCV, NIRV, NKJV
The people at a wedding
　　WE

　すると，3つのグループに大別することが出来る。第1のグループを代表してKJVを，第2のグループを代表してNLTを，第3のグループを代表してCEVを取り出せば，3つの英訳特徴を表すことが出来る。しかし，すべてをこの通りの枠にはめるわけには行かない場合も起こる。いわば，小さな特異形が出てくる。それはWEとHCSである。そういう時は，この両者も表示する。さらに必要に応じて，他の英訳聖書を参照する場合もある。

慣用句と比喩表現

　大胆な言い方をすれば，比喩表現が死ぬと慣用句になるが，他方，慣用句は生きて永らえている。それは，慣用句化された比喩表現は固定化され，自由と柔軟性は失われているものの，そのままの形で，その持つ意味が適切な文脈でいつまでも使えるからである。

　慣用句は外心構造（exocentric construction）である。すなわち，慣用句を構成する各部分の意味を集めても，全体の意味を構成しないで，各部分の意味の集合とはまったく異なる意味を造り出すからである。他方，中心の意味を構成する語句が存在して，それを中心とした意味構成をする内心構造（endocentric construction）というものがある。

　両構造の例を挙げてみよう。kick the bucket を die（死ぬ）と捉えれば，各部分の集合の意味ではないから外心構造で慣用句であるが，個々の意味を生かして，「バケツをける」の意味で用いれば，内心構造で慣用句ではない。

はしがき

原語からの聖書慣用語句

　アラム語はキリストの公生涯で使われていた言語で，キリストの教えの中で，特にその寓話に現れる表現形式にはアラム語慣用語句が駆使されたと思われる。当然，その正確な理解なしには，聖書を正しく解釈出来ないと言えるが，2つの問題がある。1つは，キリストの生存中アラム語は話し言葉であったこと。つまり，歴史的に残る文字化されたアラム語聖書からの英訳聖書が存在しないということである。第2は，英語の慣用語句を問題とする場合は，アラム語聖書慣用語句＝英語聖書慣用語句の関係になっていなければならないが，多くの場合，このイコール関係は成立しない。

　しかしながら，少しの可能性を求めて，George M. Lamsa: *Idioms in the Bible Explained and a Key to the Original Gospels*（1985）に基づいて調査してみた。彼が挙げるアラム語聖書慣用語句は今日の英語から見て，慣用語句的ではないものが多い。しかし，ギリシャ語やラテン語訳聖書にアラム語がそのまま残って定着している箇所がかなりあり，その流れで慣用化された英語の原点の存在ともいえるのである。

　つぎに，旧約聖書はヘブル語で書かれていた。当時の一般庶民であるユダヤ人には話し言葉のアラム語で解釈されていたので，ヘブル語が英語慣用語句として残る余地は少ないと思われる。しかしながら，当時の翻訳者がヘブル語慣用語句を残し，たまたまそのまま英語慣用語句になったケースもある。Wayne Leman: *Biblical Idioms in the Hebrew Scriptures*（2008）を参照しながら，現代の英語慣用語句とマッチしたものをピックアップしてみたい。

　新約聖書ではキリストはアラム語を駆使して聴衆のユダヤ人に語りかけていたが，それを記述した弟子たちは自力ないし他力の助けを借りてギリシャ語に翻訳している。その過程でアラム語慣用語句→ギリシャ語慣用語句→英語慣用語句化したかどうかは興味ある問題である。しかも，多くの新約聖書ギリシャ語慣用語句はヘブル語慣用語句の文字通りの翻訳であることを勘案すると，複雑である。パウロ書簡はその点特異である。パウロはアラム語を意識しながら，自らギリシャ語を使って書いていたから，アラム語慣用語句を取り入れたと考えられる（Lamsa: 上掲書 p. 76 参照）。本書では，Brent Hudson and Wayne Leman: *Greek*

Idioms（2009）を参照する。

以上を考慮して，本書では，英語聖書慣用語句にアラム語，ヘブル語，ギリシャ語がどのように関与してきたかを探ってみた。各項目に可能な限り「アラム語慣用語句の意味」，「ヘブル語慣用語句の意味」，「ギリシャ語慣用語句の意味」として追記した。参考にされたい。

例文

英語慣用語句は文学はもとより，いろいろな社会的分野で使われている。これの理解と実践なしには英語を十分に駆使することができない。従って，英語慣用語句がどのようなものであるかを解説すると同時に，例文がどのように使われてきたかを提示しないと，この種の本は不十分である。

幸いなことに，市河三喜氏が古典的な聖書英語の研究書を残してくれた。それが『聖書の英語』（1949，研究社）である。そこに引用されている文学作品等からの例文は大変有用であり，可能な限り原典を確認の上，活用させていただいた。

上記『聖書の英語』以後の現代の書籍，新聞・雑誌等からの例文は，慣用句を扱った辞書類やデラウエア大学の語彙に関する検索網なども手がかりにしながら，収集した。さらに，各種インターネット検索網を利用してネット上の用例を収集した。特に，Phrase Finder, Wikipedia（英語版）が有用であった。

そのほかに，英語話者と協議して作成した例文もあり，これについては出典欄に［¶］記号を使って示した。

おわりに

最後に，一言付け加えたいのは，この種の辞書につきものの不充実感である。すべて網羅的にという宿命を負っているにもかかわらず，かなり欠けている可能性があるので，時間が許すならばさらに研究して，完璧なものを目指したいと願っている。しかしながら，この領域に関して，啓蒙的な目的は十分に達したと思っている。読者がこの本を契機として興味を持ち，この本の不足点をカバーしてくだされば，この上ない幸いである。

末筆ながら，大修館書店編集第二部部長の飯塚利昭氏には一方ならぬお世話になった。2007年に拙書『英語類義語動詞の構文事典』を出したときに，「研究・教育・参考書分野では，おそらく最後になる」と決別の辞を述べたにもかかわらず，またしてもわがままを言って飯塚氏を困らせたが，出版を快諾してくださった。ここに深く感謝申し上げる。校正の段階では，元同社編集部勤務の藤田侊一郎氏に大変お世話になった。編集技術上の優秀さばかりでなく，博学で，小生が見逃した社会的情報をも提供してくれた。多大の援助である。感謝申し上げる。

　2011年春

小 野 経 男

略記号リスト

●参考書目の略記号

〈I〉	=市河三喜：聖書の英語（1949, 研究社）
L	= George M. Lamsa: *Idioms in the Bible explained and a key to the original gospels*（1985, HarperCollins）
WL	= Wayne Leman: *Biblical Idioms in the Hebrew Scriptures*（2008, MS）
HL	= Brent Hudson and Wayne Leman : *Greek Idioms*（2009, MS）
LDOCE	= *Longman Dictionary of Contemporary English*（2005, Longman）

●主な英訳聖書の略記号

CEV	= Contemporary English Version（1995）
ASV	= American Standard Version（1901）
ESV	= English Standard Version（1971）
KJV	= King James Version（1611）
21KJV	= 21th King James Version（1994）
NAS	= New American Standard Version（1995）
NIV	= New International Version（1983）
NLT	= New Living Translation（1984）
HCS	= Holman Christian Standard Bible（2003）
WE	= Worldwide English New Testament（1998）

（注）なお，引用する日本語訳聖書は，とくに断り書きがない限り，照合の便利を勘案して新改訳聖書（日本聖書刊行会）を中心とする。

参考書目

BibleGateway.com（Christianbook.com, Christian）
eBible Japan
The Phrase Finder（http://www.phrases.org.uk/meanings/proverbs.html）
University of Delaware（htttp://www.udel.edu/）
Hudson, B. & Leman, W. 2009. *Greek Idioms*.
Lamsa, G. M. 1985. *Idioms in the Bible Explained and a Key to the Original Gospels*.
Leman, W. 2008. *Biblical Idioms in the Hebrew Scriptures*.
Longman Dictionary of Contemporary English. Longman, 2005.
The Oxford Dictionary of English Etymology. Oxford, 1966.
市河三喜　1949.『聖書の英語』　研究社
『ジーニアス英和大辞典』大修館書店，2001.
新改訳聖書　日本聖書刊行会，2003.

聖書書名（および略語）

＊聖書名は以下のように示した。略記したものについては元の書名を＝以下に記した。

●旧約
創世記
出エジプト記
レビ記
民数記
申命記
ヨシュア記
士師記
ルツ記
Ⅰサムエル記　＝サムエル記第一（新改訳），サムエル記上（新共同訳）
Ⅱサムエル記　＝サムエル記第二（新改訳），サムエル記下（新共同訳）
Ⅰ列王記　＝列王記第一（新改訳），列王記上（新共同訳）
Ⅱ列王記　＝列王記第二（新改訳），列王記下（新共同訳）
Ⅰ歴代誌　＝歴代誌第一（新改訳），歴代誌上（新共同訳）
Ⅱ歴代誌　＝歴代誌第二（新改訳），歴代誌下（新共同訳）
エズラ記
ネヘミヤ記
エステル記
ヨブ記
詩篇
箴言
伝道者　＝伝道者の書（新改訳），コヘレトの言葉（新共同訳）
雅歌
イザヤ書
エレミヤ書
哀歌
エゼキエル書

ダニエル書
ホセヤ書
ヨエル書
アモス書
オバデヤ書
ヨナ書
ミカ書
ナホム書
ハバクク書
ゼパニヤ書　＝ゼパニヤ書（新改訳），ゼファニヤ書（新共同訳）
ハガイ書
ゼカリヤ書
マラキ書

●新約

マタイの福音書　＝マタイの福音書（新改訳），マタイによる福音書（新共同訳）

マルコの福音書　＝マルコの福音書（新改訳），マルコによる福音書（新共同訳）

ルカの福音書　＝ルカの福音書（新改訳），ルカによる福音書（新共同訳）

ヨハネの福音書　＝ヨハネの福音書（新改訳），ヨハネによる福音書（新共同訳）

使徒の働き　＝使徒の働き（新改訳），使徒言行録（新共同訳）

ローマ人への手紙　＝ローマ人への手紙（新改訳），ローマの信徒への手紙（新共同訳）

Ⅰコリント人への手紙　＝コリント人への手紙第一（新改訳），コリントの信徒への手紙一（新共同訳）

Ⅱコリント人への手紙　＝コリント人への手紙第二（新改訳），コリントの信徒への手紙二（新共同訳）

ガラテヤ人への手紙　＝ガラテヤ人への手紙（新改訳），ガラテヤの信徒への手紙（新共同訳）

エペソ人への手紙　＝エペソ人への手紙（新改訳），エフェソの信徒への手紙（新共同訳）

ピリピ人への手紙　＝ピリピ人への手紙（新改訳），フィリピの信徒への手紙（新共同訳）

コロサイ人への手紙　＝コロサイ人への手紙（新改訳），コロサイの信徒への手紙（新共同訳）

I テサロニケ人への手紙　＝テサロニケ人への手紙第一（新改訳），テサロニケの信徒への手紙一（新共同訳）

II テサロニケ人への手紙　＝テサロニケ人への手紙第二（新改訳），テサロニケの信徒への手紙二（新共同訳）

I テモテへの手紙　＝テモテへの手紙第一（新改訳），テモテへの手紙一（新共同訳）

II テモテへの手紙　＝テモテへの手紙第二（新改訳），テモテへの手紙二（新共同訳）

テトスへの手紙

ピレモンへの手紙　＝ピレモンへの手紙（新改訳），フィレモンへの手紙（新共同訳）

ヘブル人への手紙　＝ヘブル人への手紙（新改訳），ヘブライ人への手紙（新共同訳）

ヤコブの手紙

I ペトロの手紙　＝ペトロの手紙第一（新改訳），ペトロの手紙一（新共同訳）

II ペトロの手紙　＝ペトロの手紙第二（新改訳），ペトロの手紙二（新共同訳）

I ヨハネの手紙　＝ヨハネの手紙第一（新改訳），ヨハネの手紙一（新共同訳）

II ヨハネの手紙　＝ヨハネの手紙第二（新改訳），ヨハネの手紙二（新共同訳）

III ヨハネの手紙　＝ヨハネの手紙第三（新改訳），ヨハネの手紙三（新共同訳）

ユダの手紙

黙示録　＝ヨハネの黙示録（新改訳，新共同訳）

聖書に由来する
英語慣用句の辞典

A

[Abraham]

Abraham's bosom アブラハムの胸 →死後善人が行くところ，天国

KJV And it came to pass that the beggar died, and was carried by the angels into **Abraham's bosom**. The rich man also died, and was buried. ［ルカの福音書 16:22］さて，この貧乏人は死んで，御使いたちによって**アブラハムのふところ**に連れて行かれた。金持ちも死んで葬られた。

[用例] This habit of walking is kept up by the Englishmen to a very advanced age ... when they knock off, it is to take to their beds, and prepare to go and sleep in **Abraham's bosom**. [Max O'Rell, *John Bull and his Island*] この散歩の習慣は高齢になるまで英国人は続ける。散歩をやめるのは床に就き，**天国**に行って永眠する準備を整えるときである。

[他の英訳聖書] KJV の bosom を避けて，CEV と HCS では side を，NLT では with Abraham を使っている。いずれも具体的な描写である。The time came when the beggar died and the angels carried him to **Abraham's side**. (アブラハムのそば) The rich man also died and was buried. <CEV>／ One day the poor man died and was carried away by the angels to **Abraham's side**. (アブラハムのそば) The rich man also died and was buried. <HCS>／ Finally, the poor man died and was carried by the angels to be **with Abraham**. (アブラハムとともに) The rich man also died and was buried. <NLT>

[account]

put it on my account それを私に請求してくれ →それを私のつけにしてくれ

KJV If he hath wronged thee, or oweth thee aught, **put that on mine**

account.［ピレモンへの手紙 1:18］もし彼があなたに対して損害をかけたか，負債を負っているのでしたら，**その請求は私にしてください**。

[用例] 現代英語では，この比喩的意味で put it on my account は使われていない。だだし，on one's own account（自分の責任で；自分のために）が類似した意味で使われている。

I don't like you, my dear, to alter your coat **on my account**. [¶] ねえ君，**私のために**君のコートの仕立て直しをしてほしくない。

[他の英訳聖書] この慣用句の比喩的意味はアラム語に起因しているから，英訳聖書ではすべて文字通りに解釈している。そのため，CEV も NLT も，多少語句を変えてはいるが，文字通りの表現を保つ。

If he has cheated you or owes you anything, **charge it to my account**.（それを私に請求してくれ）<CEV>／If he has wronged you in any way or owes you anything, **charge it to me**.（それを私に請求してくれ）<NLT>

[アラム語慣用語句の意味] Forget it（忘れろ）と Lamsa (1985) は訳しているが，責任の転嫁といった意味合いは消えている。

[all]

all in all すべての人の中ですべての働き →全体的に，概して

KJV And there are diversities of operations, but it is the same God which worketh **all in all**. [I コリント人への手紙 12:6] 働きにはいろいろの種類がありますが，**神はすべての人の中ですべての働きをなさる**同じ神です。

[用例] And the love of the dearest friends grow small — But the glory of the Lord is **all in all**. [R. D. Blackmore, *Dominus Illuminatio Mea*] 最愛の友の愛さえも減少する。しかし，主の栄光は**すべてに行き渡る**。

All in all, it's pretty exciting to be part of a family that has just welcomed a new generation within it. [*Woman's Own*, 1974] **概して**，新たに赤ちゃんが生まれ，その家族の一員であることはかなりわくわくするものだ。

[他の英訳聖書] all in all が抽象過ぎるきらいがあるので，変化にと

んだパラフレーズを各英訳聖書はしている。CEV は「助ける」ことを，HCS では「神の能動性」を主眼に強調し，NLT はほぼ KJV を踏襲している。

And we can each do different things. Yet the same God works **in all of us and helps us in everything we do**. (私たちすべてに働いて私たちの働きを助けてくれる) <CEV>／God works in different ways, but it is the same God who does the work **in all of us**. (私たちのすべての中に) <NLT>／And there are different activities, but the same God is **active in everyone and everything**. (すべての人に働いてすべてをなしてくださる) <HCS>

all things to all men　すべての人にすべてのもの →すべてのひとに広く対応

KJV To the weak became I as weak, that I might gain the weak. I am made **all things to all men**, that I might by all means save some. [Ⅰコリント人への手紙 9:22] 弱い人々には，弱い者になりました。弱い人々を獲得するためです。**すべての人に，すべてのものとなりました。それは，何とかして，幾人かでも救うためです。**

[用例] However, I showed no sign of wonder or disapproval; for I remembered that to be **all things to all men** was one of the injunctions of the Gentile Apostle, which for the present I should do well to heed. [S. Butler, *Erewhon*] しかし，私は驚き，ないし非難を少しも表さなかった。なぜなら，**すべての人に広く対応する**ことは非ユダヤ人使徒の指図のひとつで，当面十分に気をつけるのが賢明だと思い起こしたからである。

[他の英訳聖書] 現代英語では all things to all men は分かりにくい。そこで，CEV では live を中心にして，NLT では share を用いてすべての人々に対応する術を述べている。

When I am with people whose faith is weak, I **live as they do** (彼らのように生きる) to win them. I do everything I can to win everyone I possibly can. <CEV>／When I am with those who are weak, I **share their weakness** (彼らの弱さを共有する), for I want to bring the weak to Christ. Yes, I try to find common ground with everyone, doing everything I can to save some. <NLT>

[alpha]

the alpha and omega アルファとオメガ（ギリシャ語の最初と最後のアルファベット），初めと終わり →すべてのもの，最重要の部分

KJV "I am **the Alpha and the Omega**, the Beginning and the End," saith the Lord, "who is and who was and who is to come, the Almighty."［黙示録1:8］今いまし，昔いまし，後に来られる方，万物の支配者がこう言われる。「わたしは**アルファであり，オメガである**。」

[用例] The election of a government by the people is **the alpha and omega** of a parliamentary democracy.［¶］国民による政府の選出は議会制民主主義の**要諦部分**である。

[他の英訳聖書] 該当箇所を意訳している英訳聖書はない。

[アラム語慣用語句の意味] Lamsa (1985) の英語のパラフレーズは The first and the last; the beginning and the end とあり，文字通りギリシャ語の「はじめと終わり」である。アラム語で aleph and tau と書かれ，英語慣用語句の「最重要の部分」の意は隠されている。

[apple]

the apple of one's eye 自分のひとみ →愛する大切な人

KJV He found him in a desert land and in the waste howling wilderness; He led him about, He instructed him, He kept him as **the apple of His eye**.［申命記32:10］主は荒野で，獣のほえる荒地で彼を見つけ，これをいだき，世話をして，ご**自分のひとみ**のように，これを守られた。

[用例] Poor Richard was to me as an eldest son, **the apple of my eye**.［Sir Walter Scott, *Old Mortality*］リチャードは私にとって長男で，**愛する大事な人**だった。《［注］この例文は引用された最古のもの。》

The semi-barbaric king had a daughter as blooming as his most florid fancies, and with a soul as fervent and imperious as his own. As is usual in such cases, she was **the apple of his eye**, and was loved by him above all humanity.［F. R. Stockton, *The Lady or the Tiger*］その半ば野蛮な王様には一人の娘がいた。彼女は彼の華麗すぎる空想

のように華やかで，彼と同じように熱烈なそして傲慢な魂の持ち主であった。そういう場合にありがちなように，彼女は彼の**掌中の珠**で，だれにもまして彼に愛されていた。

[他の英訳聖書]　HCS のように apple を pupil に変えているものもあるが，大勢として KJV 風慣用句の語句形式をとるか，あるいは CEV のように one's own eyes に平易化されるかのどちらかである。

He found him in a desolate land in a barren, howling wilderness; He surrounded him, cared for him, and guarded him as **the pupil of His eye**. (彼の瞳) <HCS>／ Israel, the LORD discovered you in a barren desert filled with howling winds. God became your fortress, protecting you as though you were **his own eyes**. (彼の自身の瞳) <CEV>

[アラム語慣用語語句の意味]　アラム語慣用句は He loved and took care of him as a man would care for his precious eyes. とあり，自分の目を大切にするように愛するという動作自体に力点があるようである。

[ark]

touch/lay one's hands on the ark　神の箱を押さえる →聖なるものをぞんざいに扱う

KJV And when they came to Nachon's threshing floor, Uzzah **put forth his hand to the ark of God and took hold of it**, for the oxen shook it.［II サムエル記 6:6］こうして彼らがナコンの打ち場まで来たとき，ウザは**神の箱に手を伸ばして，それを押えた**。牛がそれをひっくり返しそうになったからである。

[用例] Nay, we have known one such heretic go so far as to **lay his hands upon the ark** itself, so to speak, and to defend the startling paradox that even in physical beauty, man is the superior.［T. H. Huxley, *Emancipation*］いや，**神聖なものに手を出す**ような一人の異教徒を知っている。彼は肉体の美しさの点でも男性のほうが優れているという驚くべきパラドックスを擁護するのだ。

If I **lay my hands on his notebook**, I'll let you know it in detail. [¶] 彼のノートを見つけたら，詳細を知らせるよ。《[注] touch/lay one's hands on the ark の the ark の部分を他の語句に代えた用法

が現代英語にはよく見かけられる。意味もネガティブではなく、「見つける、手に入れる」と肯定的に一般化されている。》

[他の英訳聖書] 文学書で使われる慣用句は KJV のものと同じではない。したがって、KJV 以降に新たに作られたものであろう。当然、CEV も NLT も他の用法を使っている。

But when they came to Nacon's threshing-floor, the oxen stumbled, so Uzzah **reached out and took hold of the sacred chest**.（手を伸ばして聖なる箱をつかんだ）<CEV>／But when they arrived at the threshing floor of Nacon, the oxen stumbled, and Uzzah **reached out his hand and steadied the Ark of God**.（手を伸ばして神の箱を安定させた）<NLT>

[axe]

lay the axe to the root of ... 斧を木の根元に置く →破壊を始める

KJV And now also **the ax is laid unto the root of the trees**; therefore every tree which bringeth not forth good fruit is hewn down and cast into the fire.［マタイの福音書 3:10］斧もすでに木の根元に置かれています。だから、良い実を結ばない木は、みな切り倒されて、火に投げ込まれます。

[用例] It was not till I saw **the axe laid to the root**, that I found the full extent of what I had to lose and suffer.［Hazlitt, *Essays*］破壊が始まって初めて自分が失って苦しむものがどんなに大きいかが分かった。

During the mid-1850s, Young instituted a Mormon Reformation, intending to "**laying the axe at the root** of the tree of sin and iniquity."［Wikipedia, *Mountain Meadows Massacre*］1850 年代半ば、ヤングはモルモン宗教改革を実施し、罪と不正の**根絶**を図った。

[他の英訳聖書] KJV の比喩的意味はそのまま持ち越されているが、語句は平易化されている。NLT では God's judgment という注釈まで挿入されている。

An ax is ready to cut the trees down at their roots.（斧が木々の根元から切るように置かれている）Any tree that doesn't produce good fruit will be chopped down and thrown into a fire. <CEV>／ Even now **the ax is ready to strike the root of the trees**! (斧が木々の根を打つように置かれている) Therefore every tree that doesn't produce good fruit will be cut down and thrown into the fire. <HCS>／ Even now **the ax of God's judgment is poised, ready to sever the roots of the trees**. (今や神の裁きの斧が置かれ，木々の根元が断ち切られようとしている) Yes, every tree that does not produce good fruit will be chopped down and thrown into the fire. <NLT>

B

[beam]

beam/mote in one's own eye 自分の目の中の梁(はり)/ちり →自分の無視している咎(とが)

KJV And why beholdest thou **the mote that is in thy brother's eye**, but considerest not **the beam that is in thine own eye**? [マタイの福音書 7:3] また，なぜあなたは，**兄弟の目の中のちり**に目をつけるが，**自分の目の中の梁**には気がつかないのですか。

[用例] But I do like to point out **the beam in other people's eyes**, even if I fail to recognize **the mote in my own**. [Sir Oliver Lodge, *Points of View*] しかし，**自分自身の小さな咎**さえ見つけられなくても，ほんとうに私は**他人の咎**を見つけたがる。

[他の英訳聖書] speck (=mote), log (=beam) のように代えているが，ほとんどの英訳聖書が KJV を踏襲している。

You can see **the speck in your friend's eye** (友人の目の中のしみ)，but you don't notice **the log in your own eye**. (あなた自身の目の中の梁) <CEV>

[beat]

beat the air/wind 空を打つ →むなしく努力する

KJV I therefore so run, but not with uncertainty; I so fight, but not as one that **beateth the air**. [Ｉコリント人への手紙 9:26] ですから，私は決勝点がどこかわからないような走り方はしていません。**空を打つ**ような拳闘もしてはいません。

[用例] It is just **beating the air** to try and persuade a miser like him to give a penny to anything. [Lyell, *Principles of Geology*] 彼みたいなけちを説得して１円でも寄付させようとするのは**むなしい努力**だ。

He cared little about contemporary politics, which he regarded as

beating the wind. [Froude, *Carlyle*, II, xvii.] 彼は当時の政治に無頓着だった。なぜなら，それは**努力してもむなしい**と看做していたからだ。

[他の英訳聖書] KJV の慣用句を残さず，他の語句を用いてすべて意訳されている。NLT にいたってはボクシングの用語まで使っている。HCS はそれを KJV と同じように節を用いて表している。

I don't run without a goal. And I don't box by **beating my fists in the air**. (拳で空(くう)を打つ) <CEV>／ So I run with purpose in every step. I am not just **shadowboxing**. (シャドーボクシング) <NLT>／ Therefore I do not run like one who runs aimlessly, or **box like one who beats the air**. (むなしく打つ者のように打つ) <HCS>

[blind]

the blind leading the blind　盲人を手引きする盲人　→無鉄砲な危険な話

KJV Let them alone: they be blind leaders of the blind. And if **the blind lead the blind**, both shall fall into the ditch. [マタイの福音書 15:14] 彼らのことは放っておきなさい。彼らは盲人を手引きする盲人です。もし，**盲人が盲人を手引きする**なら，ふたりとも穴に落ち込むのです。

[用例] The Clergy of the neighbourhood ... listened with unaffected tedium to his consultations, and advised him, as the solution of such doubts, to "drink beer and dance with the girls." **Blind leaders of the blind**! [Carlyle, *Sartor Resartus*] 近所の牧師は無表情で退屈して彼の相談事を聴いていて，そのような疑いの解決として「ビールを飲み，娘っ子たちとダンスしろ」と忠告した。**盲人が盲人の手を引くとはこのことだ**。

The **Blind Leading the Blind** is an oil painting by Pieter Bruegel the Elder: There are six blind men going forward one after the other. A blind guide goes first and falls in a hole with his staff. The next blind man trips over the first one. The third connected with the second with a staff follow his predecessors. The fifth and the sixth don't yet know what is happening but will fall into the hole at the end.

[Wikipedia, *The Blind Leading the Blind*, Jan. 11, 2010] **盲人が盲人の手を引く**というのは父親のほうのピーター・ブリューゲルの描いた油絵で，6人の盲人が列になってあとについて行きます。盲人のガイドが先に行き，杖と一緒に穴に落ちます。次の盲人が最初の盲人に躓きます。三番目の盲人は杖を持った二番目の盲人と繋がっていて，先に行った者の後を追います。五番目と六番目は何が起こったのかまだ分かりませんで，終わりには穴に落ち込んでしまいます。

[他の英訳聖書]　有名な慣用句なので，KJV が踏襲されているが，NLT のように，手引きしているのがガイドだと説明しているのがある。

Stay away from those Pharisees! They are like **blind people leading other blind people**（盲人が他の盲人の手引きをする）, and all of them will fall into a ditch. <CEV>／So ignore them. They are **blind guides leading the blind**（盲人を手引きする盲目のガイド）, and if one blind person guides another, they will both fall into a ditch. <NLT>

【 block 】

a stumbling block　つまずきの石塊 →行為の妨げ

KJV Therefore let us not judge one another anymore, but rather resolve this, not to put **a stumbling block** or a cause to fall in our brother's way.［ローマ人への手紙 14:13］ですから，私たちは，もはや互いにさばき合うことのないようにしましょう。いや，それ以上に，兄弟にとって**妨げになるもの**，つまずきになるものを置かないように決心しなさい。

[用例] The big **stumbling block** to starting a new business is that we are short of money and qualified people.［¶］新しい事業を始める上で大きな**障害**になるのは資金不足と資格者の不足だ。

After thirteen years the ... tragic battle over Britain's thalidomide children is over. It finished yesterday when Premier Wilson and the Cabinet swept away the last **stumbling block** over the multi-million pound payout.［*Daily Mirror*, 1974］13 年経って，英国におけるサリドマイド禍の子どもたちをめぐる，悲劇的な戦いは終わった。そ

れは昨日，ウィルソン内閣が数百万ポンドの支払いという最後の**妨げ**を取り去ったときに終わりを告げた。

[**他の英訳聖書**] KJV の stumbling block が実際にどういうものであるかを示しているのが CEV と NLT である。

We must stop judging others. We must also make up our minds not to **upset**（動揺させる）anyone's faith. <CEV>／So let's stop condemning each other. Decide instead to live in such a way that you will not **cause another believer to stumble and fall**.（他の信者をつまずかせ堕落させる）<NLT>

[blood]

one's blood be upon the head 血が頭上にふりかかれ →罪の責任は自分に降りかかれ

KJV And when they opposed themselves, and blasphemed, he shook his raiment, and said unto them, **Your blood be upon your own heads**; I am clean; from henceforth I will go unto the Gentiles［使徒の働き 18:6］しかし，彼らが反抗して暴言を吐いたので，パウロは着物を振り払って，「**あなたがたの血は，あなたがたの頭上にふりかかれ**。私には責任がない。今から私は異邦人のほうに行く」と言った。

[用例] God judge betwixt us! And **your blood**, if you fall, **be on you own head**.［Scott, *Kenilworth*］神はわれわれの間を裁かれる。あなたが過ちをすれば，**その責任は自分に降りかかる**。

You refused my help when you were in trouble, so the failure was **upon your head** and not mine.［¶］君は困っている時，私の助けを断った。だから失敗は**君の責任**で，私の責任ではない。

《[注] 現代英語では，主語の blood を除いた be upon the head が独立し，「～の責任だ」という一般的な意味となっている。》

[**他の英訳聖書**] 多くの英訳聖書は NLT のように KJV を踏襲しているが，CEV のように現代英語の文体に変えているものもある。

Finally, they turned against him and insulted him. So he shook the dust from his clothes and told them, "Whatever happens to you will **be your own fault**!（あなた自身の過ちである）I am not to blame. From now on I am going to preach to the Gentiles." <CEV>／But when they opposed and insulted him, Paul shook the dust from his clothes and said, "**Your blood is upon your own heads**（あなたがたの血は，あなたがたの頭上にふりかかる）— I am innocent. From now on I will go preach to the Gentiles." <NLT>

[ギリシャ語慣用語句の意味]　HL はこの語句をパラフレーズして you yourselves must take the blame for it!（あなた自身その責めを負わなければならない）としている。CEV はこの点，ギリシャ語慣用語句に忠実な意訳である。

[bowl]

The golden bowl is broken　金の器は打ち砕かれる →望みがなくなる

KJV Or ever the silver cord be loosed, or **the golden bowl be broken**, or the pitcher be broken at the fountain, or the wheel broken at the cistern —．［伝道者 12:6］こうしてついに，銀のひもは切れ，**金の器は打ち砕かれ**，水がめは泉のかたわらで砕かれ，滑車が井戸のそばでこわされる。

[用例] The mood, Miss Gallander, the precious mood, is shattered; **the golden bowl**, Felton, **is broken**. [J. B. Priestley, *The Good Companions*] 雰囲気だよ，ガランダーさん，貴重な雰囲気が壊されたのだ。フェルトンさん，**望みがない**のだ。

[他の英訳聖書]　KJV の比喩的語句はそのまま他の英訳聖書に引き継がれている。ただし，動詞の態が CEV と NLT の対比のように違っている。

The silver cord snaps, **the golden bowl breaks**（金の器が壊れる）; the water pitcher is smashed, and the pulley at the well is shattered. <CEV> / Yes, remember your Creator now while you are young, before the silver cord of life snaps and **the golden bowl is broken**.（金の器が壊れる）Don't wait until the water jar is smashed at the spring and the pulley is broken at the well. <NLT>

[アラム語慣用語句の意味]　微妙な違いが存在する。Lamsa の説明は Life comes to an end. とあり，「いのちの終わり」としている。「望みがなくなる」のは終わりまでは行っていない。

[bowel]

bowels of 〜　〜の深部 →〜の深いこころ

KJV Put on therefore, as the elect of God, holy and beloved, **bowels of mercies, kindness, humbleness of mind, meekness, longsuffering**. [コロサイ人への手紙 3:12] それゆえ，神に選ばれた者，聖なる，愛されている者として，あなたがたは**深い同情心，慈愛，謙遜，柔和，寛容**を身に着けなさい。

[用例] And at least it would be a face worth seeing: the face of a man who was without **bowels of mercy**: a face which had but to show itself to raise up ... a spirit of enduring hatred. [Stevenson, *Dr. Jekyll and Mr. Hyde*] 少なくとも観察してみるだけのことがある顔であろう。**深い同情心**のない男の顔である。首を持ち上げるだけで分かる永久に憎しみを持ったこころの顔である。

[他の英訳聖書]　KJV の bowels の比喩はすべての英訳聖書でこころの深さを表す形容詞ないし動詞で言い換えられているが，CEV のみそのまま形容詞の羅列に任せている。

God loves you and has chosen you as his own special people. So **be gentle, kind, humble, meek, and patient**. (優しく，そして親切で，謙虚で，柔和で，寛容であれ) <CEV>／ Since God chose you to be the holy people he loves, you must **clothe yourselves with tenderhearted mercy, kindness, humility, gentleness, and patience**. (優しいこころを持った同情心，それに親切さ，謙虚さ，柔和さ，寛容で身を包みなさい) <NLT>

[bread]

our daily bread　日々の糧 →日々の食事

KJV "Give us this day **our daily bread**." [マタイの福音書 6:11] 私たちの**日ごとの糧**をきょうもお与えください。

[用例] ... accustomed, that is, as we are to **the daily bread** which we eat, without much thought or appetite, but cannot do without. [S. Grand, *The Winged Victory*] 慣れているのです。つまり，**日々の食事**と同じことです。というのも，あれこれ考えず，特に食べたいとも思わずに食べるわけですが，無くてはならないものなわけです。

It drives me up the wall. **His daily bread** comes partly from — surprise, surprise! — public relations. [Phrase Finder, *Our Daily Bread*] それには腹が立ちます。彼の**毎日の飯の種**は驚いたことに宣伝活動なのです。

[他の英訳聖書] bread が food を表していることを CEV と NLT ははっきり示し，daily のパラフレーズも現代的である。他の英訳聖書は KJV を踏襲。

Give us **our food for today**. (今日の食べ物) <CEV>／ Give us **today the food we need**. (今日必要とする食べ物) <NLT>

eat the bread of idleness 怠惰のパンを食べる →怠ける

KJV She looketh well to the ways of her household, and **eateth not the bread of idleness**. [箴言 31:27] 彼女は家族の様子をよく見張り，**怠惰のパンを食べない**。

[用例] You cannot **eat the bread of idleness** on board of a man-of-war. [F. Marryat, *Newton Forster*] 軍艦に乗っていて**怠ける**ことはできない。

[他の英訳聖書] 明確に意訳されている。eat the bread「生活する」が確立していて，後に来る idleness だけを生かせばよいからであろう。

She takes good care of her family and **is** never **lazy**. (怠ける) <CEV>／ She carefully watches everything in her household and suffers nothing from **laziness**. (怠けること) <NLT>

bread of life いのちのパン →精神的糧

KJV And Jesus said unto them, "I am **the Bread of Life**. He that cometh to Me shall never hunger, and he that believeth in Me shall never thirst. ..." [ヨハネの福音書 6:35] イエスは言われた。「わたしが**いのちのパン**です。わたしに来る者は決して飢えることがなく，わたしを信じる者はどんなときにも，決して渇くことがありません。…」

[用例] A second man I honour, and still more highly: Him who is seen toiling for the spiritually indispensable; not daily bread, but **the bread of life**. [Carlyle, *Sartor Resartus*] 別の男性を尊敬します。しかももっと高く尊敬します。彼は精神的に不可欠なもの求めて労

苦しているのが見て分かります。日々の食べるパンではなく，**精神的糧**を求めているのです。

[他の英訳聖書] bread が肉体的にも精神的にも「糧」ととらえられているので，すべての英訳聖書でそのまま生かされている。ただし，CEV のように，節に書き直しているものもある。

I am **the bread that gives life**! (いのちを与えるパン) No one who comes to me will ever be hungry. No one who has faith in me will ever be thirsty. <CEV> / I am **the bread of life**. (いのちのパン) Whoever comes to me will never be hungry again. Whoever believes in me will never be thirsty. <NLT>

[アラム語慣用語句の意味] Lamsa (1985) は eternal truth (永遠の真理) としている。比喩的には「糧」も「真理」に近いといえるが，明確な形で言明している英訳聖書はない。現代英語の慣用語句としては圧倒的に「心の糧」として使われている。

cast bread upon the waters パンを水の上に投げる →返礼を求めずに与える

KJV **Cast thy bread upon the waters**: for thou shalt find it after many days. [伝道者 11:1] あなたの**パンを水の上に投げよ**。ずっと後の日になって，あなたはそれを見いだそう。

[用例] The writer ... believes that the printers ... were misunderstood benefactors of their kind, **casting their bread upon the waters** out of pure zeal, and with no hope of pecuniary return. [Baikie, *The English Bible*] その作家は，その印刷業者たちは恩恵を与える類の人の中でもきちんと理解されていない人たちだったのだと思っている。というのも，彼らは純粋に熱意から，金銭的見返りも望まずに**返礼を求めずに善行を行う**のだから。

[他の英訳聖書] 比較的 KJV に似ているのは HCS で，パンが水面に投げられる状況が記述されている。しかし，これは伝統的な英訳聖書に見られる現象で (ASV, NIV, ESV など)，現代版とも言うべき英訳聖書は CEV のように大胆に意訳している。

Be generous (寛大であれ), and someday you will be rewarded. <CEV> / **Send your grain across the seas** (穀物を海面に投げ入れなさい),

and in time, profits will flow back to you. <NLT>／ **Send your bread on the surface of the waters**（パンを水面に投げ入れなさい）, for after many days you may find it. <HCS>

[アラム語慣用語句の意味] Lamsa (1985) には Give charity and you will get it back.（慈善を行いなさい，そうすればあとでそれが戻る）と説明している。KJV の比喩的意味と同じなので，この慣用語句はもともとアラム語が語源だと分かる。

Man does not live by bread alone　人はパンのみに生きるにあらず →人には心の拠(よりどころ)もある

KJV But he answered and said, It is written, **Man shall not live by bread alone**, but by every word that proceedeth out of the mouth of God. [マタイの福音書 4:4] イエスは答えて言われた。「『**人はパンだけで生きるのではなく**，神の口から出る一つ一つのことばによる。』と書いてある。」

[用例] They seem trying to do their best to save money, but **man cannot live by baked beans alone**. [¶] 彼らはお金を貯めようと最善の努力をしているようだが，それ以外に**心の問題もある**。

[他の英訳聖書] わずかな違いはあるが，ほとんどの英訳聖書は NLT のような語句を連ねている。その中で，CEV は bread ではなく，明瞭に「食べ物」を対称物にしている点が特異である。

Jesus answered, "The Scriptures say: '**No one can live only on food**.（だれも食べ物だけで生きているのではない）People need every word that God has spoken.'" <CEV>／ But Jesus told him, "No! The Scriptures say, '**People do not live by bread alone**, but by every word that comes from the mouth of God.'" <NLT>

[breathe]

breathe into one's nostrils the breath of life　鼻孔に息を吹き込む →生かす

KJV And the LORD God formed man of the dust of the ground, and **breathed into his nostrils the breath of life**; and man became a living soul. [創世記 2:7] その後，神である主は，土地のちりで人を形造り，**その鼻にいのちの息を吹き込まれた**。そこで，人は，生きもの

となった。

> [用例] Mr. Hardy starts out with an idea, and it is a pity that he cannot mould his idea, shape it, **breathe into it the breath of life**. [G. Moore, *Confessions of a Young Man*] ハーディ氏はアイデアを出すが，残念なことに，そのアイデアを練って形作り，**命を吹き込む**ことができない。

[他の英訳聖書] ほとんどの英訳聖書は KJV と大差はなく，NLT と同じように目的語の語順が異なるだけである。

The LORD God took a handful of soil and made a man. God **breathed life into**（命を吹き込まれた）the man, and the man started breathing. <CEV>／ Then the LORD God formed the man from the dust of the ground. He **breathed the breath of life into the man's nostrils**（人の鼻孔にいのちの息を吹き込まれた）, and the man became a living person. <NLT>

[brick]

make bricks without straw わらなしでれんがを作る →材料なしでものをつくる

KJV Ye shall no more give the people **straw to make brick**, as heretofore: let them go and gather straw for themselves. [出エジプト記 5:7] おまえたちは**れんがを作るわら**を，これまでのようにこの民に与えてはならない。自分でわらを集めに行かせよ。

> [用例] "How can you blame your gardener when you won't spend money on seed or manure or even the most common gardening implements? D'you expect him to **make bricks without straw**? Don't be so unreasonable." [Lyell, *Principles of Geology*] 種や肥料，またごく普通の庭仕事の道具をケチっていて，どうして庭師を責めることができますか。**材料なしでものを作らせる**つもりなのですか。無茶を言っては困ります。

[他の英訳聖書] この慣用句はそのままの形では KJV に現れていないから，その意味を込めた語句が自由に作れる。CEV と NLT はその典型例。

Don't give the slaves any more **straw to put in their bricks**. (れんが

に入れるわら）Force them to find their own straw wherever they can. <CEV>／Do not supply any more **straw for making bricks**.（れんがを作るためのわら）Make the people get it themselves! <NLT>

[brother]

Am I my brother's keeper? 私は自分の弟の番人なのか →私が世話しなければならないのか

KJV And the LORD said unto Cain, "Where is Abel thy brother?" And he said, "I know not. **Am I my brother's keeper?**"［創世記4:9］主はカインに,「あなたの弟アベルは,どこにいるのか」と問われた。カインは答えた。「知りません。**私は,自分の弟の番人なのでしょうか**。」

〔用例〕'I don't know where he is,' she replied. '**I'm not his keeper**. He can go anywhere as he pleases, now that he is a grown-up.'［¶］「彼がどこにいるのか知りません。**彼の面倒は見ません**。彼は大人ですから好きなところにいけるのです」と彼女は答えた。

Last night, I went in to a gas station to buy a couple of things. Two friendly, African workers helped me. At the cashier station, they asked me if **I was my brother's keeper**. I hadn't heard the term before and I had some difficulty understanding due to their accent. I asked them to repeat the phrase, and they continued to explain. I had a nice conversation with both of them for a while, somewhat holding up the line.［Phrase Finder, *Am I my brother's keeper?*］昨夜ガソリンスタンドに行って2,3のものを買ったとき,2人の親切なアフリカ系の労働者が私の手助けをしてくれた。勘定をするとき,彼らは**私が弟の世話をしている**のかと聞いてきた。そのことば使いを聞いたことがなかったし,彼らのアクセントのため,理解しにくかったが,少しの間,列を滞らせながら,その2人と会話が弾んだ。

[他の英訳聖書] KJVのkeeperは「保護者,番人,監視人,看守,経営者,記録員など」広範囲な意味があって,特定しがたいが,その点,CEVは動詞語句で,NLTとHCSは別の名詞で代用している。

Afterwards the LORD asked Cain, "Where is Abel?" "How should I know?" he answered. "**Am I supposed to look after my brother?**"（私

は弟の世話をしなければならないのか) <CEV>／Afterward the LORD asked Cain, "Where is your brother? Where is Abel?" "I don't know," Cain responded. "**Am I my brother's guardian?**"（私は弟の番人ですか) <NLT>, <HCS>

[build]

build on sand　砂の上に建てる →不安定な（ぐらつく）ものを建てる

KJV And every one that heareth these sayings of Mine and doeth them not, shall be likened unto a foolish man, who **built his house upon the sand**.［マタイの福音書7:26］また，わたしのこれらのことばを聞いてそれを行なわない者はみな，**砂の上に自分の家を建てた**愚かな人に比べることができます。

[用例] It is dangerous, in the end it must be fatal, to sustain the entire structure of life and thought on the illusions of romance. But that was what Lang did ... he **built his house upon the rainbow**.［Gosse, *Andrew Lang*］ロマンスの幻想で人生と思考の全体を支えるのは危険だ。最後には致命傷になるに違いない。しかし，これはラングが行った事で，**自分の家を虹という不安定な土台に建てた**のであった。

My response is to say that it is better to **build on what might conceivably be sand** but has so far given no signs of weakness than not to build at all.［Phrase Finder, *Not to build at all*］私の返事はこうです。おそらく**不安定だと思われるものの上に建てる**のでも，これまでに弱点が見えなければ，全然建てないよりよいということです。

［他の英訳聖書］すべての英訳聖書はKJVを踏襲している。それだけこの慣用句は定着していることなのであろう。

Anyone who hears my teachings and doesn't obey them is like a foolish person who **built a house on sand**.（砂の上に家を建てる) <CEV>

[burden]

burden/dust and heat (of the day)　一日の労苦と焼けるような暑さ →一日の激しい労働

KJV These last have wrought but one hour, and thou hast made them equal unto us who have borne **the burden and the heat of the day**. ［マタイの福音書 20:12］この最後の連中は一時間しか働かなかったのに，あなたは私たちと同じにしました。私たちは**一日中，労苦と焼けるような暑さ**を辛抱したのです。

[用例] He had gone to the battlefield, stood **the dust and heat of the day**. [Trollope, *Barchester Towers*] 彼は戦場に出向いて，**一日激しい戦い**に耐えた。

Through **the heat of the day and the burden**,
And thro' sweat and thro' toil without guerdon,
To dishonour we shall not be lured in;
We will answer when Duty shall call. [College anthem by V. E. Vance, St. Francis' College, Idia, established in 1885] **一日の激しい労働**を経験し，汗して，報酬なき労苦をしても，誘惑されて不名誉に走らない。神の務めのお召しがあれば，それに応える。

[他の英訳聖書] KJV の慣用句は CEV, NLT ともに意訳されて具体的な口語訳になっている。HCS は burden を残している。

The ones who were hired last worked for only one hour. But you paid them the same that you did us. And we worked **in the hot sun all day long**! (一日中暑い陽の下で) <CEV>／Those people worked only one hour, and yet you've paid them just as much as you paid us who worked **all day in the scorching heat**. (一日中焼け付くような太陽のもとで) <NLT>／These last men put in one hour, and you made them equal to us who bore **the burden of the day and the burning heat!**' (丸一日の労苦と焼けつく暑さ) <HCS>

[bury]

bury my father　私の父を葬る →最後まで父の面倒をみる

KJV And another of His disciples said unto Him, "Lord, suffer me first to go and **bury my father**." ［マタイの福音書 8:21］また，別のひと

りの弟子がイエスにこう言った。「主よ。まず行って，**私の父を葬ることを許してください。**」

[用例] 次の例文は表現形式は同じでも，意味は文字通りのものである。OED や Webster's のような大きな辞書でも，この比喩的意味は載っていない。アラム語源の慣用句は KJV で採用しない限り，英語の慣用句にはなりえないのである。

　Last week she came home after a long absence and **buried her father** with her children. [¶] 長いこと留守してから彼女は先週家に帰り，子供たちと一緒に**父親を埋葬した。**

[他の英訳聖書]　もともとアラム語からの KJV の慣用句は比喩的表現として受け取られていなかった。そのため，顕著な違いを表す CEV や NLT でさえも文字通りの解釈をしている。

Another disciple said to Jesus, "Lord, let me wait till I **bury my father**."（父を葬る）<CEV>／Another of his disciples said, "Lord, first let me return home and **bury my father**." <NLT>

[アラム語慣用語句の意味]　Lamsa (1985) には take care of my father until he dies とあり，KJV の文字通りの意味とは違っているが，この意味は慣用句として残らなかった。

C

[calf]

kill the fatted calf　肥えた子牛を殺す　→最高のもてなしをする

KJV And **bring hither the fatted calf and kill it**, and let us eat and be merry. [ルカの福音書 15:23] そして**肥えた子牛を引いて来てほふりなさい。食べて祝おうではないか。**

[用例] Sometimes I have a mind to go home; my mother ... would receive her prodigal, and **kill tha fatted veal** for me. [Thackeray, *The Newcomes*] 時々家に帰る気になります。そうすれば，母は放蕩息子を受け入れ，**最高のもてなしをしてくれるでしょう。**

We'll **kill the fatted calf** tonight, so stick around, you're gonna hear electric music, solid walls of sound. [Bernie Taupin, *Bennie and the Jets*, 1973] 今晩最高のもてなしをしようじゃないか。みんな集まれ。エレキの音楽とガンガンするすばらしい音を聞こう。

[他の英訳聖書]　比喩の中心部分である the best (or fattened) calf は残り，他の動詞部分が変わっているだけである。したがって，KJV の中心語句はそのまま踏襲されている。

Get the best calf and prepare it（最高の子牛を持ってきて料理しなさい）, so we can eat and celebrate. <CEV>／ And **kill the calf we have been fattening**.（太らせてきた子牛を殺しなさい）We must celebrate with a feast. <NLT>／ Then **bring the fattened calf and slaughter it**（太らせた子牛を持ってきて殺しなさい）, and let's celebrate with a feast. <HCS>

[cheek]

turn the other cheek　他方の頬を出す　→やらせたままで復讐しない

KJV But I say unto you that ye resist not evil, but whosoever shall smite thee on thy right cheek, **turn to him the other also**. [マタイの

福音書5:39] しかし，わたしはあなたがたに言います。悪い者に手向かってはいけません。あなたの右の頬を打つような者には，**左の頬も向けなさい**。

[用例] Keeping the principle of nonviolence does not mean, however, **turning the other cheek**. [¶] しかしながら，非暴力の原則を守るということは**やらせたままで復讐しない**ということではない。

The bombings have made me change my mind about capital punishment. We should bring back hanging. It is time to stop **turning the other cheek**. [*The Sun*, 1974] その爆破によって死刑に関しての私の考えは変わった。絞首刑を復活すべきだ。**やらせたままで復讐しない**のをやめるときが来た。

[他の英訳聖書] CEVとNLTは動詞語句を代えてはいるものの，基本的にはKJVの踏襲である。

But I tell you not to try to get even with a person who has done something to you. When someone slaps your right cheek, **turn and let that person slap your other cheek**. (向きを変えてその人に他方の頬を打たせなさい) <CEV>／ But I say, do not resist an evil person! If someone slaps you on the right cheek, **offer the other cheek also**. (他方の頬も向けなさい) <NLT>／ But I tell you, don't resist an evildoer. On the contrary, if anyone slaps you on your right cheek, **turn the other to him also**. (他方も彼に向けなさい) <HCS>

[アラム語慣用語句の意味] Lamsa (1985) は Don't start a quarrel or fight. Be humble (喧嘩を始めるな。謙虚になれ) としている。しかし，このアラム語の意味では聖書の意図が生かされないのではないかと思う。

[choose]

Many are called but few are chosen 呼ばれる者は多いが選ばれる者は少ない →特別扱いの人は少ない

KJV For **many are called, but few are chosen**. [マタイの福音書22:14] **招待される者は多いが，選ばれる者は少ない**のです。

[用例] This kind of information is valuable and available only to **the chosen few**. [¶] この種の情報は価値があり，**選ばれし少数の人**

のみが得られるものです。

[他の英訳聖書] 定型化しているので，圧倒的に多くの英訳聖書はKJVを踏襲しているが，CEVはfewをa fewに代えて肯定的内容にしている。

Many are invited, but only a few are chosen.（招待されるものは多いが，2, 3の人だけが選ばれるのです）<CEV>／For **many are called, but few are chosen**. <NLT>

[cleave]

cleave to the roof of the mouth　（舌が）上あごにつく →黙る

KJV If I do not remember thee, let my tongue **cleave to the roof of my mouth**, if I prefer not Jerusalem above my chief joy.［詩篇137:6］もしも，私がおまえを思い出さず，私がエルサレムを最上の喜びにもまさってたたえないなら，私の舌が**上あごについてしまう**ように。

[用例] His heart began to sink within him; he endeavoured to resume his psalm tune, but his parched tongue **clove to the roof of his mouth**, and he could not utter a stave. [Irving, *Sketch Book*, "Sleepy Hollow."] 彼の心は消沈し始めた。彼は賛美の歌を再び歌おうとしたが，**舌が乾ききって黙ってしまい**，一節も歌えなかった。

I want you to know, with all due respect to everybody, it ain't so. It never happened. I will deny it until my tongue **cleaves to the roof of my mouth** and I can't get enough breath to say another word. [John Dale, in his Sunday morning sermon, 2006] 失礼な言い方だが，知ってほしいのです。そんなことはありません。決してそんなことは起こりませんでした。私は**黙りこくって別な言葉が出てこなくなるまで**否定します。

[他の英訳聖書] すべての英訳聖書がKJVを踏襲するか，CEVとHCSのように動詞を代えている。この語句の慣用化が徹底されているようである。

Let my tongue **stick to the roof of my mouth**（上あごにくっつく），if I don't think about you above all else. <CEV>／May my tongue **stick to the roof of my mouth** if I do not remember you. <HCS>

[coal]

heap coals of fire on one's head　人の頭に燃える炭火を積む →悪に対し善を返し悔恨を促す

KJV If thine enemy hunger, feed him; if he thirst, give him drink. For in so doing thou shalt **heap coals of fire on his head**.［ローマ人への手紙12:20］もしあなたの敵が飢えたなら，彼に食べさせなさい。渇いたなら，飲ませなさい。そうすることによって，あなたは**彼の頭に燃える炭火を積む**ことになるのです。

[用例] But one day, as I was crossing the hospital square, Sir John stopped me, and **heaped coals of fire on my head** by telling me that he had tried to get me one of the resident appointments ...［Huxley, *Autobiography*］しかし，ある日，病院広場を横切っていると，ジョン卿に呼び止められ，私のために医学実習生の予約を取るよう努力してくれたと告げられ，私の**悪意にもかかわらず親切にしてくれた**ことで，私は**悔恨の念**をもった。

[他の英訳聖書]　動詞と coals の前の修飾語に違いが見られるが，中心語の coals は残している。ただし，NLT は shame を挿入して意味の明確化を図っている。

If your enemies are hungry, give them something to eat. And if they are thirsty, give them something to drink. This will be the same as **piling burning coals on their heads**.（彼らの頭に燃えている炭火を積む）<CEV>／If your enemies are hungry, feed them. If they are thirsty, give them something to drink. In doing this, you will **heap burning coals of shame on their heads**.（彼らの頭に恥の燃えている炭火を積む）<NLT>

[アラム語慣用語句の意味]　Lamsa (1985) の cause them to regret（悔い改めさせる）は KJV の比喩的な意味と同じである。ということは，KJV を書く前に翻訳者たちはアラム語慣用語句を理解していたのであろう。

[ギリシャ語慣用語句の意味]　HL はこれをギリシャ語慣用語句としているが，そうだとすれば，アラム語慣用語句からギリシャ語慣用語句になったものであろう。これを HL は you will be very kind to him

(彼にとても親切になる)としているが,短略すぎるパラフレーズであろう。

[countenance]

One's countenance fell 顔を伏せた →顔に落胆の色が浮かんだ

KJV But unto Cain and to his offering He had not respect. And Cain was very wroth, and **his countenance fell**. [創世記 4:5] だが,カインとそのささげ物には目を留められなかった。それで,カインはひどく怒り,**顔を伏せた**。

[用例] "For artists?" said the landlord. **His countenance fell** and the smile of welcome disappeared. [Stevenson, *New Arabian Nights*]「芸術家のためだって」と家主は文句を言って**落胆を示し**,歓迎の微笑みは消えていた。

[他の英訳聖書] 多くが KJV の慣用語句を踏襲している中で,CEV, NLT, NIV はまったく意訳していて,現代的な表現になっている。

But not with Cain and his offering. This made Cain so angry that he could **not hide his feelings**. (彼の感情を隠さなかった) <CEV>／But he did not accept Cain and his gift. This made Cain very angry, and he **looked dejected**. (落胆した表情を見せた) <NLT>／But on Cain and his offering he did not look with favor. So Cain was very angry, and **his face was downcast**. (彼はうつむいた) <NIV>

[crackling]

crackling of thorns under a pot なべの下でいばらがはじける音 →ばか者の高笑い

KJV For as is **the crackling of thorns under a pot**, so is the laughter of the fool. This also is vanity. [伝道者 7:6] 愚かな者の笑いは,**なべの下のいばらがはじける音**に似ている。これもまた,むなしい。

[用例] Laughter means sympathy; good laughter is not "**the crackling of thorns under the pot**." [Carlyle, *Shakespeare*] 笑いの意味しているところは同情である。よい笑いは「**ばか者の高笑い**」ではない。

[他の英訳聖書] KJV をそのまま踏襲しているのもあるが,多くは CEV や NLT のように,crackling を動詞化(分詞)し,pot の代わり

に fire を使っている。

Foolish laughter is stupid. It sounds like **thorns crackling in a fire**. (火の中でいばらがはじける)<CEV>／A fool's laughter is quickly gone, like **thorns crackling in a fire**. This also is meaningless. <NLT>

[crystal]

clear as crystal　水晶のように透き通った →透明な，明白な

KJV Having the glory of God: and her light was like unto a stone most precious, even like a jasper stone, **clear as crystal**. [黙示録 21:11] 都には神の栄光があった。その輝きは高価な宝石に似ており，**透き通った碧玉のようであった**。

[用例] Such an investigation made it **crystal clear** that he, filled with bias against the rich, had a plan for blowing up the millionaire's house. [¶] そのような調査の結果，彼が金持ち階級に偏見を持っていて，その百万長者の家を爆破しようとする計画を持っていたことは**明白**であった。

In this pleasant humour I came down the hill to where Goudet stands in a green end of a valley, with Chateau Beaufort opposite upon a rocky steep, and the stream, **as clear as crystal**, lying in a deep pool between them. [Robert Louis Stevenson, *Travels with a Donkey in the Cévennes*, 1879] このような気持よい気分になって，私は丘を降りてグーデ村が渓谷の緑の端に位置しているところへ来た。対岸の岩の断崖の上にはボーフォール城があり，**透明な**小川が両者の間に深い池となって横たわっていた。

[他の英訳聖書] 2通りに分かれる。NLT のように KJV の流れにあるものと，CEV のように crystal clear という現代英語風に代えるものとである。

The glory of God made the city bright. It was dazzling and **crystal clear** like a precious jasper stone. <CEV>／It shone with the glory of God and sparkled like a precious stone-like jasper **as clear as crystal**. <NLT>

[cross]

take up one's cross　自分の十字架を負う　→苦難に耐える

　KJV　Then Jesus said unto His disciples, "If any man will come after Me, let him deny himself and **take up his cross** and follow Me."［マタイの福音書 16:24］それから，イエスは弟子たちに言われた。「だれでもわたしについて来たいと思うなら，自分を捨て，**自分の十字架を負い**，そしてわたしについて来なさい。」

　［用例］We want to keep back part of the price; and we continually talk of **taking up our cross**, as if the only harm in a cross was the weight of it...［Ruskin, *The Mystery of Life and its Arts*］代価は一部隠したままにしておきたい。その口で，**十字架を背負う**という話を延々とするわけです。まるで，十字架の困ったところは重いということだけでもあるかのように。

［他の英訳聖書］　すべての英訳聖書は CEV のように KJV を踏襲している。この慣用句はパターン化している。

If any of you want to be my followers, you must forget about yourself. You must **take up your cross**（自分の十字架を負う）and follow me. <CEV>

［ギリシャ語慣用語句］　HL はこの語句を be prepared to suffer, including death（死ぬことを含めて，いつでも苦難に耐えること）とパラフレーズしている。

[cup]

drink of the cup　杯を飲む　→どんな悲しみにも耐える

　KJV　But Jesus answered and said, "Ye know not what ye ask. Are ye able to **drink of the cup** that I shall drink of?" They said unto Him, "We are able."［マタイの福音書 20:22］けれども，イエスは答えて言われた。「あなたがたは自分が何を求めているのか，わかっていないのです。わたしが飲もうとしている**杯を飲む**ことができますか。」彼らは「できます」と言った。

　［用例］How'll she feel just the same for me as she does now, when we eat o' the same bit, and **drink o' the same cup**, and think o' the same things from one day's end to another?［Eliot, *Silas Marner*］私

たちが，一日の終わりから次の日まで，同じものを食べ，**同じ悲しみを共有し**，同じことを思考するときに，彼女は今のように私に対して全く同じ感情をもつだろうか。

[他の英訳聖書]　the cup の前の前置詞は異なっても，多くは KJV のパターンを踏襲しているが，NLT はその cup に説明的修飾語句をつけている。

Jesus answered, "Not one of you knows what you are asking. Are you able to **drink from the cup**（杯を飲む）that I must soon drink from?" James and John said, "Yes, we are!" <CEV>／But Jesus answered by saying to them, "You don't know what you are asking! Are you able to **drink from the bitter cup of suffering**（悲しみの苦い杯を飲む）I am about to drink?" <NLT>

[アラム語慣用語句の意味]　Lamsa (1985) には載っていないが，同じ章の 23 節の語句は載っている。意味的には同じレベルのものなので，ここに説明を加える。My cup you shall drink.（あなたがたはわたしの杯を飲みはします）[マタイの福音書 20:23] の箇所を You shall die as I die.（あなたがたは私のように死ぬ）としている。KJV の意訳より激しい解釈である。

One's cup is full/runs over　杯があふれている →大変な喜び/悲しみを味わう

KJV　Thou preparest a table before me in the presence of mine enemies; Thou anointest my head with oil; **my cup runneth over**. [詩篇 23:5] 私の敵の前で，あなたは私のために食事をととのえ，私の頭に油をそそいでくださいます。**私の杯は，あふれています。**

[用例] To marry a Papist! This was all that was wanted to make **poor Tom's cup of bitterness run over**. [Thackeray, *The Newcomes*] カトリック教徒と結婚するんだって。それを聞けば間違いなく**可哀想なトムの苦い運命は耐えがたくなったよ**。

[他の英訳聖書]　本来 cup の意味は中立で，「喜び」でも「悲しみ」でもその器になりうる。詩篇 23:5 は文脈から判断して「喜び」であるが，例文では「悲しみ」の器になる。その点，NLT は blessings を挿入して意味を明瞭にしている。CEV は語句を易しくしているが，

KJV の踏襲であり,多くの英訳聖書はこれに倣っている。

You treat me to a feast, while my enemies watch. You honor me as your guest, and you **fill my cup until it overflows**.(あふれるばかりに私の杯をいっぱいにする)<CEV>／You prepare a feast for me in the presence of my enemies. You honor me by anointing my head with oil. **My cup overflows with blessings**.(私の杯は祝福であふれる)<NLT>

D

[daughter]
daughter of the horseleech　蛭(ひる)の娘 →貪欲な人

KJV The horseleech hath two daughters, crying, "Give, give!" There are three things that are never satisfied, yea, four things that say not, "It is enough". [箴言 30:15] 蛭にはふたりの娘がいて,「くれろ,くれろ」と言う。飽くことを知らないものが,三つある。いや,四つあって,「もう十分だ」と言わない。

> [用例] Such and many such like were the morning attendants of the Duke of Buckingham — all genuine descendants of **the daughter of the horseleech**, whose cry is "Give, give." [Scott, *Peveril of the Peak*] そのような多くの人々はバッキンガム公爵の朝の付添い人でみんな真正な**貪欲**家系に属していた。彼らの叫ぶ声は「くれ,くれ」ばかりであった。
>
> With outstretched hands and hungry looks, these beribboned **daughters of the horseleech** are round you. [*Punch* 1881] 手を差し出して,ひもじい顔つきをして,このリボンで飾った**貪欲な娘**たちが周りにいる。

[他の英訳聖書]　NLT のパターンを取る英訳聖書が多い。KJV の踏襲であるが,horseleech をより一般的な leech に代えている。daughter of はヘブル語法で,このほかに daughters of music(歌う女性)のように使う。<I>

Greed has twins(貪欲には双子がいる), each named "Give me!" There are three or four things that are never satisfied. <CEV>／**The leech has two suckers**(蛭には二人の乳飲み子がいる) that cry out, "More, more!" There are three things that are never satisfied — no, four that never say, "Enough!" <NLT>

[day]

day of small things　小さな出来事の日 →少しの数・金額

KJV For who hath despised **the day of small things**? For they shall rejoice and shall see the plummet in the hand of Zerubbabel with those seven. They are the eyes of the LORD, which run to and fro through the whole earth.［ゼカリヤ書4:10］だれが，その日を小さな事としてさげすんだのか。これらは，ゼルバベルの手にある下げ振りを見て喜ぼう。これらの七つは，全地を行き巡る主の目である。

[用例] I am but the incumbent of a poor country parish; my aid must be of the humblest sort. And if you are inclined to despise **the day of small things**, seek some more efficient succour than such as I can offer.［C. Brontë, *Jane Eyre*］私は田舎の貧しい教区の牧師に過ぎない。私の援助はほんのわずかなもので，**ちっぽけな額**だとけなすつもりなら，私の提供するものよりももっと効率的な援助を求めなさい。

[他の英訳聖書] この語句は軽蔑的要素を含んでいるが，CEVもNLTも事（神殿工事）の始まりとして，「小さな事」ととらえている。KJVでは時間よりも内容からの軽蔑感を示している。そのパターンをHCSも採っている。

Those who have made fun of **this day of small beginnings**（この小さな始まりを）will celebrate when they see Zerubbabel holding this important stone. Those seven lamps represent my eyes — the eyes of the LORD — and they see everything on this earth. <CEV> ／ Do not despise **these small beginnings**（この小さな始まりを）, for the LORD rejoices to see the work begin, to see the plumb line in Zerubbabel's hand.（The seven lamps represent the eyes of the LORD that search all around the world.）<NLT> ／ For who scorns **the day of small things**?（この小さなことを）These seven eyes of the LORD, which scan throughout the whole earth, will rejoice when they see the plumb line in Zerubbabel's hand. <HCS>

[dead]

Let the dead bury their dead　死人に自分たちの死人を葬らせよ　→過去のことは過去のこと

KJV But Jesus said unto him, "Follow Me, and **let the dead bury their dead**."［マタイの福音書8:22］ところが，イエスは彼に言われた。「わたしについて来なさい。**死人たちに彼らの中の死人たちを葬らせなさい。**」

[用例] And all her things, everything that could remind him of her, had been put away. It was **the dead burying its dead**.［May Sinclair, *The Token*］そしてすべて彼女のもの，すべて彼に彼女のことを思い出させるものは片付けられた。**過去のことは過去のことなのだ。**

A: "There must have been numerous decisions made or not made during the New Orleans disaster by non-feasant public servants that would have been better had their bosses or colleagues said, 'Yeah, yeah, yeah, let's cross that bridge when we come to it.'"

B: "Not too dissimilar in intent are the expressions 'Don't borrow trouble,' and '**Let the dead bury their dead**.'"［Phrase Finder, *Don't cross the bridge...*］A:「ニューオリンズの災害の折，不作為の公務員の多くの決定がなされたに違いないし，あるいはなされなかったに違いない。それらはもし彼らの上司なり，同僚が「そうだ，そうだ，その橋に着いたら渡ろう（取り越し苦労はやめて，その時になったら決めよう）」と言っていたら，よい結果になっていたであろう。」B:「意図的にはあまり違いはない表現に「わざわざ面倒を引き寄せるな」と「**過去のことは過去のこと**」というのがある。」

[他の英訳聖書]　NLT を除いて，すべての英訳聖書は KJV を踏襲している。NLT は spiritually を挿入して死人が霊的に死んだ者だと明示している。

But Jesus told him, "Follow me now. **Let the spiritually dead bury their own dead**."（霊的に死んだ者は自分自身の死を葬らせよ）<NLT>

[アラム語慣用語句の意味]　8章21節に And another of His disciples

said unto Him, "Lord, suffer me first to go and bury my father."(また，別のひとりの弟子がイエスにこう言った。「主よ。まず行って，私の父を葬ることを許してください。」)とあって，bury my father の説明からはじめる。Lamsa (1985) はここの意味を Take care of my father until he dies (父が死ぬまで面倒を見る) の意であるとしている。そうすると，22節の bury their dead の意味が通らなくなる。Lamsa は dead のアラム語は metta で，これが town のアラム語 matta と混同したのではないかと主張している。当時の筆写者の技術や材料から起こっても当然だと考えられる。

　もし，イエスの弟子の一人の父親が死んだのであれば，イエスは何らかのかかわりを持ち，当日説教をしていなかったかもしれない。そして会葬者の一人になっていたのかもしれない。この dead が town の誤記だとすれば，当時の慣習で町が死人を葬っていたので，イエスは Let the town bury the dead. (死人は町に葬らせればよい) と言ったのかもしれない。

dead letter　古い文字 →役に立たない規律

KJV But now we are delivered from the law, that being dead wherein we were held; that we should serve in newness of spirit, and not in **the oldness of the letter**. [ローマ人への手紙 7:6] しかし，今は，私たちは自分を捕えていた律法に対して死んだので，それから解放され，その結果，**古い文字**にはよらず，新しい御霊によって仕えているのです。

[用例] Then came the devastating thought that Elfride's childlike, unreasoning, and indiscreet act in flying to him [=Knight] only proved that the proprieties must be **a dead letter** with her. [Hardy, *A Pair of Blue Eyes*] 騎士のところに跳んでいった，エルフライドの子供じみた，非理性的な，無分別な行為によって，彼女にとって礼儀作法はもう**役に立たない規律**だという衝撃的な思いが起こってきた。

　Arthur M. Schlesinger has written ... what amounts to an elegy on the Constitution of his country. Naturally he does not assume it to be **a dead letter**. [*The Listener*, 1974] アーサー・M・シュレシンガーは自分の国の憲法を挽歌に譬えられるものを書いたが，当然のこと

[他の英訳聖書] 文字通りに dead letter は存在しないが，コンテクストからこの意味が浮かび上がってくる。CEV も NLT も多少表現は違うが噛み砕いた口語体である。

But the Law no longer rules over us. We are like dead people, and it cannot have any power over us. Now we can serve God in a new way by obeying his Spirit, and not in the old way by **obeying the written Law**.（書かれた律法に従うこと）<CEV>／But now we have been released from the law, for we died to it and are no longer captive to its power. Now we can serve God, not in the old way of **obeying the letter of the law**（律法の文字に従うこと），but in the new way of living in the Spirit. <NLT>

[deep]

Deep calls unto deep　淵が淵を呼び起こす →全地を震撼する

KJV **Deep calleth unto deep** at the noise of Thy waterspouts; all Thy waves and Thy billows have gone over me.［詩篇 42:7］あなたの大滝のとどろきに，淵が淵を呼び起こし，あなたの波，あなたの大波は，みな私の上を越えて行きました。

[用例] There was a fearful, sullen sound of rushing waves and broken surges. **Deep called unto deep**.［Irving, *Sketch Book*］波が押し寄せ砕ける，恐ろしい，鈍い音があった。**すべてを揺るがす音であった**。

I recently ran across this phrase in the movie "Infamous"(the second Truman Capote movie). The Harper Lee character says that when Capote told her about the Clutter murders it was **deep calling unto deep**.［Phrase Finder, *Deep calls unto deep*］私は最近，映画「悪名」（2番目のトルーマン・カポーティ作品）でこの語句に出くわした。ハーパー・リー役がカポーティがクラター一家の殺人について彼女に語った時，それは**全地を揺るがすほどの衝撃**だったと言っています。

[他の英訳聖書] 詩的な KJV に比べて，CEV と NLT は動的な描写である。

Your vicious waves have swept over me like **an angry ocean or a roaring waterfall**. (怒り狂った大洋かとどろく滝) <CEV>／I hear **the tumult of the raging seas** (怒り狂った海の激動) as your waves and surging tides sweep over me. <NLT>

[delight]

delight to honor　栄誉を与える →敬意を払う，喜ばせる

KJV So Haman came in. And the king said unto him, "What shall be done unto the man whom the king **delighteth to honor**?" Now Haman thought in his heart, "To whom would the king delight to do honor more than to myself?" [エステル記 6:6] ハマンがはいって来たので，王は彼に言った。「王が**栄誉を与えたい**と思う者には，どうしたらよかろう。」そのとき，ハマンは心のうちで思った。「王が栄誉を与えたいと思われる者は，私以外にだれがあろう。」

[用例] But butchers, also, and butchers of the bloodiest badge have been all Martial Commanders whom the world invariably **delights to honor**. [Melville, *Moby Dick*] しかし，殺し屋，もっとも血まみれなバッジをつけた殺し屋はみな軍隊の司令官で世の人は例外なく**敬意を払う**のさ。

We are **delighted to honor** in this manner an individual whose very name is synonymous with corporate and financial integrity. [University of Delaware, *Messenger*, 2003] このようにして，氏名それ自体が共同的，財政的規準と一致する個人の方に**敬意を払う**。

[他の英訳聖書] KJV の格調高い表現が CEV と NLT ではごく普通の表現に代えられている。そのままで口語体だともったいぶった言い方になるのであろう。

When Haman entered the room, the king asked him, "What should I do for a man I **want to honor**?" (敬いたい) Haman was sure that he was the one the king wanted to honor. <CEV>／ So Haman came in, and the king said, "What should I do **to honor** (尊敬する) a man who truly pleases me?" Haman thought to himself, "Whom would the king wish to honor more than me?" <NLT>

[dog]

dead dog 死んだ犬 →無価値なもの

KJV After whom has the king of Israel come out? After whom dost thou pursue? After a **dead dog**, after a flea! ［Ⅰサムエル記 24：14］「イスラエルの王はだれを追って出て来られたのですか。あなたはだれを追いかけておられるのですか。それは**死んだ犬**のあとを追い，一匹の蚤を追っておられるのにすぎません。」

[用例] "Come down," he shouted. "You're no more use than a **dead dog**. We'll just have to go along the reef till we find the opening."［W. S. Maugham, *Red*］「降りて来い」と彼は叫んだ。「お前は**役立たず**の船乗りだ。岩礁に沿っていって出口を見つけなければならないというのに。」

[他の英訳聖書]　すべての英訳聖書が dead dog を使っている。この比喩表現はすっかり慣用語句として定着している。

Why should the king of Israel be out chasing me, anyway? I'm as worthless as a **dead dog**（死んだ犬）or a flea. I pray that the LORD will help me escape and show that I am in the right. <CEV>

[door]

at the door 戸口で →すぐそこに

KJV "If thou doest well, shalt thou not be accepted? And if thou doest not well, sin lieth **at the door**. And unto thee shall be his desire, and thou shalt rule over him."［創世記 4：7］「あなたが正しく行なったのであれば，受け入れられる。ただし，あなたが正しく行なっていないのなら，罪は**戸口**で待ち伏せして，あなたを恋い慕っている。だが，あなたは，それを治めるべきである。」

[用例] "The blame of sin lies **at the door of** the wrong-doer, and he must take the consequences."［Brewer, *Dictionary of Phrase and Fable*］悪事を働く人は罪の責めを**すぐ受け**，彼はその責任を取らなければならない。

The blame for this sorry state of affairs can be laid **at the door of** the Association of University Teachers, which has ... failed to protect its membership against the ravages of education policy and inflation.

[*The Guardian*, 1975] この悲しい事態に対する責めは大学教員組合**にある**であろう。なぜなら，教育政策とインフレの荒廃に対して組合員達を守れなかったからである。

[**他の英訳聖書**] 「すぐそばで待ち構えている」という状況が at the door にはあって，その状況を CEV は waiting を，NLT では crouching at the door を使って表している。NLT の at the door は 2 重の効果が出る。

If you had done the right thing, you would be smiling. But you did the wrong thing, and now sin is **waiting to attack** (待ち伏せて攻撃する) you like a lion. Sin wants to destroy you, but don't let it! <CEV>／ You will be accepted if you do what is right. But if you refuse to do what is right, then watch out! Sin is **crouching at the door** (戸口で待ち伏せして), eager to control you. But you must subdue it and be its master. <NLT>

[drop]

drop in/of a bucket/ocean　手おけ/大海のひとしずく →全体に比べてほんの少し

KJV Behold, the nations are as **a drop of a bucket**, and are counted as the small dust of the balance; behold, He taketh up the isles as a very little thing. [イザヤ書 40:15] 見よ。国々は，**手おけの一しずく**，はかりの上のごみのようにみなされる。見よ。主は島々を細かいちりのように取り上げる。

[用例] A."D'you know how much he owes? I've got a little money saved and I would willingly let him have it."
B."It's awfully good of you, but I'm afraid it would be **a drop in the ocean** compared to the amount he requires. Why, it must be well over a hundred thousand pounds." [Lyell, *Principles of Geology*]
A.「彼がいくら借金しているか知っていますか。少しお金を蓄えてあるので，彼に貸してあげたいのです。」B.「それはご親切に。けれども，あなたの額は彼の必要額と比べると**ほんの少し**でしょう。なにしろ，彼の必要額は 10 万ポンド以上になるに違いないから。」

On Thursday, September 30, at 7 p.m., marine scientist Joseph

Scudlark will present "Acid Rain: Just **a Drop in the Ocean**?," a free public lecture at the University's Hugh R. Sharp Campus in Lewes. Scudlark will explain what acid rain is and where it comes from, look at the long-term trends associated with acid rain in Delaware and neighboring states, and discuss its ecological consequences. [University of Delaware, *News*, 1999] 9月30日木曜日, 夜7時より, 海洋科学者ジョゼフ・スカドラーク氏が「酸性雨, **全体に比べほんの少しか?**」と題して話される。ルイスにある大学のヒュー・R・シャープキャンパスで行われる無料の講義で, 酸性雨がどんなものであるのか, どこからくるのかが説明され, デラウェアとその周辺州に降る酸性雨の長期に渡る傾向とその地球環境上の問題が討議される。

[他の英訳聖書] すべての英訳聖書は CEV のように a drop in a bucket にしている。KJV の a drop of a bucket を残さなかったのは, of の現代用法(所属・分離)を避けたのであろう。

To the LORD, all nations are merely **a drop in a bucket**(手おけのひとしずく)or dust on balance scales; all of the islands are but a handful of sand. <CEV>

[dust]

lick the dust　ちりをなめる →前に倒れる, 降参する

KJV They that dwell in the wilderness shall bow before him, and his enemies shall **lick the dust**. [詩篇72:9] 荒野の民は彼の前にひざをつき, 彼の敵は**ちりをなめます**ように。

[用例] He found the surly innkeepers **licked the very ground** before him now. [Reade, *The Cloister & the Hearth*] 彼はぶっきらぼうな居酒屋の主人たちが今や彼に**降参した**と知った。《[注] 口語体では bite/kiss the dust の方がよく用いられ, 「病気になる, 死ぬ」の意でも使われる。しばしばユーモラスな表現とされる。》

In Westerns, where Indians were routinely portrayed as the bad guys, Indians were said **to bite the dust** when they were shot and fell to the ground. [Phrase Finder, *Bite the dust*] 西部劇ではインディアンはいつも悪いやつとして描かれ, 撃たれて地面に倒れる

と，くたばったとされた。

[他の英訳聖書] KJV の比喩表現中の lick（なめる）が CEV と NLT では具体的な表現となり，分かりやすくなっているが，文学的味わいが欠けている。

Force the desert tribes to accept his rule, and make his enemies **crawl in the dirt**.（ちりに這う）<CEV>／ Desert nomads will bow before him; his enemies will **fall before him in the dust**.（彼の前でちりに倒れる）<NLT>

shake off the dust of one's feet ／ shake the dust from one's feet　足のちりを払い落とす　→怒って立ち去る

KJV And whosoever shall not receive you, nor hear your words, when ye depart out of that house or city, **shake off the dust of your feet**.［マタイの福音書 10:14］もしだれも，あなたがたを受け入れず，あなたがたのことばに耳を傾けないなら，その家またはその町を出て行くときに，**あなたがたの足のちりを払い落としなさい**。

[用例] Could John Hewson ever hope to **shake off the dust of cobbling** among the neighbors who knew him so well?［W. A. Eddy, *The Wits vs. John Partridge, Astrologer*］ジョン・ヒューソンは彼をよく知っている近所の人々から**怒って立ち去る**なんて望んだのであろうか。

In Biblical times, when leaving Gentile cities, pious Jews often **shook the dust from their feet** to show their separation from Gentile practices.［Wikipedia, *Shaking the dust from the feet*］聖書時代に，敬虔なユダヤ人は異邦人の町を離れるとき，異邦人の習慣とは異なることを表すために**足のちりを払った**。《[注] 必ずしも「怒って」行う行為ではなく，習慣の異なることをあらわす目的もあった。》

[他の英訳聖書] 現代風に of を from に代えているが，KJV に忠実なのは NLT で，CEV は at them をつけて敵対関係を明らかにしている。 If someone won't welcome you or listen to your message, leave their home or town. And **shake the dust from your feet at them**.（彼らに対して足からちりを払い落とす）<CEV>／ If any household or town refuses to welcome you or listen to your message, **shake its dust from**

your feet（足からちりを払い落とす）as you leave. <NLT>

[アラム語慣用語句の意味]　微妙な意味の違いがある。Lamsa (1985) は have nothing to do with them; leave them alone.（彼らと関係ない。ほっておけ）としている。文脈からすると，アラム語慣用語句の方が適しているようにも思えるが，KJV はユダヤ人の習慣を表していて，定着している。

dust and heat（of the day） ⇒ burden

E

[eat]

Eat, drink, and be merry 食べて，飲んで，陽気になれ →くよくよしないで今のときを楽しめ

KJV Then I commended mirth, because a man hath no better thing under the sun than **to eat and to drink and to be merry**, for that shall abide with him from his labor the days of his life, which God giveth him under the sun.［伝道者 8:15］それゆえ，わたしは快楽をたたえる。太陽の下，人間にとって**飲み食いし，楽しむ**以上の幸福はない。それは，太陽の下，神が彼に与える人生の日々の労苦に添えられたものなのだ。

[用例] A whole generation had been infected by the **eat-drink-and-be-merry**-for tomorrow-we-die spirit which accomapanied the departure of the soldiers to the training camps and the fighting front.［F. L. Allen, *Only Yesterday*］若い同世代の人々は**くよくよしないで今のときを楽しめ**，明日は死ぬ身だから，という風潮に毒されてきた。それは兵士が訓練キャンプや前線に出発するときに起こる感情であった。

[他の英訳聖書] CEV のように噛み砕いて記述すると，比喩性が完全に消えてしまう。NLT のように KJV の基幹部分を残せば，比喩性は少し残るが，語句を変えたので慣用句的ではなくなっている。

So I think we should get as much out of life as we possibly can. There is nothing better than **to enjoy our food and drink and to have a good time**. (飲食を喜び，楽しく過ごす) Then we can make it through this troublesome life that God has given us here on earth. <CEV>／ So I recommend having fun, because there is nothing better for people in this world than **to eat, drink, and enjoy life**. (食べて，飲んで，人生を楽しむ) That way they will experience some happiness along with all the hard work God gives them under the sun. <NLT>

[eleventh]

at the eleventh hour 11時に →最後の機会で

KJV And **about the eleventh hour** he went out and found others standing idle, and said unto them, 'Why stand ye here all the day idle?'［マタイの福音書20:6］また，**五時ごろ**出かけてみると，別の人たちが立っていたので，彼らに言った。「なぜ，一日中仕事もしないでここにいるのですか。」

[用例] Now God be praised that He has saved you **at the eleventh hour**.［Shaw, *Saint Joan*］神は称えるべきかな。あなたを**最後の機会**で救いなさった。

"Old saved **at the eleventh hour**," said my aunt, quoting one of the less successful advertisements of Tono-Bungay.［H. G. Wells, *Tono-Bungay*］「年寄りが**最後の機会**で救われた」と叔母が言い，あまり成功しなかったインチキ売薬のトーノバンゲイの例を引用した。

At the eleventh hour Mr. Len Murray, the TUG General Secretary, ... managed to get the Amalgamated Union of Engineering Workers to withdraw its resolution against the social contract.［*The Guardian*, 1974］**最後の時**になってTUGの書記長，レン・マレー氏は技術者の合同組合にその売買契約に反対する決意を引っ込めさせた。

[他の英訳聖書]　KJVでは「十一時」とあって，それを忠実に踏襲しているのはNASである。多数の他の聖書は「午後五時」としている。NASでも，「午後五時」という注記があり，当時の時刻と現代の時刻の名称の違いである。《[注] 当時は12時間を朝の6時（または日の出）から夕方6時（または日没）までで数えたので，11時は現代の夕方5時ということになる。》

Finally, **about five in the afternoon**（午後五時ごろ）the man went back and found some others standing there. He asked them, "Why have you been standing here all day long doing nothing?" <CEV>／ And **about the eleventh hour**（十一時ごろ）he went out and found others standing around; and he said to them, 'Why have you been standing here idle all day long?' <NAS>

[enough]

enough and to spare 有り余っている →いやというほどたくさん

KJV And when he came to himself, he said, 'How many hired servants of my father's have bread **enough and to spare**, and I perish with hunger!' ［ルカの福音書 15:17］しかし，我に返ったとき彼は，こう言った。「父のところには，パンの**あり余っている**雇い人が大ぜいいるではないか。それなのに，私はここで，飢え死にしそうだ。」

［用例］ "We'll go on a picnic in the country.""OK, have you got enough food?""Surely we've got **enough and to spare**." ［¶］「郊外にピクニックに行きますよ。」「いいとも，十分食糧を持ったかい？」「もちろんだとも。**いやというほどいっぱい**ね。」

The Haight was hit hard by the Depression, as was much of the city. Residents with **enough money to spare** left the declining and crowded neighborhood for greener pastures within the growing city limits, or newer, smaller suburban homes in the Bay Area. ［Wikipedia, *Haight-Ashbury*］ヘイト地区は大恐慌でひどくやられた。町の多くも同様であった。**十分お金に余裕の**あった住人は下落していく人口増加の近隣を離れ，成長する郊外の緑豊かな牧草地に移るか，ベイエリアにある狭いが，新しい家に移っていった。

[他の英訳聖書] KJV の用法は辞書にはあるが，学者ぶった言い方で，現代語では enough to spare の方が多く（例文参照），NLT や CEV（類似表現）もそれを使っている。HCS は more than enough というありふれた語句を使っている。

Finally, he came to his senses and said, "My father's workers have **plenty to eat**（たくさんの食べ物）, and here I am, starving to death!" <CEV>／ When he finally came to his senses, he said to himself, 'At home even the hired servants have food **enough to spare**（有り余る）, and here I am dying of hunger!' <NLT>／ When he came to his senses, he said, 'How many of my father's hired hands have **more than enough**（有り余る）food, and here I am dying of hunger!' <HCS>

[enter]

enter into another's labor 他人の労苦の実を得る →他人の利益を手に入れる

KJV I sent you to reap that whereon ye bestowed no labor; other men labored, and ye have **entered into their labors**. [ヨハネの福音書4：38] わたしは，あなたがたに自分で労苦しなかったものを刈り取らせるために，あなたがたを遣わしました。ほかの人々が労苦して，あなたがたは**その労苦の実を得ている**のです。

[用例] Men, nations, poets, artisans, women, all have worked for him (=Shakespeare), and he **enters into their labors**. [Emerson, *Representative Men*] 男性たち，国家群，詩人たち，女性たち，すべてが彼（シェイクスピア）のために働き，彼は**その利益を手に入れて**いる。

[他の英訳聖書] KJVの比喩的表現をCEVとNLTは「労働」と「収穫」に分けて具体的に叙述している。HCSはKJV的ではあるが，動詞を変えて慣用語句を消している。

I am sending you to **harvest crops** in fields where **others have done all the hard work**. (他人があらゆる重労働をして作った収穫を得る) <CEV>／ I sent you to harvest where you didn't plant; **others had already done the work, and now you will get to gather the harvest**. (他人がすでに労働をなして，その収穫をあなたは得ようとする) <NLT>／ I sent you to reap what you didn't labor for; others have labored, and you have **benefited from their labor**. (他人の労働から利益を得た) <HCS>

[entertain]

entertain an angel unawares 御使いを知らずにもてなす →大切な人をそれとは知らずにもてなす

KJV Be not forgetful to entertain strangers, for thereby some have **entertained angels unawares**. [ヘブル人への手紙13：2] 旅人をもてなすことを忘れてはいけません。こうして，ある人々は**御使いたちを，それとは知らずにもてなし**ました。

[用例] You have made an old man very happy; and I may say, indeed, that I have **entertained an angel unawares**. [R. L. Stevenson, *Prince Otto*] あなたのおかげで一人の老人が大変幸せになりました。実際，**大切な人をそうとは知らずにもてなしていたケース**といったほうがいいかもしれないです。

[他の英訳聖書] 動詞と without 以下の語句の違いこそあれ，すべての英訳聖書は KJV の unawares のみを代えて踏襲している。

Be sure to welcome strangers into your home. By doing this, some people have **welcomed angels as guests, without even knowing it**. (知らずに御使いをもてなした) <CEV> ／ Don't forget to show hospitality to strangers, for some who have done this have **entertained angels without realizing it**! (知らずに御使いをもてなした) <NLT>

[アラム語慣用語句の意味] 聖句の前半部分の entertained angels のみ Lamsa (1985) は entertaining pious or holy men (敬虔な，あるいは聖なる人々をもてなす) としていて，unawares の部分が欠けているので，全体の比喩的意味が欠けてしまう。

[eye]

eye for eye and tooth for tooth 目には目，歯には歯を →同じ程度に報復する

KJV And if any misfortune follow, then thou shalt give life for life, **eye for eye, tooth for tooth**, hand for hand, foot for foot, burning for burning, wound for wound, stripe for stripe. [出エジプト記 21:23-25] しかし，殺傷事故があれば，いのちにはいのちを与えなければならない。**目には目。歯には歯。手には手。足には足。やけどにはやけど。傷には傷。打ち傷には打ち傷。**

《[注] 似たような表現に see eye to eye がある。文字通り訳せば，「目には目を物言わせる」となって，報復を暗示するようであるが，これはイザヤ書 52:8, Thy watchmen shall lift up the voice; with the voice together shall they sing: for they shall **see eye to eye**, when the LORD shall bring again Zion. (聞け。あなたの見張り人たちが，声を張り上げ，共に喜び歌っている。彼らは，主がシオンに帰られるのを，**まのあたりに見る**からだ。) にあって，報復の意味とはまったく異なる。》

[用例] Oh, I owe him so much. On only one condition can I hope to forgive him. It is, if I may take **an eye for an eye, a tooth for a tooth**; for every wrench of agony return a wrench: reduce him to my level. [E. Brontë, *Wuthering Heights*] ああ，彼には借りがたくさんある。たった一つだけ彼を許す条件があると思う。それは，「**目には目を，歯には歯を**」とやれれば，ということね。つまり，苦しみをねじりこまれればねじり返して，彼を私と同じレベルに下げてやる，ということよ。

I did not believe in the death penalty — **an eye for an eye** — but how else can we stop this sort of thing? [*Daily Mail*, 1974] 私は受けた**被害と同じ程度に報復する**ような，死刑のあり方を信じないが，ほかにどうしたらこの種の犯罪を止められるのか。

[**他の英訳聖書**] この慣用句は定型化していて，すべての英訳聖書に共通している。

But if she is seriously injured, the payment will be life for life, **eye for eye, tooth for tooth**, hand for hand, foot for foot, burn for burn, cut for cut, and bruise for bruise. <CEV>

Eye is evil 目が悪い →憎しみを持つ

KJV The light of the body is the eye: if therefore thine eye be single, thy whole body shall be full of light. But if **thine eye be evil**, thy whole body shall be full of darkness. If therefore the light that is in thee be darkness, how great is that darkness! [マタイの福音書 6:22-23] からだのあかりは目です。それで，もしあなたの目が健全なら，あなたの全身が明るいが，もし，**目が悪ければ**，あなたの全身が暗いでしょう。それなら，もしあなたのうちの光が暗ければ，その暗さはどんなでしょう。

[用例] No eye at all is better than an **evil eye**, dark master! [Dickens, *Christmas Carol*] **憎しみの目**ほど悪い目は全くありませんよ，闇の旦那！

When I gave my big police dog the **evil eye** like this he liked to collapse, went out and nearly got himself killed by the neighbour's pet poodle pooch. [Oakland Tribune, *Double Whammy*, 1941] うちの大

きな警察犬にこんなふうに**憎しみの目**を向けたら，犬はへなへなと座り込んで，表に出て行き，自ら進んで近所の愛玩犬のプードルに殺されそうになった。

[他の英訳聖書] KJV の evil を bad に代えた英訳聖書が圧倒的に多く，NKJV や ESV でさえも bad に代えている。

Your eyes are like a window for your body. When they are good, you have all the light you need. But when **your eyes are bad**（目が悪い），everything is dark. If the light inside you is dark, you surely are in the dark. <CEV>／The lamp of the body is the eye. If therefore your eye is good, your whole body will be full of light. But if **your eye is bad**（目が悪い），your whole body will be full of darkness. If therefore the light that is in you is darkness, how great is that darkness! <NKJV>

[ギリシャ語慣用語句の意味] HL によると，22 節の your eye is good は you are generous（気前がよい）の意であり，23 節の your eye is bad は you are stingy（けち）の意であるという。20 節から「天に宝を積む」という話が続いていたので，意味のつながりがあって，一応の納得が得られるが，22 節からは別の話が始まっているという説もある。

lift up eyes　目を上げる →見上げる

KJV I will **lift up mine eyes** unto the hills, from whence cometh my help.［詩篇 121:1］私は山に向かって**目を上げる**。私の助けは，どこから来るのだろうか。

用例 He (Tom) was just then close upon the roaring dam: but he presently turned, and, **lifting up his eyes**, saw the figure whose worn look and loneliness seemed to him a confirmation of his worst conjectures.［Eliot, *The Mill on the Floss*］彼（トム）はちょうどそのときとどろくダムの近くにいた。彼がすぐに振り向いて**見上げた**とき，目に入った人物のやつれた顔つきと寂しさによって，彼の最悪の推測が当たっていたように思えた。

[他の英訳聖書] KJV の lift up を一様に look (up) to に代えている以外はすべての英訳聖書で定型化されている。

I **look to the hills**!（山を見る）Where will I find help? <CEV>／I **look**

up to the mountains（山を見上げる）— does my help come from there? <NLT>

[ヘブル語慣用語句の意味]　WL はヘブル語の意味を look up toward（〜の方に見上げる）としている。これは典型的なヘブル語イデオムで，市河氏は「一体 "lift up" という expression が Hebrew 的否東洋的なので，古事記の「言挙げせぬ国」などいうのも Chamberlain は "lift up words" と訳しておる位である」と言っている。<I, p. 253>

F

[face]

the face of the earth 地の面 →地球上

KJV Of fowls also of the air by sevens, the male and the female; to keep seed alive upon **the face of all the earth**. [創世記7:3] また空の鳥の中からも雄と雌,七つがいずつを取りなさい。それはその種類が**全地の面**で生き残るためである。

[用例] I wish they would exterminate every cur of them (dogs) off **the face of the earth**. [Thackeray, *The Newcomes*] **地球上**から野良犬をすべてなくしてしまえばなあ。

The critical zone is the interface between the materials that comprise the planet and the biotic world, and it sustains life on **the face of the Earth**. [University of Delaware, *Critical Zone*, 2006] 臨界ゾーンとは地球を構成する物質と生物界の間の境界面で,**地球上**の生命を支えているものである。

[他の英訳聖書] KJVの慣用語句をほぼそのまま踏襲しているESV,HCSのような伝統的な英訳聖書もあるが,多くはCEVのように,faceを削っている。

Also take seven pairs of every kind of bird with you. Do this so there will always be animals and birds **on the earth**. (地上) <CEV>／And seven pairs, male and female, of the birds of the sky — in order to keep offspring alive on **the face of the whole earth**. (全地表) <HCS>

[ヘブル語慣用語句の意味] 市河氏<I>もこれをHebraism(ヘブル語法)としているが,すっかり英語化している。*LDOCE4*はin the world(世界中)の強調語法だとして,つぎの例を挙げている。

If she was the last woman on **the face of the earth**, I still wouldn't be interested! (彼女が世界中で最後の女性であっても,私は関心がないだろう)

[fall]

fall on stony ground　岩地に落ちる →無駄である/意に介しない

KJV Some **fell upon stony places** where they had not much earth; and forthwith they sprang up, because they had no deepness of earth. And when the sun was up they were scorched, and because they had no root they withered away.［マタイの福音書 13:5f］また，別の種が土の薄い**岩地に落ちた**。土が深くなかったので，すぐに芽を出した。しかし，日が上ると，焼けて，根がないために枯れてしまった。

[用例] He (my father) hated to see youngsters waste time. The seed of the lesson did not **fall on stony ground**. I grew more and more addicted to the organization of my time.［A. Bennett, *John O'London's Weekly*］父は若者が時間を浪費するのが嫌いだった。その教訓は**無駄**ではなかった。私は自分の時間を組織立てることにますます夢中になった。

This is the seed-corn **falling on stony ground**. But this defence, in its turn, brings back all the old charges of Ranterism — that a sin is no sin if the intentions are pure.［Wikipedia, *John Saddington*］これは穀物の粒が**無駄**になるケースである。しかし，この守りの姿勢は今度は原始メソジスト主義に対する古くからの非難を蒸し返すことになる。それは，意図が純粋なら罪は罪ではないというものである。

［他の英訳聖書］　KJV の比喩的意味を CEV も NLT も踏襲しているが，後者の英訳聖書はより描写的である。

Other seeds **fell on thin, rocky ground**（土の薄い岩地に落ちた）and quickly started growing because the soil wasn't very deep. But when the sun came up, the plants were scorched and dried up, because they did not have enough roots. <CEV> ／ Other seeds **fell on shallow soil with underlying rock**.（底が岩の薄い土地に落ちた）The seeds sprouted quickly because the soil was shallow. But the plants soon wilted under the hot sun, and since they didn't have deep roots, they died. <NLT>

fall among ～　～間に落ちる →～に遭遇する

KJV And Jesus answering said, A certain man went down from Jerusalem to Jericho, and **fell among thieves**, which stripped him of his raiment, and wounded him, and departed, leaving him half dead.［ルカの福音書10:30］イエスは答えて言われた。「ある人が，エルサレムからエリコへ下る道で，**強盗に襲われた**。強盗どもは，その人の着物をはぎとり，なぐりつけ，半殺しにして逃げて行った。」

[用例] Then came an even worse reflection; how if he had **fallen among material thieves as well as spiritual ones**? [Butler, *The Way of All Flesh*] それからもっと悪い想いさえ起こった。もし**泥棒に遭遇して**，物ばかりでなく，精神的なものまで取られてしまっていたらどうしただろうかと。

[他の英訳聖書] fall among という慣用語句を使った英訳聖書は ESV のような伝統を重んじるタイプの英訳聖書に見られるが，ごく少なく，HCS のように fall を使っても fall into the hands of 〜になったり，CEV や NLT のように現代風に attack を使ったりしている。

As a man was going down from Jerusalem to Jericho, **robbers attacked him**（強盗が彼を襲った）and grabbed everything he had. They beat him up and ran off, leaving him half dead. <CEV>／Jesus replied with a story: A Jewish man was traveling on a trip from Jerusalem to Jericho, and he **was attacked by bandits**.（追いはぎに襲われた）They stripped him of his clothes, beat him up, and left him half dead beside the road. <NLT>／A man was going down from Jerusalem to Jericho and **fell into the hands of robbers**.（強盗の手に落ちた）They stripped him, beat him up, and fled, leaving him half dead. <HCS>／A man was going down from Jerusalem to Jericho, and he **fell among robbers**, who stripped him and beat him and departed, leaving him half dead. <ESV>

[fat]

the fat of the land　地の最もよいもの →最高に贅沢なもの

KJV And take your father and your households, and come unto me; and I will give you the good of the land of Egypt, and ye shall eat **the fat of the land**.［創世記45:18］あなたがたの父と家族とを連れて，私のもとへ来なさい。私はあなたがたにエジプトの最良の地を与え，地

の最も良い物を食べさせる。

[用例] He did not seem to be refusing a little mutton and tart, but a gigantic host of dishes; waving away **the very fat of the land**. [J. B. Priestley, *The Good Companions*.] 彼は小さな羊肉やパイを拒んでいるようには思えなかったが，豪勢な料理は拒否した。すなわち，**最高の贅沢なものは遠ざけていた**。

How long was he going to put up with me living off **the fat of the land** in his kitchen, not pulling my weight with his other servants? [J. B. Hilton, *Gamekeeper's Gallows*, 1976] 私がほかの召使たちと共に自分の分を働かないで，キッチンの**最高の贅沢なもの**を食べて生活していることに，どれだけ彼は我慢できるだろうか。

[**他の英訳聖書**] KJVのfatには「肥沃」とか「丸々と太った，おいしそうなさま」の意味があり，この意味がNLTではthe bestとなって現れ，HCSではrichnessとなっている。他方，CEVではその意味は直接現れていないが，動詞enjoyが間接的に示している。

Have them bring their father and their families here. I will give them the best land in Egypt, and they can eat and **enjoy everything that grows on it**. (そこで育つすべてのものを楽しむ) <CEV> ／ Then get your father and all of your families, and return here to me. I will give you the very best land in Egypt, and you will eat from **the best that the land produces**. (土地が産出する最高なもの) <NLT> ／ Get your father and your households, and come back to me. I will give you the best of the land of Egypt, and you can eat from **the richness of the land**. (その地の豊かな産物) <HCS>

[fear]

fear and trembling 恐れおののいて →身を低くして

KJV Servants, be obedient to those who are your masters according to the flesh, with **fear and trembling**, in singleness of your heart, as unto Christ. [エペソ人への手紙6:5] 奴隷たちよ。あなたがたは，キリストに従うように，**恐れおののいて**真心から地上の主人に従いなさい。

[用例] Therefore I think that if my Lord — with **fear and trembling**

I say this — will cast off his hempen coat and scarf, ... [G. S. Sansom, *Translations from the "No"*] ですから，**身を低くして言う**のですが，主君が麻のコートとマフラーを脱ぎ捨てれば…と思うのです。

There is no way of making an aged art young again; it must be born anew and grow up from infancy as a new thing, working out its own salvation from effort to effort in all **fear and trembling**. [S. Butler, *Erewhon*] 古い芸術を再び若くするすべはない。それは新しく生まれ変わり，赤子から新しいものとして成長し，自身の保存を**身を低くして**努力を重ねて達成しなければならない。《[注] この用例は〈fear and trembling〉が〈working out its own salvation〉と結びついているので，[ピリピ人への手紙 2:12] からの出典と考えられる。》

[他の英訳聖書] CEV も NLT もかなり意訳している。特に CEV は KJV の fear を「畏敬」の「おそれ」と解釈し great respect と be loyal to の表現に代えている。

Slaves, you must obey your earthly masters. Show them a **great respect and be as loyal to them** (大きな尊敬を払い…忠誠になれ) as you are to Christ. <CEV>／ Slaves, obey your earthly masters with **deep respect and fear**. (深い尊敬の念と恐れ) Serve them sincerely as you would serve Christ. <NLT>

【fig】

leaves without figs いちじくの実を付かない枝 →成果のない空約束

KJV Then said he unto the dresser of his vineyard, Behold, these three years I come seeking **fruit on this fig tree, and find none**: cut it down; why cumbereth it the ground? [ルカの福音書 13:7] そこで，ぶどう園の番人に言った。「見なさい。三年もの間，やって来ては，このいちじくの実のなるのを待っているのに，なっていたためしがない。これを切り倒してしまいなさい。何のために土地をふさいでいるのですか。」

用例 A. "He has definitely promised to find me a job."

　B. "That's good; but you shouldn't rely too much on what he says.

He doesn't mean to deceive people, but he's so incurably lazy that most of his promises are **leaves without figs**." [Lyell, *Principles of Geology*] A. 「彼ははっきりと私に仕事を見つけてくれると約束してくれたのです。」B. 「それは結構だけど，彼の言うことにあまり頼ってはいけないと思うよ。彼は救いがたいほど怠け者で，彼の約束は大抵**成果をもたらさない空約束**だ。」

[他の英訳聖書] この慣用語句そのものはなく，文脈から派生したものである。そのため，KJV のパターンを保持しているか，それとも文脈から推測して自由なパターンを取るかに2分される。

So he said to the gardener, "For three years I have come looking for **figs on this tree, and I haven't found any yet**. (この木のいちじくを，しかしいまだに一つもなっていない) Chop it down! Why should it take up space?" <CEV>／ Finally, he said to his gardener, 'I've waited three years, and there hasn't been **a single fig**! (一つのいちじく) Cut it down. It's just taking up space in the garden.' <NLT>

【 fight 】

fight the good fight 立派な戦いをする →規範に従って懸命に生きる

KJV **Fight the good fight** of faith. Lay hold on eternal life, whereunto thou art also called and hast professed a good profession before many witnesses. [I テモテへの手紙 6:12] 信仰の戦いを**立派に戦い抜き**，永遠の命を手に入れなさい。命を得るために，あなたは神から召され，多くの証人の前で立派に信仰を表明したのです。(新共同訳)

[用例] A voice ... cries "Go forth, Charles Honeyman, **fight the good fight**: — [Thackeray, *The Newcomes*, p. 38] 声が起こる，「出て行け，チャールズ・ハニーマン，**懸命に生きよ**」。

She **fought the good fight**, she kept the faith, and though she knew the race for equality was not finished, she knew that the army of supporters she had hoped for long ago had become a reality that would carry and someday complete her vision. [University of Delaware, *Special Olympics*, 2009] 彼女は自分の信仰を守って**懸命に生きた**。平等へのレースはまだ終わっていないことを知っていたが，

はるか以前に望んでいた支持者の団体が現実となり，彼女の未来図を前進させ，いつの日か完成してくれるであろう。

[他の英訳聖書] 下記のように，すべての英訳聖書はKJVと同じか，類似の表現をしている。

Fight a good fight（勇敢に戦え）for the faith and claim eternal life. God offered it to you when you clearly told about your faith, while so many people listened. <CEV>／**Fight the good fight**（立派に戦え）for the true faith. Hold tightly to the eternal life to which God has called you, which you have confessed so well before many witnesses. <NLT>

[fire]

go through fire（and water） 火の中（水の中）をくぐる →最大の危険をおかす

KJV Thou hast caused men to ride over our heads; we **went through fire and through water**: but thou broughtest us out into a wealthy place. ［詩篇66:12］あなたは人々に，私たちの頭の上を乗り越えさせられました。私たちは，**火の中を通り，水の中を通りました**。しかし，あなたは豊かな所へ私たちを連れ出されました。

［用例］He used to say he would **go through fire** for his country, but I wonder how he would do it. ［¶］彼はよく国のためなら**最大の危険を冒す**と言っていたが，どのようにそれをするというのだろう。

The brothers understood each other perfectly and could **go through fire and water** for each other. However, their friendship was put to a difficult test, when one brother brought a beautiful girl from his war expedition. ［Wikipedia, *Bobolice Castle*］兄弟は相手を完璧に理解し，相手のためなら**最大の危険をも冒す**ことができた。しかし，一人が戦いの遠征先から一人の美しい娘を連れてきたとき，彼らの友情は難しい試練に直面した。

[他の英訳聖書] やや古いとはいえ，go through fire (and water) が現代英語に活きているので，多くの英訳聖書はKJVのこの語句を残している。ただ，water の代わりに flood (s) がかなり目立つ。

You sent war chariots to crush our skulls. We **traveled through fire and through floods**, but you brought us to a land of plenty. <CEV>／

Then you put a leader over us. We **went through fire and flood**, but you brought us to a place of great abundance. <NLT>／ You let men ride over our heads; we **went through fire and water**, but You brought us out to abundance. <HCS>

[flesh]

All flesh is grass　すべての人は草 →すべての生き物は朽ちてまた再生する

KJV The voice said, "Cry!" And he said, "What shall I cry?" "**All flesh is grass**, and all the goodliness thereof is as the flower of the field. The grass withereth, the flower fadeth, because the spirit of the LORD bloweth upon it; surely the people is grass.［イザヤ書 40:6f］「呼ばわれ」と言う者の声がする。私は,「何と呼ばわりましょう」と答えた。「**すべての人は草，その栄光は，みな野の花のようだ。主のいぶきがその上に吹くと，草は枯れ，花はしぼむ。まことに，民は草だ。**」

［用例］The animal eats the plant; and a new incarnation begins. **All flesh is grass**. The animal becomes part of another animal, and the reincarnation continues.［J. A. Thomson, *Introduction to Science*］動物は植物を食べ，そして新しい生命が始まる。**すべての生き物は朽ちて生まれ変わる**。動物は他の動物の一部になり，輪廻再生が続く。

But I, being fond of true philosophy, say very often to myself, "Alas! All things that have been born were born to die, and **flesh**（which Death mows down to hay）**is grass**."［Phrase Finder, *Mind in your Purse*］私は哲学が好きなので，よく自分に向かって「ああ，生まれたものはすべて死ぬために生まれたのだ。**すべての生きものは死が刈り取って干し草にするので，朽ちてまた再生するのだ**」と言う。

［他の英訳聖書］　KJV の最後の語句に the people が来ているように all flesh は「人間」を指している。そのため，CEV も NLT も「人間」を表す語句を使っていて正しいが，そうだとすると，例文の all flesh が活きてこない。英語に活きているのは flesh＝生き物のようである。 Someone told me to shout, and I asked, "What should I shout?" **We hu-**

mans are merely grass（われわれ人間は草に過ぎない）, and we last no longer than wild flowers. At the LORD's command, flowers and grass disappear, and so do we. <CEV>／ A voice said, "Shout!" I asked, "What should I shout?" "Shout that **people are like the grass**.（人は草のようだ）Their beauty fades as quickly as the flowers in a field. The grass withers and the flowers fade beneath the breath of the LORD. And so it is with people. <NLT>

[アラム語慣用語句の意味] Lamsa（1985）はアラム語慣用句では輪廻再生思想ではなく,「一時性」を表しているとして, Man's earthly life is temporal like grass（人の地上での生活は草のように一時的なもの）としている。ここでは, flesh を「人間」ととらえている。

flesh and blood 血と肉 →家族の一員

KJV Forasmuch then as the children are partakers of **flesh and blood**, he also himself likewise took part of the same; that through death he might destroy him that had the power of death, that is, the devil［ヘブル人への手紙2:14］そこで, 子たちはみな**血と肉**とを持っているので, 主もまた同じように, これらのものをお持ちになりました。これは, その死によって, 悪魔という, 死の力を持つ者を滅ぼし…

[用例] He treated his own **flesh and blood** in a way nobody expected him to do.［¶］彼は自分の**血肉を分けたもの**をだれも予想しないような方法で扱った。

[他の英訳聖書] flesh and blood は CEV, NLT, HCS の三者に共通しているが, 前後の語句の構成が異なって, 独自の構成になっている。なお, 慣用語句は聖書の他の箇所にも頻出するが, 旧約［創世記29:14, 士師記9:2など］では多くが bone and blood となっている。

We are people of **flesh and blood**. That is why Jesus became one of us. He died to destroy the devil, who had power over death. <CEV>／ Because God's children are human beings — made of **flesh and blood** — the Son also became flesh and blood. For only as a human being could he die, and only by dying could he break the power of the devil, who had the power of death. <NLT>／ Now since the children have **flesh**

and blood in common, He also shared in these, so that through His death He might destroy the one holding the power of death — that is, the Devil <HCS>

【 flood 】

before the flood　洪水の前に →大昔に

　KJV For as in the days that were **before the flood** they were eating and drinking, marrying and giving in marriage, until the day that Noah entered into the ark. [マタイの福音書 24:38] **洪水前の**日々は，ノアが箱舟にはいるその日まで，人々は，飲んだり，食べたり，めとったり，とついだりしていました。

　[用例] She appeared in black at the funeral in a dress that looked as if it had been made **before the flood**. [¶] 彼女は喪服を着て葬儀に現れたが，そのドレスは**大昔に**作ったような代物だった。

[他の英訳聖書]　比喩的意味を生かした英訳聖書はなく，原型を何らかの形で残している。

People were eating, drinking, and getting married right **up to the day that the flood came**（洪水が襲ってくる日まで）and Noah went into the big boat. <CEV>／**In those days before the flood**（洪水以前の時代に＝大昔に），the people were enjoying banquets and parties and weddings right up to the time Noah entered his boat. <NLT>

【 fly 】

a fly in the ointment　香油の中のはえ →（物事を）台無しにするもの

　KJV **Dead flies cause the ointment of the apothecary to send forth a stinking savor**; so doth a little folly in him that hath a reputation for wisdom and honor. [伝道者 10:1] **死んだはえは，調合した香油を臭くし，発酵させる。**少しの愚かさは，知恵や栄誉よりも重い。

　[用例] A Poor Relation — is the most irrelevant thing in nature, — a lion in your path, — a frog in your chamber, — **a fly in your ointment**. [Lamb, *Essays of Elia*, "Poor Relations."] 貧弱な関係とは本来最も関係ないこと，すなわち，あなたの行く道に現れるライオン，あなたの部屋に現れるカエル，あなたの**香油の中のはえ**など，

物事を台無しにするものである。

A: "I'm glad to hear you've got such a splendid job at last."

B: "It is good, isn't it? The only **fly in the ointment** is the distance I have to go to work every day. The journey will take a large part of my pay, but it can't be helped." [Lyell, *Principles of Geology*] A:「ついにそのような素晴らしい仕事に就いたそうでよかったですね。」B:「いいでしょう。ただ玉に瑕(きず)は毎日の通勤に要する時間です。その道のりが給料の大部分になります。でも仕方ないですね。」

The only **fly in the ointment** is the frosty estate manager, Miss Grose, who seems remote and unfriendly to the new arrival. [Wikipedia, *In a Dark Place*] 唯一**台無しにするもの**は白髪の農園管理者のグロースさんで，新入りによそよそしく冷たいように思える。

[他の英訳聖書] KJVを踏襲しているCEVは名詞句を温存しているが，NLTはそれを節にして，より口語体風にしている。

A few dead flies in perfume (香油の中の2，3匹のはえ) make all of it stink, and a little foolishness outweighs a lot of wisdom. <CEV>／As **dead flies cause even a bottle of perfume to stink** (死んだはえが香水びんを臭くする), so a little foolishness spoils great wisdom and honor. <NLT>

[fool]

suffer fools gladly 愚か者を喜んで耐え忍ぶ →愚か者を我慢する

KJV For ye **suffer fools gladly**, seeing ye yourselves are wise! [IIコリント人への手紙 11:19] あなたがたは賢いのに，よくも**喜んで愚か者たちをこらえています**。

[用例] She was a very strict lady who did not **suffer fools gladly**, but her sternness was mixed with love and grace. [¶] 彼女は厳しい女性で，**愚か者を我慢する**タイプではなかったが，彼女の厳しさには愛とめぐみが混じっていた。

Nimrod is an unethical scientist who does not **suffer fools gladly**. He is cruel and sadistic, as seen in his treatment of the Huldan alien creature and of the Doctor clones he created during Project: Lazarus.

[Wikipedia, *Nimrod*] ニムロドは**愚か者には我慢**ができない非倫理的な科学者で，彼自身がプロジェクト・ラザロの上演中に創造したハルダからの地球外動物やドクター・クローンの取り扱いを見て分かるとおり，残酷でサデスティックである。《[注] Nimrod は英国科学小説のテレビシリーズ，Doctor Who のプロジェクト・トワイライトとプロジェクト・ラザロに登場する人物。》

[**他の英訳聖書**]　CEV も NLT も KJV の suffer に代えてより口語的な put up with を使っている。

And since you are so smart, you will **gladly put up with a fool**. (喜んで愚か者を我慢する) <CEV>／After all, you think you are so wise, but you **enjoy putting up with fools**! <NLT>

[foot]

feet of clay　土の足 →大きな弱点

KJV Thou, O king, sawest; and behold, a great image! This great image, whose brightness was excellent, stood before thee; and the form thereof was terrible. This image's head was of fine gold, his breast and his arms of silver, his belly and his thighs of brass, his legs of iron, his feet part of iron and **part of clay**.［ダニエル書2:31-33］王さま。あなたは一つの大きな像をご覧になりました。見よ。その像は巨大で，その輝きは常ならず，それがあなたの前に立っていました。その姿は恐ろしいものでした。それは頭が純金，胸と腕が銀，腹と腿が青銅，すねは鉄，足は一部が鉄，**一部が粘土**でした。

[用例] Nowadays everybody knows that it is crystal clear that no politician can exist without **feet of clay**.［¶］今では，どんな政治家も**かなりうさんくさいところがある**ことは明白であることをみな知っている。

To find that somebody has **feet of clay** means to realize that the person is phony or at least fallible. The phrase originated with the idea of looking at a statue made of something wonderful, let's say gold, and then seeing with disappointment that the statue's feet were mere clay.［Phrase Finder, *Feet of Clay*］だれかが**土の足**を持っているのが分かるということはその人が偽者であるか，あるいは少なく

とも間違った人間であることを知ることである。この慣用語句はもともと,素晴らしい材料で,たとえば金で,創られた像を見ていて,実はその足がただの土であることが分かって,失望するという発想から生じた。《[注] この例文は現代の英語話者が feet of clay をどのように解釈しているかを示すもの。》

[他の英訳聖書] KJV では be 動詞の省略という空所化が行われているが,CEV も NLT も空所化なしで,iron と clay の併記の説明(mixture と combination)を加えている。

Your Majesty, what you saw standing in front of you was a huge and terrifying statue, shining brightly. Its head was made of gold, its chest and arms were silver, and from its waist down to its knees, it was bronze. From there to its ankles it was iron, and **its feet were a mixture of iron and clay**. (その足は鉄と粘土の混じったものでした) <CEV>／
In your vision, Your Majesty, you saw standing before you a huge, shining statue of a man. It was a frightening sight. The head of the statue was made of fine gold. Its chest and arms were silver, its belly and thighs were bronze, its legs were iron, and **its feet were a combination of iron and baked clay**. (その足は鉄とれんがの混じったものでした) <NLT>

[fullness]

the fullness　それに満ちているもの →すべてそこにあるもの

KJV The earth is the LORD'S, and **the fullness** thereof, the world and they that dwell therein. [詩篇 24:1] 地とそれに満ちているもの,世界とその中に住むものは主のものである。《[注] fullness にこの意味を担わすのはヘブル語法である。<I>》

[用例] John began to speak of his good fortune. "The earth and all **its fullness** are given into my hands," he exclaimed. "My crops are growing and ripening...." [T. F. Powys, *John Told and the Worm*] ジョンは彼の幸運について話し始めた。「この地とそこにあるすべてのものが手中にある」と彼は叫んだ。「作物は生長し,実り始めているのだ。」

[他の英訳聖書]　KJV の抽象的な表現を CEV と NLT は具象的な表現

The earth and **everything on it** (そこにあるすべてのもの) belong to the LORD. The world and its people belong to him. <CEV>／ The earth is the LORD's, and **everything in it**. The world and all its people belong to him. <NLT>

the fullness of time　定めの時　→定刻

KJV But when **the fullness of the time** had come, God sent forth His Son, made of a woman, made under the law, to redeem those who were under the law, that we might receive the adoption of sons. ［ガラテヤ人への手紙 4:4f］しかし**定めの時**が来たので，神はご自分の御子を遣わし，この方を，女から生まれた者，また律法の下にある者となさいました。これは律法の下にある者を贖い出すためで，その結果，私たちが子としての身分を受けるようになるためです。

［用例］It was a cold evening, and Reggie wandered in and out of his bed-room, in a state of betwixt and between, now clad only in a bath towel, later on in a pair of trousers and socks, in **the fullness of time** completely clothed. ［E. F. Benson, *The Babe, B. A.*］寒い朝であった。レギーは寝室からぶらぶらと出たり入ったりしていた。心ここにあらずで，今バスタオルだけを着ていたと思えば，あとでズボンとソックスをはいていたりしていて，やがて**決まった時間**にはきちっと身支度をしていた。

Players with the more severe chondral defects will probably progress to osteoarthritis in **the fullness of time**. ［University of Delaware, *Footballer's Hip*, 2005］もっと深刻な軟骨障害をもつ競技者は**決まった時**が来ると，たぶん骨関節炎に進展する。

［他の英訳聖書］先の fullness とは違い，時が満ちて事が始まることを意味し，HCS はそれを completion で表している。そのニュアンスを CEV と NLT は現代英語風に口語体で表している。

But when **the completion of the time came** (時間が満ちた), God sent His Son, born of a woman, born under the law. <HCS>／ But when **the time was right** (時が定まった), God sent his Son, and a woman gave birth to him. His Son obeyed the Law, so he could set us free from the Law, and we could become God's children. <CEV>／ But when **the right time came**（定まった時が来た）, God sent his Son, born of a woman, subject to the law. God sent him to buy freedom for us who were slaves to the law, so that he could adopt us as his very own children. <NLT>

G

[gall]

gall and wormwood 胆汁とニガヨモギ →苦い経験

KJV And I said, "My strength and my hope are perished from the LORD," remembering mine affliction and my misery, **the wormwood and the gall**.［哀歌3：18f］私は言った。「私の誉れと，主から受けた望みは消えうせた」と。私の悩みとさすらいの思い出は，**苦よもぎと苦味**だけ。

[用例] The memories of traveling to Europe were nothing but **gall and wormwood** to me, because all my belongings were stolen as soon as I got to the destination.［¶］ヨーロッパ旅行の思い出は私にとって**苦い経験**に過ぎません。なぜなら，目的地に着くや否や私の身の回りのものすべて盗まれてしまったからです。

In his diary, Chase wrote that the release of Mason and Slidell "... was like **gall and wormwood** to me. But we cannot afford delays while the matter hangs in uncertainty, the public mind will remain disquieted, our commerce will suffer serious harm...."［Wikipedia, *Trent Affair*］自分の日記に，チェイスは「メイソンとスライデルの解放は自分にとって**苦々しいこと**だったが，事態が不確かな状態にあるときに，遅らす余裕はない。なぜなら，民衆は不安な状態に置かれ，通商が深刻な打撃を受けることになるからだ」と書いている。

[**他の英訳聖書**] KJV の比喩的表現は完全に意訳され，CEV では miserable と形容詞1語に，NLT では bitter beyond words とフレーズ化されている。意訳化の大勢の中で HCS は wormwood を残し，gall を poison に代えて KJV を継承している。

I tell myself, "I am finished! I can't count on the LORD to do anything for me," just thinking of my troubles and my lonely wandering makes me **miserable**. (惨めに) <CEV>／ I cry out, "My splendor is gone! Everything I had hoped for from the LORD is lost!" The thought of my suffering and homelessness is **bitter beyond words**. (言語を絶するほどむごい) <NLT>／ Then I thought: My future is lost, as well as my hope from the LORD. Remember my affliction and my homelessness, **the wormwood and the poison**. (ニガヨモギと毒) <HCS>

[gather]

gathered to one's fathers　先祖のもとに集められた →先祖と一緒に埋葬された

 KJV And also all that generation were **gathered unto their fathers**, and there arose another generation after them who knew not the LORD nor yet the works which He had done for Israel. [士師記2:10] その同世代の者もみな，**その先祖のもとに集められた**が，彼らのあとに，主を知らず，また，主がイスラエルのためにされたわざも知らないほかの世代が起こった。

[用例] He died and **was gathered to his fathers** without our ever having thought about him at all. [Gaskell, *Cranford*] 彼は死んで**先祖とともに埋葬された**が，われわれは彼のことは以後全然思い出さなかった。

Sir Walter was struck down by paralysis, and after lingering a few months, was **gathered to his fathers**. [*Southport American*, 1843] ウォルター卿は中風で倒れ，数か月病床にあって，**亡くなり先祖のもとに埋葬された**。

[他の英訳聖書]　CEVもNLTもともにdieを使って，簡略化している。

After a while **the people of Joshua's generation died** (ヨシュアの時代の人々は死んだ), and the next generation did not know the LORD or any of the things he had done for Israel. <CEV>／ After **that generation died** (その世代は死んだ), another generation grew up who did not acknowledge the LORD or remember the mighty things he had done for Israel. <NLT>

[ghost]

give up the ghost 霊をあきらめる →死ぬ

KJV Then Abraham **gave up the ghost** and died in a good old age, an old man and full of years, and was gathered to his people.〔創世記 25: 8〕アブラハムは平安な老年を迎え，長寿を全うして**息絶えて死に**，自分の民に加えられた。

用例 Why, not even a woman now! Nothing but a kind of animalized victim! And then the supreme endless spasm, during which she **gave up the ghost** and bade good-bye to her very self.〔A. Bennett, *Old Wives' Tale*〕今は女性だって駄目なのだ。まあ野獣化した犠牲者以外は駄目だ。そうすれば終局の終わりなき発作が残り，そこで彼女は**死んで**己れ自身にさよならを言うのさ。

He explained, "I am going to **give up the ghost** of my alter-ego, Zebulon Dread, and depart for India in order to find the happiness that the liberation struggle failed to deliver".〔Wikipedia, *Zebulon Dread*〕彼は「もう一人の自分であるゼブロン・ドレッドは**死ぬ**。そして私はインドに向かい，解放闘争がもたらさなかった幸福を見つけるのだ」と説明した。

[他の英訳聖書] KJV の慣用句は平凡な現代語（died）に意訳されている。むしろ，そのあとに来る修飾語句に変化があって面白い。

Abraham **died**（死んだ）at the ripe old age of one hundred seventy-five. <CEV>／ And he **died** at a ripe old age, having lived a long and satisfying life. He breathed his last and joined his ancestors in death. <NLT>

[glass]

see as in/through a glass darkly ぼんやり映るものを見る → ぼんやりと見る

KJV For now we **see through a glass, darkly**, but then face to face. Now I know in part; but then shall I know, even as also I am known.〔I コリント人への手紙 13:12〕今，私たちは**鏡にぼんやり映るものを見ています**が，その時には顔と顔とを合わせて見ることになります。今，私は一部分しか知りませんが，その時には，私が完全に知られているのと同じように，私も完全に知ることになります。

[用例] Mr. Meek would **see himself, through in a glass darkly**, inviting her to stay and rest with him upon the hay. [T. F. Powys, *Mr. Weston's Good Wine*] ミーク氏は自分が彼女を招いて自分と一緒に干し草の上にいて安らいでいる光景をよく**幻のように見た**ものだった。

When I read this, I by no means understand what is meant, — at least I only half **see** the drift of it **through a glass darkly**. [Letters from B. H. Chamberlain to L. Hearn] これを読んだとき，私はその意味がまったく分かりませんでした。少なくともその趣旨が**ぼんやりと**半分ほど**分かった**とだけは言えます。

[他の英訳聖書]　KJV の古風な表現は CEV も NLT も明確な現代語に意訳されている。cloudy の修飾先が違っていて，強調の違いが出ている。

Now all we can **see** of God is **like a cloudy picture in a mirror**.（鏡に映るぼんやりとした絵のように見る）Later we will see him face to face. We don't know everything, but then we will, just as God completely understands us. <CEV>／Now we **see things imperfectly as in a cloudy mirror**（濁った鏡の中のように物事を見る）, but then we will see everything with perfect clarity. All that I know now is partial and incomplete, but then I will know everything completely, just as God now knows me completely. <NLT>

[glory]

in all its glory　栄華を極めて → (人が) 得意満面で，(ものが) 今を盛りに

KJV And yet I say unto you, that even Solomon **in all his glory** was not arrayed like one of these. [マタイの福音書 6:29] しかし，わたしはあなたがたに言います。**栄華を窮めた**ソロモンでさえ，このような花の一つほどにも着飾ってはいませんでした。

[用例] The morning star emerged from behind the clouds **in all its glory**. [¶] 明けの明星が**今を盛りの壮大さを示して**雲の背後から出てきた。

At this time of the year you can see a full moon **in all its glory**.

[¶] 毎年今頃この上ない見事な満月が見られる。

I am interested in the almost morbid or garish association of something alive displayed **in all its anatomical glory** under/between glass. [Phrase Finder, *Under Glass*] 私はガラスの下か，あるいはその間で**今を盛りに解剖上の輝き**をもって見せてくれる生き物の部分がほとんど病的に，あるいはどぎつく関係していることに興味を持っている。

[他の英訳聖書] NLT のように KJV の語彙の羅列を保つ英訳聖書が多いが，名詞は CEV のように wealth を使うものや，HCS のように splendor を使うものもあって，様々である。

But I tell you that Solomon **with all his wealth**（あらゆる富を持った）wasn't as well clothed as one of them. <CEV>／Yet Solomon **in all his glory** was not dressed as beautifully as they are. <NLT>／Yet I tell you that not even Solomon **in all his splendor**（豪華を極めた）was adorned like one of these! <HCS>

[go]

go the way of all flesh すべての人の行く道を行く →死ぬ

KJV And behold, this day I am **going the way of all the earth**. And ye know in all your hearts and in all your souls that not one thing hath failed of all the good things which the LORD your God spoke concerning you: all have come to pass unto you, and not one thing hath failed thereof. [ヨシュア記 23:14] 見よ。きょう，私は**世のすべての人の行く道を行こう**としている。あなたがたは，心を尽くし，精神を尽くして知らなければならない。あなたがたの神，主が，あなたがたについて約束したすべての良いことが一つもたがわなかったことを。それは，一つもたがわず，みな，あなたがたのために実現した。《[注] flesh のところで解説したように，all flesh はヘブル語法で「すべての生きもの」の意味である。市河 <I> に出てくる KJV では，標題の all flesh を守っているが，現存の KJV や 21 世紀版の 21KJV も all the earth になっている。》

[用例] The first stranger handed his neighbor the family mug — a huge vessel of brown ware, having its upper edge worn away like a

goat　　　　　　　　　　　　　　72

threshold by the rub of whole generations of thirsty lips that had **gone the way of all flesh**. [T. Hardy, *The Three Strangers*] 最初の外から来た人はその隣人に家族で使っていたマグを手渡した。それは褐色の大きな容器で，上の部分がすり減った敷居のように，先に**亡くなった**すべての人々の渇いた唇によってすり減らされてあった。

[**他の英訳聖書**]　NLTのほうがKJVに近く，最後の語句が現代風になっているだけである。しかし，CEVの人間扱いと比較すると，興味がある。

I will soon die, **as everyone must**. (すべての人がそうならざるを得ないように) But deep in your hearts you know that the LORD has kept every promise he ever made to you. Not one of them has been broken. <CEV>／Soon I will die, **going the way of everything on earth**. (地上のすべてのものの成り行きのように) Deep in your hearts you know that every promise of the LORD your God has come true. Not a single one has failed! <NLT>

【 goat 】

offer a goat for ～　いけにえとして捧げる →他人の罪のために身代わりとなる

　KJV And Aaron shall **bring the goat** upon which the LORD's lot fell, and **offer him for a sin offering**. But the goat, on which the lot fell to be the scapegoat, shall be presented alive before the LORD, to make an atonement with him, and to let him go for a scapegoat into the wilderness. [レビ記 16:9f] アロンは，主のくじに当たった**やぎをささげて，それを罪のためのいけにえとする**。アザゼルのためのくじが当たったやぎは，主の前に生きたままで立たせておかなければならない。これは，それによって贖いをするために，アザゼルとして荒野に放つためである。《[注] ユダヤ教の「あがないの日」に祭司長が象徴的に人の罪を子ヤギの上に積み重ね，それを逃がすという祭祀を行う。そのことから **scapegoat**（身代わり）という語が生れた。根拠になった聖書箇所は上記のレビ記 16:9 と 12:6 があるが，scapegoat があがないの対象を goat（ヤギ）としているので，レビ記 16:9 を採った。》

[用例] "Let Clara open the door," said he (=Mr. Huddlestone). "So, if they fire a volley, he will be protected. And in the meantime stand behind me. I am the **scapegoat**; my sins have found me out."[Stevenson, *New Arabian Nights*]「クラーラに戸をあけさせなさい」とハドルストン氏は言った。「そうすれば, 彼らが一斉射撃をしても, 彼は逃れられる。その間に, 私の背後に隠れなさい。罪が明らかにされたからには, 私は**身代わりだ**。」

Goats are also **offered** to Babaji **as a gesture for his love**. Goats are not slaughtered though; rather they are being fed and taken care of.[Wikipedia, *Baba Balak Nath*] ヤギはまたババジに**その愛のためのジェスチャーとして捧げられる**。しかし, 殺されるのではなく, むしろ育てられ面倒を見てもらえているのである。

[他の英訳聖書] 語順は違っても, 各英訳聖書は同じような語彙を使っていて, 大差ない。

After you **offer the first goat as a sacrifice for sin**(最初のヤギを罪の犠牲として捧げる), the other one must be presented to me alive, before you send it into the desert to take away the sins of the people. <CEV>／Aaron will then **present as a sin offering the goat**(罪の償いとしてヤギを捧げる) chosen by lot for the LORD. The other goat, the scapegoat chosen by lot to be sent away, will be kept alive, standing before the LORD. When it is sent away to Azazel in the wilderness, the people will be purified and made right with the LORD. <NLT>

[good]

good for nothing 役に立たない →ろくでなし

KJV Ye are the salt of the earth: but if the salt have lost his savour, wherewith shall it be salted? it is thenceforth **good for nothing**, but to be cast out, and to be trodden under foot of men.[マタイの福音書5:13] あなたがたは, 地の塩です。もし塩が塩けをなくしたら, 何によって塩けをつけるのでしょう。もう**何の役にも立たず**, 外に捨てられて, 人々に踏みつけられるだけです。

[用例] His natural instinct, like that of all very young men who are **good for nothing**, was to do as those in authority told him.[Butler,

The Way of All Flesh] 彼の持って生まれた本能は，**ろくでなしの若年者**の場合と同じで，上に立つ人の命じるままにやることであった。

Ashok is a **good-for-nothing** youth whose only aim is to enjoy life by drinking and dancing the night away with his friends. [Wikipedia, *Atputham*] アショクは**ろくでなし**の若者で，その唯一の目的は友達とともに，夜中に酒を飲み踊り明かして人生を楽しむだけである。

[他の英訳聖書] good for nothing は現代英語でも頻繁に使われているにもかかわらず，下記3つの特異の訳を示す英訳聖書では使われていない。伝統的な英訳聖書（HCS，ASV，NIV など）でも KJV のパターンを踏襲していない。恐らく，否定語が先に来るという現代英語の特徴を出したのであろう。

You are like salt for everyone on earth. But if salt no longer tastes like salt, how can it make food salty? **All it is good for** (役に立つことと言えばただ) is to be thrown out and walked on. <CEV>／ You are the salt of the earth. But what good is salt if it has lost its flavor? Can you make it salty again? It will be thrown out and trampled underfoot as **worthless**. (価値のないもの) <NLT>／ You are the salt of the earth. But if the salt should lose its taste, how can it be made salty? It's **no longer good for anything** (もはや何の役に立たない) but to be thrown out and trampled on by men. <HCS>

[grace]

fall from grace 恵みから外れる →上司の不興を買う，影響力を失う

KJV Christ is become of no effect unto you, whosoever of you are justified by the law; ye are **fallen from grace**. [ガラテヤ人への手紙 5:4] 律法によって義と認められようとしているあなたがたは，キリストから離れ，**恵みから落ちて**しまったのです。

[用例] He **fell from grace** for the first time when he made a blunder on management. [¶] 彼は経営上の大ミスを犯して，初めて**上司の不興を買った**。

If you are a sycophant to a particular person in power, when they **fall from grace**, you will be seen as part of their clique and be out of favour. [Phrase Finder, *Suckers*] もしもあなたがおべっか使いで，特定の権力者におべっかを使っていると，その権力者が**影響力を失う**と，あなたも派閥の一員とみなされて恩恵から外されるだろう。

[他の英訳聖書] HCS のように全く KJV に忠実なものもあるが，説明的語句を添えて意味を明確にしている NLT もある。CEV にいたっては，キリストと恵みを一つの対象にしてまとめている。

And if you try to please God by obeying the Law, you have **cut yourself off from Christ and his wonderful kindness**. (キリストとその素晴らしい恵みから自らを断ち切る) <CEV>／For if you are trying to make yourselves right with God by keeping the law, you have been cut off from Christ! You have **fallen away from God's grace**. (神の恵みから外れる) <NLT>／You who are trying to be justified by the law are alienated from Christ; you have **fallen from grace**! <HCS>

[grind]

grind the faces of ～　顔をすりつぶす →こき使う

KJV "What mean ye that ye beat My people to pieces and **grind the faces of** the poor?" saith the Lord GOD of hosts. [イザヤ書 3:15] なぜ，あなたがたは，わが民を砕き，貧しい者の**顔をすりつぶす**のか。―万軍の神，主の御告げ。《[注] face はヘブル語法で「人」を表し，grind は「残酷に苦しめる」を意味する。<I>》

用例 The industrious millionaire makes his money, not by **grinding the faces of** the poor, but by affording to the poor the best possible market for their labor. [*The Literary World*, 1892 (Stoffel)] その勤勉な百万長者は貧しい者を**こき使う**方法ではなく，彼らにその労働にとって最適と思われる市場(しじょう)を与えることによって，金をもうけている。

[他の英訳聖書] どこに「すりつぶす」かが CEV と NLT には明示されている。他は動詞の違いこそあれ，KJV を踏襲している。

The LORD All-Powerful says, "You have crushed my people and **rubbed in the dirt the faces of** (顔を泥の中にすりつぶす) the poor."

<CEV>／ "How dare you crush my people, **grinding the faces of** the poor **into the dust**?" demands the Lord, the LORD of Heaven's Armies. <NLT>

[ground]

down to the ground　その場で →完全に

KJV And the children of Benjamin came forth out of Gibeah, and destroyed **down to the ground** of the Israelites that day twenty and two thousand men.［士師記 20:21］ベニヤミン族はギブアから出て来て，その日，イスラエル人二万二千人を**その場で**殺した。

〔用例〕"If you had (asked me) I should have said "Yes", and you would have married a woman who loved 'ee!" "Really!" "**Down to the ground**!" she whispered vehemently. [Hardy, *Tess*]「私に尋ねていたら，「はい」と答えていたでしょう。そしてあなたはあなたを愛していた女性と結婚していたでしょう。」「やはりね」「まさしくそうですよ」と彼女は激しくささやいた。

The album's success was largely based on the second single released from the album, "Shake Your Body (**Down to the Ground**)", which became a Top 10 single in the spring of 1979. [Wikipedia, *Destiny (The Jacksons Album)*] そのアルバムの成功の基は主にそのアルバムからリリースされた第二のシングル盤の「Shake Your Body (Down to the Ground)(**徹底的に**)体を震わせよ」にあった。それは 1979 年の春のトップテンに入った。

[他の英訳聖書] KJV の慣用語句は動作の終点を表しているが，日本語訳では単なる「場所」になっている。この「場所」解釈が他の英訳聖書すべてに現れている。唯一 ESV ではその「場所」語句が省かれている。

Benjamin's soldiers came out of Gibeah and attacked, and when the day was over, twenty-two thousand Israelite soldiers lay dead **on the ground**.（地面に）<CEV>／ Then they advanced toward Gibeah to attack the men of Benjamin. But Benjamin's warriors, who were defending the town, came out and killed 22,000 Israelites **on the battlefield**（その戦場で）that day. <NLT>／ The people of Benjamin came out of

Gibeah and destroyed on that day 22,000 men of the Israelites. <ESV>

[gulf]

a great gulf fixed 大きな淵 →とてつもない隔たり

KJV And beside all this, between us and you there is **a great gulf fixed**: so that they which would pass from hence to you cannot; neither can they pass to us, that would come from thence. ［ルカの福音書 16：26］そればかりでなく，私たちとおまえたちの間には，**大きな淵**があります。ここからそちらへ渡ろうとしても，渡れないし，そこからこちらへ越えて来ることもできないのです。

> 用例 ... and, as it turned out, that his attainments in English were exactly of the same extent as hers in the Malay, there seemed to be **an impassable gulf fixed** between all communications of ideas, if either party had happened to possess any. ［De Quincey, *Confessions of an English Opium-Eater*］のちに分かったことであるが，彼の英語への造詣はマレー半島の彼女とまったく同程度だったので，どちらにも思想と呼べるものがあったとしても，すべての伝達方法には**とてつもない隔たり**があるように見えた。

[他の英訳聖書] ほとんどの英訳聖書は ditch（溝）か chasm（割れ目）を使っている。興味あることは，ASV と ESV で gulf と chasm が分かれていることである。米語と英語の**溝**なのかもしれない。

And besides, there is **a deep ditch**（深い溝）between us, and no one from either side can cross over. <CEV>／ And besides, there is **a great chasm**（大きな割れ目）separating us. No one can cross over to you from here, and no one can cross over to us from there. <NLT>／ And besides all this, between us and you there is **a great gulf fixed**, that they that would pass from hence to you may not be able, and that none may cross over from thence to us. <ASV>／ And besides all this, between us and you **a great chasm** has been fixed, in order that those who would pass from here to you may not be able, and none may cross from there to us. <ESV>

H

[hair]

Hairs of one's head are all numbered　髪の毛もみな数えられている →神の深い愛顧を受けている

KJV But **the very hairs of your head are all numbered**. Fear ye not therefore, ye are of more value than many sparrows.［マタイの福音書 10:30f］また，**あなたがたの頭の毛さえも，みな数えられています**。だから恐れることはありません。あなたがたは，たくさんの雀よりもすぐれた者です。

[用例] "... It's Christmas Eve, boy. Be good to me, ... Maybe **the hairs of my head were numbered**," she went on with a sudden serious sweetness, "but nobody could even count my love for you ..." [*Eng. Short Stories*]「ねークリスマスイブだよ。私に親切にしておくれ。私は**髪の毛が数えられているほど神の深い愛顧を受けていた**のだけれど」と彼女は急に本気に優しくなって，「けれどね，だれもお前にたいする私の愛を数えることはできないと思うよ」と続けて言った。

[他の英訳聖書]「数える」の意味の動詞 count と number の違いこそあれ，すべて KJV のパターンを踏襲して比喩的に使われている。比喩そのものの解釈が厄介なため，そのまま残したものと思われる。

Even the hairs on your head are counted. So don't be afraid! You are worth much more than many sparrows. <CEV>／ And **the very hairs on your head are all numbered**. So don't be afraid; you are more valuable to God than a whole flock of sparrows. <NLT>

[halt]

halt between two opinions　どっちつかずにいる →疑っている

KJV And Elijah came unto all the people and said, "How long **halt ye between two opinions**? If the LORD be God, follow Him; but if Baal, then follow him." And the people answered him not a word. [I 列王記 18:21] エリヤはみなの前に進み出て言った。「あなたがたは，いつまでどっちつかずによろめいているのか。もし，主が神であれば，それに従い，もし，バアルが神であれば，それに従え。」しかし，民は一言も彼に答えなかった。

[用例] Never do I remember to have **halted more between two opinions** than on my journey to Battersby upon this unhappy errand. [Butler, *The Way of All Flesh*] 私が覚えている限り，この不幸な使いでバターズビーに行く途中でほどどっちつかずで迷ったことはない。

[**他の英訳聖書**] KJV の慣用句を CEV は現代風に意訳し，NLT にいたっては感情の描写が生き生きとしている。

Elijah stood in front of them and said, "How much longer will you try to **have things both ways**? (二股かけて物事をやる) If the LORD is God, worship him! But if Baal is God, worship him!" The people did not say a word. <CEV> ／ Then Elijah stood in front of them and said, "How much longer will you **waver, hobbling between two opinions**? (迷って二つの意見の間をふらふらしている) If the LORD is God, follow him! But if Baal is God, then follow him!" But the people were completely silent. <NLT>

[hand]

take somebody by the hand　手を引く → (注意深く) 手をとる

KJV Not according to the covenant that I made with their fathers in the day when I **took them by the hand** to lead them out of the land of Egypt; because they continued not in my covenant, and I regarded them not, saith the Lord. [ヘブル人への手紙 8:9] それは，わたしが**彼らの父祖たちの手を引いて**，彼らをエジプトの地から導き出した日に彼らと結んだ契約のようなものではない。彼らがわたしの契約を守り通さないので，わたしも，彼らを顧みなかったと，主は言われる。

[用例] I **took her by the hand** and stepped into the dark house, but nobody was there, only a cat. [¶] 私は**彼女の手を注意深く取って**暗い家の中に入っていったが，一匹の猫以外はだれも居なかった。

[他の英訳聖書] すべての英訳聖書は KJV を踏襲している。ただし、ギリシャ語原典のニュアンスを生かしているのはない。文脈依存で OK としているのかもしれない。

It won't be like the agreement that I made with their ancestors, when I **took them by the hand** and led them out of Egypt. They broke their agreement with me, and I stopped caring about them! <CEV>

[ギリシャ語慣用語句の意味] HL はこの語句を carefully guide 〜（用心深く案内する）としている。確かに、このニュアンスは文脈で読み取れるが、現代英語ではこの意味はない <LDOCE4>。

wash one's hands of ... …の手を洗う →…の責任を拒否する

KJV When Pilate saw that he could not prevail, but rather that a tumult was beginning, he took water and **washed his hands** before the multitude, saying, "I am innocent of the blood of this just person. See ye to it." ［マタイの福音書 27:24］そこでピラトは、自分では手の下しようがなく、かえって暴動になりそうなのを見て、群衆の目の前で水を取り寄せ、**手を洗って**、言った。「この人の血について、私には責任がない。自分たちで始末するがよい。」

［用例］ "If, of course, you're going to regard every suggestion I make as a criticism," he said..."then I **wash my hands of** the whole matter." ［Angus Wilson, *Anglo-Saxon Attitudes*］もちろんあなたが私のすべての提案を批判ととるつもりなら、私はこの事柄についてまったく**責任を取りません**。

A related saying is "sometimes you have to get your hands dirty," meaning detachment from difficult situations is not always possible. There is also the saying that someone "has blood on their hands", implicating or accusing a person of being an enabler or passive participant in wrongdoing, and that a person "**washes one's hands of**" something, meaning a person disavows responsibility for something. ［Wikipedia, *Dirty Hands*］関係した諺に「時には手を汚さなければならない」というのがある。困難な状況から完全に逃れることはいつも可能というわけではないという意味である。また、「手に血をつけている」というものがある。だれかが悪行の能動的または受動

的加担者であると示唆し，非難するとき使う。また，「**あることの手を洗う**」というのがあり，責任を否認する場合に使う。

[**他の英訳聖書**]　すべての英訳聖書は KJV を踏襲している。易しい比喩表現であるからであろう。ただ，CEV はすぐこのあとで，同じ内容の won't have anything to do with ～ を導入している点，興味がある。

Pilate saw that there was nothing he could do and that the people were starting to riot. So he took some water and **washed his hands**（手を洗った）in front of them and said, "I won't have anything to do with killing this man. You are the ones doing it!" <CEV>／ Pilate saw that he wasn't getting anywhere and that a riot was developing. So he sent for a bowl of water and **washed his hands** before the crowd, saying, "I am innocent of this man's blood. The responsibility is yours!" <NLV>

put one's hand to the plough　手を鋤につける →長くて困難な仕事を始める

KJV And Jesus said unto him, "No man, having **put his hand to the plow** and looking back, is fit for the Kingdom of God."［ルカの福音書 9:62］するとイエスは彼に言われた。「だれでも，**手を鋤につけてから，うしろを見る者は，神の国にふさわしくありません。**」

[用例] But Mr. Povey disregarded all appeals. He had **put his hand to the plough**, and he would not look back.［A. Bennett, *The Old Wives' Tale*］しかし，ポヴェイ氏はすべての懇願を無視した。彼は**長くてたいへんな仕事を始めた**ので，後ろを振り向く気はなかった。

Now that Japan has **put her hand to the plough**, she will not look back. (*Ephemeral Literature*) 日本は**長くてたいへんな仕事を始めた**からには，後ろを振り向くことはあるまい。

[**他の英訳聖書**]　KJV の比喩表現は継承されているが，CEV は put one's hand を具体的に start に代えて，比喩性を緩めている。

Jesus answered, "Anyone who **starts plowing**（耕し始める）and keeps looking back isn't worth a thing to God's kingdom!" <CEV>／ But Jesus told him, "Anyone who **puts a hand to the plow**（手を鋤につける）

and then looks back is not fit for the Kingdom of God." <NLT>

[アラム語慣用語句の意味] この語句自体ではなく、そのあとの looking back がアラム語の慣用句で、a lazy worker となっている。「長くてたいへんな仕事を始めてから、それを怠ける」という意となる。

Do not let one's left hand know what one's right hand does 右の手のしていることを左の手に知られるな →善行はひそかに行え

KJV But when thou givest alms, **let not thy left hand know what thy right hand doeth**. [マタイの福音書6:3] あなたは、施しをするとき、右の手のしていることを左の手に知られないようにしなさい。

[用例] Bees will not work except in darkness; Thought will not work except in Silence: neither will Virtue work except in Secrecy. **Let not thy left hand know what thy right hand doeth!** [Carlyle, *Sartor Resartus*] 蜂は暗いところ以外は働かない。思考は沈黙のところ以外は働かない。同様に美徳は隠れたところ以外は働かない。**善行はひそかに行うものだ。**

It's a pity the BBC planners decided to screen 'Battle of Britain' and Engelbert (a singer) at the same time. **Their left hand does not seem to know what their right hand is doing**. [*Daily Mirror*, 1974] BBC の企画者が「英国(ブリテン)の戦い」と歌手のエンゲルベルトを同時に放映しようと決めたことは残念なことである。**双方がお互いのよい企画のことを知らなかったようである。**《[注] この例文のように、教訓的な意味よりも、「二つのよい企画がうまくかみ合わない」ことを表すこともある。》

[他の英訳聖書] NLT は KJV の踏襲であるが、CEV はその比喩表現の基本形を残しながら、半分ほど意訳している。

When you give to the poor, **don't let anyone know about it**. (そのこと(=施すこと)をだれにも知らすな) <CEV>／But when you give to someone in need, **don't let your left hand know what your right hand is doing**. (右の手のしていることを左の手に知らせるな) <NLT>

[アラム語慣用語句の意味] アラム語の方がより具体的である。Lamsa (1985) はアラム語の意味は Don't advertise your giving (与え

ることを宣伝するな）としている。例文にもあるように，KJVの比喩性は他の善行にも当てはまって，敷衍化されている。

bound hand and foot 手足を縛られたまま →自由にできないで

KJV And he that was dead came forth, **bound hand and foot** with graveclothes: and his face was bound about with a napkin. Jesus saith unto them, Loose him, and let him go.［ヨハネの福音書11:44］すると，死んでいた人が，**手と足を長い布で巻かれたままで**出て来た。彼の顔は布切れで包まれていた。イエスは彼らに言われた。「ほどいてやって，帰らせなさい。」

[用例] You know that I would do anything to assist you if it was in my power, but I am **bound hand and foot** by my agreement with my present Company not to take on any other work, so I am helpless in the matter.［Lyell, *Principles of Geology*］ご存知のように，できるならお助けするために何なりともするのですが，現会社との協定で，他の仕事は引き受けないようにされているので，**好きなようにはできない**のです。その件では無力です。

Bound hand and foot, he was thrown alive into a mould in which a block of concrete was about to be made.［Wikipedia, *San Geronimo*］**手足を縛られて，自由にできないまま**，彼はコンクリートブロックが作られようとしている鋳型の中に生きたまま投げこまれた。

[他の英訳聖書] KJVの慣用語句を踏襲したHCSのような例はまれで，多くの英訳聖書では語彙，用法とも変化に富んでいる。

The man who had been dead came out. His hands and feet were **wrapped with strips of burial cloth**（埋葬用の布で包まれて）, and a cloth covered his face. Jesus then told the people, "Untie him and let him go." <CEV>／ And the dead man came out, **his hands and feet bound in graveclothes**（手足を経帷子(かたびら)で包まれて）, his face wrapped in a headcloth. Jesus told them, "Unwrap him and let him go!" <NLT>／ The dead man came out **bound hand and foot** with linen strips and with his face wrapped in a cloth. Jesus said to them, "Loose him and let him go." <HCS>

with both hands 両手で →全力で，巧みに

KJV That they may do evil **with both hands** earnestly, the prince asketh, and the judge asketh for a reward; and the great man, he uttereth his mischievous desire: so they wrap it up. [ミカ書 7:3] 彼らの**手は**悪事を働くのに**巧みで**，役人は物を求め，さばきつかさは報酬に応じてさばき，有力者は自分の欲するままを語り，こうして事を曲げている。

[用例] You couldn't deny that, if you tried **with both hands**. [L. Carroll, *Through the Looking-glass*] **全力で**やっても，それを否定できないでしょう。

[他の英訳聖書] KJV の慣用語句は表面的には「巧みさ」の意味が出てこない。市河 <I, p.234> では (*fig.*) with all one's might (全力を尽くして) とあり，『ジーニアス英和大辞典』にもこの意味は出ているが，「巧みさ」の意はない。

People **cooperate** (協力して) to commit crime. Judges and leaders demand bribes, and rulers cheat in court. <CEV>／ **Both their hands are equally skilled** (両手はともに巧みで) at doing evil! Officials and judges alike demand bribes. The people with influence get what they want, and together they scheme to twist justice. <NLT>／ **Both hands are good** (両手はともに巧みで) at accomplishing evil: the official and the judge demand a bribe; when the powerful man communicates his evil desire, they plot it together. <HCS>

have clean hands 清い手を持つ →潔白である

KJV He that **hath clean hands**, and a pure heart; who hath not lifted up his soul unto vanity, nor sworn deceitfully. [詩篇 24:4] **手がきよく**，心がきよらかな者，そのたましいをむなしいことに向けず，欺き誓わなかった人。

[用例] "**Clean hands** and a pure heart" were required of all who would approach the holy hill either of Zion or of Parnassus. [Butcher, *The Greek Idea of the State*] 「**潔白**で純真な者」という条件がシオンであれパルナッソスであれ，聖なる山に近づこうとするものすべてに要求された。《[注] 現代では His hands are clean と言えば，「公

金に手をつけない者」の意味で使われると市河 <I, p.235> には出ている。また,『ジーニアス英和大辞典』には with clean hands(正直に)の成句が載っている。》

[他の英訳聖書] HCS のように KJV を引き継いでいるものもあれば,CEV のように hand も heart も使用してないものもある。NLT はその中間的なものである。

Only those who **do right for the right reasons**(正しい理由で正しいことをする), and don't worship idols or tell lies under oath. <CEV>／Only those whose **hands and hearts are pure**(手と心が清い), who do not worship idols and never tell lies. <NLT>／ The one who **has clean hands and a pure heart**, who has not set his mind on what is false, and who has not sworn deceitfully. <HCS>

[ヘブル語慣用語句の意味] WL によれば,clean hands は act purely(潔白な振る舞いをする)という意味を持っていたそうである。KJV の慣用語句はここから来たものと思われる。

strengthen the hand(s) of ～　～の手を強める →～を励ます

KJV And Jonathan Saul's son arose, and went to David into the wood, and **strengthened his hand** in God. [I サムエル記 23:16] サウルの子ヨナタンは,ホレシュのダビデのところに来て,神の御名によってダビデを**力**づけた。

[用例] If the public as a whole know that you're in agreement with him, it'll **strengthen his hands** enormously. Won't you write him a letter to that effect? [Lyell, *Principles of Geology*] もしもあなたが彼に同意していることを大衆全体が知ったら,大衆は彼を大いに**励ま**すでしょう。彼に手紙を書いてその旨を伝えたらいかがですか。《[注] 逆に weaken the hand (s) of ～(～の手を弱める)は「落胆させる」の意となる。》

[他の英訳聖書] KJV の hand にあたる部分が下記の英訳聖書ばかりでなく,ほとんどの英訳聖書から消えている。この比喩を使わなくても encourage 一語で十分だからであろう。

But Jonathan went to see David, and God helped him **encourage David**.(ダビデを励ました)<CEV>／ Jonathan went to find David and encouraged him to stay strong（彼を励まして強くあれと言った）in his faith in God. <NLT>／ Then Saul's son Jonathan came to David in Horesh and **encouraged him** in ［his faith in］ God. <HCS>

give the right hand(s) of fellowship　右手を出して交際する → 友情の印として握手する

KJV And when James, Cephas, and John, who seemed to be pillars, perceived the grace that was given unto me, they **gave** to me and Barnabas **the right hands of fellowship**; that we should go unto the heathen, and they unto the circumcision.［ガラテヤ人への手紙 2:9］そして，私に与えられたこの恵みを認め，柱として重んじられているヤコブとケパとヨハネが，私とバルナバに，**交わりのしるしとして右手を差し伸べました**。それは，私たちが異邦人のところへ行き，彼らが割礼を受けた人々のところへ行くためです。

［用例］He is reformed in every respect, apparently: quite a Christian: **offering the right hand of fellowship** to his enemies all around!［E. Brontë, *Wuthering Heights*］彼は見たところは，すべての点で改心した完全なクリスチャンで，周囲にいる敵に**友情ある握手をする**。

［他の英訳聖書］ KJV の意訳そのままを表したのが CEV で，NLT では encourage 一語に簡潔化している。他方，KJV を踏襲している HCS のような伝統訳の少数派もある。

James, Peter, and John realized that God had given me the message about his undeserved kindness. And these men are supposed to be the backbone of the church. They even **gave** Barnabas and me **a friendly handshake**.（友情ある握手をした）This was to show that we would work with Gentiles and that they would work with Jews. <CEV>／ In fact, James, Peter, and John, who were known as pillars of the church, recognized the gift God had given me, and they accepted Barnabas and me as their co-workers. They **encouraged**（励ました）us to keep preaching to the Gentiles, while they continued their work with the Jews. <NLT>／ When James, Cephas, and John, recognized as pillars, acknowledged the grace that had been given to me, they **gave the right hand of fellowship** to me and Barnabas, ［agreeing］ that we should go to the Gentiles and they to the circumcised. <HCS>

One's right hand has lost/forgotten its cunning　右手がその巧みさを失う　→昔の熟練を消耗する

KJV If I forget thee, O Jerusalem, let **my right hand forget her cunning**.［詩篇 137：5］エルサレムよ。もしも，私がおまえを忘れたら，私の右手がその巧みさを忘れるように。

[用例] Above all, the hand of the courtier **had lost its cunning**; he could no longer perform upon the lute.［Rylands, *Words and Poetry*］とりわけ，その廷臣はかっての**熟練さを失っており**，もはやリュートを弾くことはできなかった。

[他の英訳聖書]　KJV の cunning の使い方が厄介で，多くの英訳聖書は他の語句に代えている。特に NLT はその意訳部分を解説している感じがする。

Jerusalem, if I forget you, let **my right hand go limp**.（右手が利かなくなる）<CEV>／If I forget you, O Jerusalem, let **my right hand forget how to play the harp**.（右手がハープの弾き方を忘れる）<NLT>／If I forget you, Jerusalem, may **my right hand forget its skill**.（右手がその技術を忘れる）<HCS>

[heart]

after one's own heart　自分の心にかなうような　→自分の好みにしたがって

KJV But now thy kingdom shall not continue. The LORD hath sought Him a man **after His own heart**, and the LORD hath commanded him to be captain over His people, because thou hast not kept that which the LORD commanded thee.［I サムエル記 13：14］今は，あなたの王国は立たない。主はご**自分の心にかなう**人を求め，主はその人をご自分の民の君主に任命しておられる。あなたが，主の命じられたことを守らなかったからだ。

[用例] Each woman will have her own particular house and home, furnished **after her own heart** in her own manner ― with a little balcony.［H. G. Wells, *Tono-Bungay*］それぞれの女性は独自の方法で**自分の好みにしたがって**家具を備え付け，それに小さなバルコ

heart　　　　　　　　　　　　　　　88

ニーのついた自分の家を持つであろう。

[他の英訳聖書]　KJV の慣用句はほとんどの英訳聖書で引き継がれているが，CEV は平易な語句に意訳していて，該当語句を探すのに苦労するほどである。

But no, you disobeyed, and so the LORD won't choose anyone else from your family to be king. In fact, he has already chosen the one he **wants**（望む）to be the next leader of his people. <CEV>／ But now your kingdom must end, for the LORD has sought out a man **after his own heart**.（自分の心にかなう）The LORD has already appointed him to be the leader of his people, because you have not kept the LORD's command. <NLT>

soft heart　臆病 →優しい心

KJV For God maketh my **heart soft**, and the Almighty troubleth me.［ヨブ記 23:16］神は私の**心を弱くし**，全能者は私をおびえさせた。

[用例] He has a **soft heart** although he always keeps silent and grim-faced.［¶］彼はいつも黙っていてしかめっ面をしているが，**優しい心**の持ち主だ。

In a letter to his wife, Stefi, Schmid described his horror at the sight of mass murder and of children being beaten on the way. He went on: "You know how it is with my **soft heart**. I could not think and had to help them."［Wikipedia, *Anton Schmid*］奥さんのシュテフィへ送った手紙の中で，シュミットは大量殺人と子供たちが（キャンプに送られる）途中で鞭打たれる光景を目にして，彼の恐怖を語っている。「それが私の**優しい心**にどう響いたか分るだろう。私は考えられなかったし，彼らを助けてやらなければならないと思った」と書き続けた。

[他の英訳聖書]　KJV の語句を踏襲している英訳聖書はない。一番近い NKJV でさえ，soft の代わりに weak を使っている。

Merely the thought of God All-Powerful makes me **tremble with fear**.（恐怖で震える）<CEV>／ God has made me **sick at heart**;（心を悩ます）the Almighty has terrified me. <NLT>／ For God made my **heart** weak（心を弱くする）, and the Almighty terrifies me. <NKJV>

[ヘブル語慣用語句] これはヘブル語の fearful <WL> からきて，その比喩的表現が残ったものである。しかし，現代語のイデオムは「優しい」という意味しかない。

[hewer]

hewers of wood（and drawers of water） たきぎを割る者（水を汲む者）→下等労働する愚かな者

KJV And the princes said unto them, "Let them live, but let them be **hewers of wood and drawers of water** unto all the congregation, as the princes had promised them."［ヨシュア記 9:21］族長たちが全会衆に，「彼らを生かしておこう」と言ったので，彼らは全会衆のために，**たきぎを割る者，水を汲む者**となった。族長たちが彼らに言ったとおりである。

[用例] The staff, a mixture of ex-teachers and subject specialists, ... hanker after status. Most of all, they do not want to be confused with lecturers in technical colleges ... who deal only with **hewers of wood**.［*The Guardian*, 1974］もと教師とテーマの専門家たちから成る教授陣は社会的地位を熱心に求めている。ほとんどは専門学校の講師と混同されるのを嫌っている。なぜなら連中は**下等のくだらんもの**を扱っているからである。

No longer shall we be **hewers of wood**. Arise! ye sons of the Baymen's clan: Put on your armour, clear the land!［Wikipedia, *Hewers of Wood*］もはや我々は**下等労働をする愚か者**ではない。汝らベイメン族の子孫たちよ。武具をつけてわが地を解放せよ。

[他の英訳聖書] 動詞表現と名詞表現の違いがあるが，CEV も NLT も意訳せず，KJV の比喩表現を生かしている。

"We promised these people in the name of the LORD God of Israel that we would let them live, so we must not harm them. If we break our promise, God will punish us. We'll let them live, but we'll make them **cut wood and carry water**（たきぎを割り，水を汲む）for our people." <CEV>／ "Let them live." So they made them **woodcutters and water carriers**（きこりや水運搬人）for the entire community, as the

Israelite leaders directed. <NLT>

[hip]

smite hip and thigh 腰関節部分を強打する →打ちのめす

KJV And he **smote** them **hip and thigh** with a great slaughter. And he went down and dwelt in the top of the rock of Etam. ［士師記 15:8］ そして，サムソンは彼らを取りひしいで，**激しく打った**。それから，サムソンは下って行って，エタムの岩の裂け目に住んだ。

[用例] Seldom has a club triumphed so completely as did the Vegetarian Club. The meat-eaters were **smitten hip and thigh** and great joy reigned in the vegetarian camp. [*The Herald of the Golden Age*, 1911] 菜食主義者クラブのように完全に勝利したクラブはめったになかった。肉食主義者たちは**打ちのめされ**，菜食主義者陣営は大きな喜びが溢れていた。

Hooker had his blood boiled, (saying) "I felt myself a dastard; now I saw my advantage — I swore to myself I would **smite** that Amalekite Sam **hip and thigh**." [Wikipedia, *Reaction to Darwin's Theory*] フッカーは怒り狂って言った。「自分が卑劣漢になったと感じた。今では自分が有利になったことを認め，あのアマレクの子孫のサムを**打ちのめしてやる**と誓った。」

[他の英訳聖書] KJV の日本語版では，すでに意訳が行われ，その意訳の英語版が CEV と NLT に見られる。さらに，NLT には感情要素がこめられている。

Then Samson started **hacking them to pieces**（彼らをめった切りする）with his sword. Samson left Philistia and went to live in the cave at Etam Rock. <CEV>／So he **attacked the Philistines with great fury and killed many of them**.（ペリシテ人を激しくたたき，その多くを殺した）Then he went to live in a cave in the rock of Etam. <NLT>

[hold]

hold forth 堅く握る →公然と話す →意見を長々と述べる

KJV **Holding forth** the word of life; that I may rejoice in the day of Christ, that I have not run in vain, neither laboured in vain. ［ピリピ人への手紙 2:16］ いのちのことばを**しっかり握って**，彼らの間で世の

光として輝くためです。そうすれば，私は，自分の努力したことがむだではなく，苦労したこともむだでなかったことを，キリストの日に誇ることができます。

[用例] When she went downstairs Paul was lying back in an armchair, **holding forth** with much vehemence to Agatha. [D. H. Lawrence, *Sons and Lovers*] 彼女が階下に下りると，ポールが肘掛け椅子に仰向けに寝ながら，アガサに熱心に**長々としゃべっていた**。

The speaker was **holding forth** on the collapse of the present government. [¶] 演説者は現政府の崩壊について**長々と話していた**。

... he was **holding forth** emphatically about repentance, the wrath to come, and the uncomfortable prospects for sinners. [John Wyndham, *The Day of the Triffids*] 彼は熱心に悔い改めと来たるべき神の怒り，それに罪びとたちにとって心地よくない予測を**長々と述べていた**。

[他の英訳聖書] 「堅く握る」から「意見を長々と述べる」への推移を理解するのは難しい。実際，他の英訳聖書はほとんど hold firmly (堅く保つ) と意訳している。市河 <I> には hold forth = to preach; to speak publicly (usually somewhat contemptuously) (説教する；公然と話す（通常は多少軽蔑して）) とある。思うに，「いのちの言葉を差し出す」意からいのちの言葉を堂々と話し，それが長く続くのであろう。

Try to shine as lights among the people of this world, as you **hold firmly** (堅く保持する) to the message that gives life. Then on the day when Christ returns, I can take pride in you. I can also know that my work and efforts were not useless. <CEV>／ As you **hold out** (長く持ちこたえる) the word of life-in order that I may boast on the day of Christ that I did not run or labor for nothing. <NIV>

[hope]

hope against hope 望みえないときに望みを抱く →わずかの可能性にすがる

[KJV] Abraham, **against all hope**, believed in hope, that he might become the father of many nations, according to that which had been spoken, "So shall thy seed be."［ローマ人への手紙 4:18］彼は**望みえないときに望みを抱いて**信じました。それは，「あなたの子孫はこのようになる」と言われていたとおりに，彼があらゆる国の人々の父となるためでした。

[用例] Though she had been told that he was not to come, instinct had kept her there; or the pathetic, aching **hope against hope** which lovers never part with. [Galsworthy, *Best Short Stories*, ed. Kairyudo] 彼女は彼が来ることはないと言われていたが，本能的にそこにとどまった。あるいは本能でなければ，恋人たちが決して手離さない痛々しい，**わずかの可能性にすがって**そこにとどまったのである。

[他の英訳聖書] KJV の慣用句はすべて意訳され，嚙み砕いた用法で現代語表現に直されている。

God promised Abraham a lot of descendants. And **when it all seemed hopeless, Abraham still had faith in God**（すべてが望みないと思えたときでも，アブラハムは依然として神を信頼していた）and became the ancestor of many nations.<CEV>／ **Even when there was no reason for hope, Abraham kept hoping**（希望するすべがないときでも，アブラハムは希望を持っていた）— believing that he would become the father of many nations. For God had said to him, "That's how many descendants you will have!" <NLT>

[horn]

exalt/lift up one's horn 角を上げる →自らを誇る

KJV **Lift not up your horn** on high; speak not with a stiff neck. [詩篇 75:5]「おまえたちの**角を高く上げるな**。横柄な態度で語るな。」と言う。Cf. All the horns of the wicked will I also cut off, but **the horns of the righteous shall be exalted**. [同 10 節] 悪者どもの角をことごとく切り捨てよう。しかし，**正しい者の角は，高く上げられる**。

[用例] It would, he said, all come right some day, and **Kim's horn would be exalted** between pillars — monstrous pillars — of beauty and strength. [R. Kipling, *Kim*] いつかすべてはうまく収まっていくだろう。そうすれば，**キムは美と力の巨大な塔の間で自らを誇る**

[**他の英訳聖書**]　CEV と NLT では元の語句を完全に意訳している。特に NLT は動作の描写が生き生きとしていて，違った形で KJV の本来の描写表現を残している。

Stop bragging!（誇るのをやめよ）Quit telling me how great you are. .... Our Lord, you will destroy the power of evil people, but you will **give strength to**（力を与える）those who are good. <CEV>／Don't **raise your fists in defiance**（こぶしをふりあげて反抗するな）at the heavens or speak with such arrogance. .... For God says, "I will break the strength of the wicked, but I will **increase the power**（力を増す）of the godly." <NLT>

[**ヘブル語慣用語句の意味**]　WL はこの語句の意味を defy God（神に反抗する）としている。意訳している他の英訳聖書はこの意味を含意しているようである。

[house]

set one's house in order　家を整理する →事態を正す

KJV Thus saith the LORD: '**Set thine house in order**, for thou shalt die and not live.' ［Ⅱ列王記 20:1］主はこう仰せられる。「**あなたの家を整理せよ。あなたは死ぬ。直らない。**」

[用例] ... and rather brusque letters to Native Princes, telling them to **put their houses in order**, to refrain from kidnapping women, or filling offenders with pounded red pepper, and eccentricities of that kind. [Kipling, *Plain Tales from the Hills*] 土着民の王子様たちにやや無愛想な手紙を送り，**彼らの事態を正し**，女性を誘拐したり，犯罪者にすりつぶした唐辛子を食べさせる様な極端な行為をやめさせるように告げた。

The One Mighty and Strong was said by Joseph Smith Jr. to be one who would "**set in order the house of God**" and arrange for the "inheritances of the [Latter Day] Saints". [Wikipedia, *One Mighty and Strong*] 巨大で強力な人とはモルモン教創立者のジョゼフ・スミスによって言及された人で，**神の事態を正し**モルモン教の継承を整える人である。

[他の英訳聖書] KJV の比喩表現を CEV も NLT も意訳している。NLT はもとの houses を的確に affairs に言い換えている。

The LORD says you won't ever get well. You are going to die, so you had better start **doing what needs to be done**.（なすべき必要なことをする）<CEV>／ This is what the LORD says: **Set your affairs in order**（自分の事態を正せ）, for you are going to die. You will not recover from this illness. <NLT>

[housetop]

proclaim from the housetops　屋上で言い広める →公に宣言する

KJV Therefore whatsoever ye have spoken in darkness shall be heard in the light; and that which ye have spoken in the ear in closets shall **be proclaimed upon the housetops**.［ルカの福音書 12:3］ですから，あなたがたが暗やみで言ったことが，明るみで聞かれ，家の中でささやいたことが，**屋上で言い広められます**。

用例 ... why surely a person may say, even **proclaim upon the housetops**, that it hurts and grieves. [Hardy, *Jude the Obscure*] まあ，確かに人の口はうるさく，**みんなに言い広められて**人の感情を害し，人を悲しませるでしょう。

[他の英訳聖書] どの英訳聖書も housetops を生かしている。それはこの地方の家は屋根が平らで，夏など夕涼みに出ることが多く，大きな声で隣近所の会話がなされるからである。<I>

Whatever you say in the dark will be heard when it is day. Whatever you whisper in a closed room will **be shouted from the housetops**.（屋上から大声で言われる）<CEV>／ Whatever you have said in the dark will be heard in the light, and what you have whispered behind closed doors will **be shouted from the housetops for all to hear**!（みんなに聞こえるように屋上から大声で言われる）<NLT>

I

[iron]

with a rod of iron　鉄の杖で →過酷な仕方で

KJV Thou shalt break them **with a rod of iron**; thou shalt dash them in pieces like a potter's vessel. [詩篇2:9] あなたは**鉄の杖で**彼らを打ち砕き，焼き物の器のように粉々にする。

[用例] The man is colossal. He is brilliantly clever, in spite of his vulgarity and lack of education: he is remorseless, and he rules his little kingdom **with a rod of iron**. [Edgar Wallace, *The Law of the Four Just Men*] その男は巨大である。彼は下品で教育もなかったが非常に賢い。また冷酷で自分の小さな王国を**過酷な仕方で**支配している。

The Paradise Club focuses upon two brothers, Frank & Danny Kane who ran the South Side **with a rod of iron**. Frank has become a priest but leaves the church; he inherits The Paradise Club on the death of their mother and returns to London to try and steer Danny away from crime. [Wikipedia, *The Paradise Club*]「楽園クラブ」という劇は2人の兄弟フランク・ケインとダニー・ケインが主人公で，ロンドンのサウス・サイドを**過酷な仕方で**縄張りとしていた。フランクは司祭になったが教会を去る。彼は母の死によって楽園クラブを引き継ぎ，ロンドンに戻ってダニーを犯罪から引き戻そうとする。

[他の英訳聖書]　代表としてCEVを選んだが，みな一様にKJVに倣っている。

You will smash them **with an iron rod** and shatter them like dishes of clay. <CEV>

[itching]

have itching ears　自分に都合のよい発言を好む →他人の悪評を好む

KJV For the time will come when they will not endure sound doctrine; but **having itching ears**, they shall heap to themselves teachers in accordance with their own lusts. ［II テモテへの手紙 4:3］というのは，人々が健全な教えに耳を貸そうとせず，**自分につごうの良いことを言ってもらうために**，気ままな願いをもって，次々に教師たちを自分たちのために寄せ集める。

[用例] A: "Who told you that?"
B: "Johnson."
A: "I thought so. If ever a fellow **has itching ears**, he has ..." [¶]
A:「だれがあなたにそれを言ったのですか。」B:「ジョンソンさんです。」A:「そう思った。**他人の悪評を好む**人がいるとすれば，彼です…」

[他の英訳聖書]　CEV も NLT もかなり意訳しているが，ともに itching は共通に残している。

The time is coming when people won't listen to good teaching. Instead, they will look for teachers who will please them by **telling them only what they are itching to hear**. (聞きたくてたまらないことだけを話す) <CEV>／For a time is coming when people will no longer listen to sound and wholesome teaching. They will follow their own desires and will look for teachers who will **tell them whatever their itching ears want to hear**. (うずうずする耳が聞きたいことは何でも話す) <NLT>

J

[Jerusalem]

New Jerusalem　新しいエルサレム →理想郷

KJV And I, John, saw the holy city, **New Jerusalem**, coming down from God out of Heaven, prepared as a bride adorned for her husband. ［黙示録21:2］私はまた，聖なる都，**新しいエルサレム**が，夫のために飾られた花嫁のように整えられて，神のみもとを出て，天から下って来るのを見た。

[用例] Youthful men, not having taken a deep root, give up their hold of life so easily! And saintly men, who walk with God on earth, would fain be away, to walk with him on the golden pavements of the **New Jerusalem**. [Harthorne, *The Scarlet Letter*] 若々しい人々は，まだ深く根を下ろしていないのに，人生の足場をいとも簡単にはずしてしまう。他方，聖人のような人々はこの世で神とともに歩み，喜んで世を去って**理想郷**の黄金の道を神とともに歩みたがるのだ。

This election campaign can't be much fun for the idealists and visionaries among us. At first glance there seems to be a distinct shortage of ... **New Jerusalems**. [*Daily Mirror*, 1974] 今度の選挙キャンペーンは我々の中の理想主義者や夢想家にはあまり愉快のものであるはずがない。一瞥しても，**理想郷**の話題がはっきりと欠けているようだからだ。

[他の英訳聖書]　意訳している聖書を見かけない。恐らく，「新しいエルサレム」という表現がユダヤ民族の一般的な概念なので，意訳する必要がないのであろう。

Then I saw **New Jerusalem**（理想郷）, that holy city, coming down from God in heaven. It was like a bride dressed in her wedding gown and ready to meet her husband. <CEV>／ And I saw the holy city, the **new Jerusalem**, coming down from God out of heaven like a bride beautifully dressed for her husband. <NLT>

K

【kick】

kick against the pricks／goads とげのついた棒をける →権威者に反抗してかえって自分の傷を深くする

[KJV] And when we had all fallen to the earth, I heard a voice speaking unto me, and saying in the Hebrew tongue, 'Saul, Saul, why persecutest thou Me? It is hard for thee to **kick against the goads**.'［使徒の働き 26:14］私たちはみな地に倒れましたが，そのとき声があって，ヘブル語で私にこう言うのが聞こえました。「サウロ，サウロ。なぜわたしを迫害するのか。**とげのついた棒をける**のは，あなたにとって痛いことだ。」

[用例] What happened happened, and it was no good **kicking against the pricks**.［D. H. Lawrence, *Sons and Lovers*］起こったことは起こったことだ。**抵抗してもかえって自分の傷を深くする**だけだ。

You'll find that this agitation that you're trying to stir up, will be a case of **kicking against the pricks**. The only effect it'll have will be your own dismissal.［Lyell, *Principles of Geology*］あなたが巻き起こそうとしているこの煽動は**自分の傷を深くする**ケースだ。結局は自分自身が首になるだけだ。

Actually, since youths must all eventually claim their freedom, they all must sooner or later **kick over the traces** of obedience in home and school.［Phrase Finder, *Kick over the Traces*］実際のところ若者たちは結局みな自由を主張するに違いないから，家庭や学校で遅かれ早かれ**権威者に反抗して**からおとなしくなるに違いない。《［注］OED によると，kick against the pricks と kick over the traces とは同じ意味で，現代では後者の方がよく使われているようである。》

[他の英訳聖書] pricks や goads が何であるかが CEV や NLT では明確に示されている。意訳の効果である。KJV を忠実に継承している

HCSと比べてみるとその差が明瞭である。

We all fell to the ground. Then I heard a voice say to me in Aramaic, "Saul, Saul, why are you so cruel to me? It's foolish to **fight against me**!"（私に反抗する）<CEV>／We all fell down, and I heard a voice saying to me in Aramaic, 'Saul, Saul, why are you persecuting me? It is useless for you to **fight against my will**.'（私の意志に反抗する）<NLT>／When we had all fallen to the ground, I heard a voice speaking to me in the Hebrew language, 'Saul, Saul, why are you persecuting Me? It is hard for you to **kick against the goads**.'（とげのついた棒をける）<HCS>

[kind]

after one's kind　その種類に従って →それと同じ性質の/に

　KJV And God said, "Let the earth bring forth the living creature **after his kind**: cattle and creeping thing and beast of the earth **after his kind**"; and it was so. ［創世記 1:24］神は仰せられた。「地が，**種類にしたがって**，生き物を生ぜよ。家畜や，はうもの，野の獣を，**種類にしたがって**。」そのようになった。

　用例 The evil principle deprecated in that religion, is the orderly sequence by which the seed brings forth a crop **after its kind**. ［Eliot, *Silas Marner*］その宗教で非難される邪悪な原則は種が**その性質と同じ**作物を生む規則正しい連作のことである。

[他の英訳聖書]　KJV の意味を CEV は簡略化して all kinds of としている。NLT はむしろさらに詳細化して every sort of と of the same kind を併記している。

God said, "I command the earth to give life to **all kinds of**（あらゆる種類の）tame animals, wild animals, and reptiles." And that's what happened. <CEV>／Then God said, "Let the earth produce **every sort of** animal, each producing offspring **of the same kind**（あらゆる種類の／同じ性質を持った）— livestock, small animals that scurry along the ground, and wild animals." And that is what happened. <NLT>

[kingdom]

blow/send to kingdom come　御国に送る →爆死させる

　KJV **Thy Kingdom come**. Thy will be done on earth, as it is in Heaven.［マタイの福音書6:10］**御国が来ますように**。みこころが天で行なわれるように地でも行なわれますように。

[用例] The policeman was **blown to kingdom come** when he tried to touch the unexploded bomb taken away from the building. [¶] その警官は建物から取り出した不発弾に触ろうとして**爆死した**。

In February the battleship returned to Norfolk. There Ziegler complained to his wife about the morale, training, and safety situation aboard Iowa, stating, "We're shorthanded. Chiefs with seventeen years of service are quitting. I've got to teach these kids to push the right button, or they'll **blow us to kingdom come**! My butt is on the line!" [Wikipedia, *USS Iowa Turret Explosion*] 2月，戦艦アイオワはノーフォークに戻ってきた。ジーグラーは妻にアイオワの士気，訓練，安全状況を述べて，「人員が足りないのだ。17年の経験のあるチーフたちがやめようとしているのだ。おれはあの若い連中に正しいボタンの押し方を教えなければならないのだ。さもないと，連中は我々を**爆死させる**からな。俺は危険にさらされているのだ」と言った。

[**他の英訳聖書**] 比喩的意味は全体の文脈から出てくるので，個々には意訳されてない。

Come and set up your kingdom（来て，貴方の王国を立ててください）, so that everyone on earth will obey you, as you are obeyed in heaven. <CEV>／**May your Kingdom come soon.**（すぐに貴方の王国を来させてください）May your will be done on earth, as it is in heaven. <NLT>

until/till kingdom come 王国がくるまで →無駄に長く

KJV 上記と同じ聖書の箇所。

[用例] It's no use sitting there blowing through your nostrils. You can blow through your nostrils **till kingdom come** ... you're still not getting any housekeeping money. [*Daily Mirror*, 1974] そこに座って鼻を鳴らしていても無駄だ。**いつまでも鳴らしているがよい**。そうしていても家計の足しにならぬ。

L

[labor]
a labor of love 愛の労苦 →報酬を期待しない仕事

KJV We give thanks to God always for you all, making mention of you in our prayers, remembering without ceasing your work of faith, and **labor of love**, and patience of hope in our Lord Jesus Christ, in the sight of God and our Father, knowing, brethren beloved, of your election by God. [Ⅰテサロニケ人への手紙 1:2-4] 私たちは，いつもあなたがたすべてのために神に感謝し，祈りのときにあなたがたを覚え，絶えず，私たちの父なる神の御前に，あなたがたの信仰の働き，**愛の労苦**，主イエス・キリストへの望みの忍耐を思い起こしています。神に愛されている兄弟たち。あなたがたが神に選ばれた者であることは私たちが知っています。

[用例] I dislike cleaning floors myself, but my younger brother has been fond of doing it since his childhood. It is **a labor of love** to him. [¶] 私自身は床を掃除するのが嫌いだが，弟は少年のころから好きだった。その掃除は彼にとって**好きな無報酬労働**だ。

In the 1920s there was hardly any translating done at all except as **a labour of love**, and even Proust was a name and nothing more. [*Punch*, 1974] 1920年代は**報酬を期待しない仕事**としてならともかく，何の翻訳も全く無かったと言ってよい。フランスの作家プルーストでさえ名前だけ知られていて，翻訳は何もなかった。

[他の英訳聖書] 意訳に走らないで，何らかの形で原義を生かしている。

We thank God for you and always mention you in our prayers. Each time we pray, we tell God our Father about your faith and **loving work**（愛する仕事）and about your firm hope in our Lord Jesus Christ. <CEV> ／ We always thank God for all of you and pray for you constantly. As we pray to our God and Father about you, we think of your faithful work, your **loving deeds**（愛する行い）, and the enduring hope you have because of our Lord Jesus Christ. <NLT>

[lamb]

like/as a lamb to the slaughter　ほふり場に引かれていく小羊のように →死の危険に気づかず/観念した

KJV He was oppressed, and He was afflicted, yet He opened not his mouth; He is brought **as a lamb to the slaughter**; and as a sheep before her shearers is dumb, so He openeth not His mouth.［イザヤ書53:7］彼は痛めつけられた。彼は苦しんだが，口を開かない。**ほふり場に引かれて行く小羊のように，毛を刈る者の前で黙っている雌羊のように，彼は口を開かない。**

[用例] The plane with three terrorists on board was approaching New York. All the passengers aboard it were sitting still **like lambs to the slaughter**.［¶］3人のテロリストが乗っていた飛行機はニューヨークに近づいていた。乗客はみな**死の危険に気づかず**じっと座っていた。

Smith reluctantly agreed and submitted to arrest, further quoted as saying "I am going **like a lamb to the slaughter**; but I am calm as a summer's morning."［Wikipedia, *Death of Joseph Smith*］スミス［モルモン教教主］は不承不承同意して捕縛に身をゆだねた。さらに「私は**死の危険に観念した**小羊のように行こう。しかし，夏の朝のように私の心は静かだ」と言ったといわれている。

[他の英訳聖書]　CEVだけ具体的にkillという言葉を使っている。他はほとんどKJVの模倣。

He was beaten down and punished, but he didn't say a word. He was **like a lamb being led to be killed**.（連れて行って殺される羊のように）He was quiet, as a sheep is quiet while its wool is being cut; he never opened his mouth. <CEV>／He was oppressed and treated harshly, yet he never said a word. He was led **like a lamb to the slaughter**.（ほふり場に引かれていく小羊のように）And as a sheep is silent before the shearers, he did not open his mouth. <NET>

[アラム語慣用語句の意味] Lamsa (1985) によれば，Gentle, not protesting の意味を持つという。しかし，このアラム語の慣用句では「死」のイメージがない。KJVにはもっと暗い意味合いがある。

[land]

a land of milk and honey 乳と蜜の流れる地 →豊かな楽しい場所

KJV And I have come down to deliver them out of the hand of the Egyptians, and to bring them up out of that land unto a good land and a large, unto **a land flowing with milk and honey**, unto the place of the Canaanites and the Hittites, and the Amorites and the Perizzites, and the Hivites and the Jebusites. [出エジプト記 3:8] わたしが下って来たのは，彼らをエジプトの手から救い出し，その地から，広い良い地，**乳と蜜の流れる地**，カナン人，ヘテ人，エモリ人，ペリジ人，ヒビ人，エブス人のいる所に，彼らを上らせるためだ。

[用例] The batch of recruits dispatched to the front would hope to soon return to their homes, in **a land of milk and honey**. [¶] 前線に派遣された一団の新兵はすぐに**豊かな楽しい場所**である郷里に帰りたいと願っていたであろう。

Rothblatt proposes a "two-star" solution: Two Stars for Peace. "When America welcomes Israel and Palestine as the 51st and 52nd states of the union, the age-old dream of peace and prosperity in **the land of milk and honey** will have been achieved. As America re-sews her flag with a 51st and 52nd star, the entire world will applaud the arrival of this fine new design." [Wikipedia, *Two Stars for Peace Solution*] ロスブラット博士は「二つの星」解決案を提案する。平和の二つの星である。「アメリカがイスラエルとパレスチナを合衆国の51番目と52番目の州として歓迎すれば，**乳と蜜の流れる地であり，本来豊かな楽しい場所**であるべきところに平和と繁栄の長年の夢が実現するだろう。アメリカが51番目と52番目の星を国旗に縫いつけるとき，全世界はこの素晴らしい新しいアイデアの到来を歓迎するだろう」と述べた。

[他の英訳聖書] 多少の変化はあるが，ほとんど KJV に倣ったもの。

I will bring my people out of Egypt into a country where there is **good land, rich with milk and honey**（乳と蜜の豊かな良い土地）I will give them the land where the Canaanites, Hittites, Amorites, Perizzites, Hivites, and Jebusites now live. <CEV>／ So I have come down to rescue them from the power of the Egyptians and lead them out of Egypt into their own fertile and spacious land. It is **a land flowing with milk and honey**（乳と蜜の流れる土地）— the land where the Canaanites, Hittites, Amorites, Perizzites, Hivites, and Jebusites now live. <NLT>

[**ヘブル語慣用語句の意味**] ヘブル語にこれに似た flowing with milk and honey <WL> があり，意味は fertile（肥沃な）である。milk and honey はもともとヘブル語を基にした慣用語句であったのであろう。

the land of Nod　ノデの地　→眠り，さまよいの境地

KJV And Cain went out from the presence of the LORD, and dwelt in **the land of Nod** to the east of Eden. ［創世記 4:16］それで，カインは，主の前から去って，エデンの東，**ノデの地**に住みついた。

　[用例] He looked so comfortable in **the land of Nod** that I hesitated to call him. ［¶］彼は**眠り，さまよいの境地**でとても気持ちよさそうに見えたので，私は声をかけるのを躊躇した。

[**他の英訳聖書**] ノデは本来特定の地域を指すのではなく，神の前から逃れたカインの心的境地を表し，「放浪，逃亡」の比喩的意味となったもの。その比喩的意味を表すのは CEV のみ。

But Cain had to go far from the LORD and live in **the Land of Wandering**（さまよいの土地），which is east of Eden. <CEV>／ So Cain left the LORD's presence and settled in **the land of Nod**（ノデの地），east of Eden. <NLT>

the land of the living　生ける者の地　→生活の場

KJV He was taken from prison and from judgment; and who shall declare His generation? For He was cut off out of **the land of the living**; for the transgression of My people was He stricken. ［イザヤ書 53:8］しいたげと，さばきによって，彼は取り去られた。彼の時代の者で，だれが思ったことだろう。彼がわたしの民のそむきの罪のために打たれ，**生ける者の地**から絶たれたことを。

[用例] For three months after her husband passed away she remained alone in her house, seldom going out for shopping. But when her children came back home and comforted her, she finally was back in **the land of the living**. [¶] 夫が亡くなってから3か月間，彼女は家に一人でいて，めったに外に買いものに出かけなかった。しかし，子供たちが家に戻って彼女を元気づけると，ようやく彼女は**生活の場**に戻った。

[**他の英訳聖書**] CEV と NLT の意訳が目立ち，ともに節表現に代えて具体化している。

He was condemned to death without a fair trial. Who could have imagined what would happen to him? **His life was taken away** (彼のいのちは取り去られた) because of the sinful things my people had done. <CEV> / Unjustly condemned, he was led away. No one cared that he died without descendants, that **his life was cut short in midstream**. (彼のいのちは中途で終った) But he was struck down for the rebellion of my people. <NLT>

the promised land　誓われた地　→待ち望む地，素晴らしい地

KJV All the commandments which I command thee this day shall ye observe to do, that ye may live and multiply, and go in and possess **the land which the LORD swore** unto your fathers. [申命記 8:1] 私が，きょう，あなたに命じるすべての命令をあなたがたは守り行なわなければならない。そうすれば，あなたがたは生き，その数はふえ，**主があなたがたの先祖たちに誓われた地**を所有することができる。

[用例] Her ambition was always to come to England which she thought of as **a promised land**. [*Nova*, 1974] 彼女の野心はいつも英国にやってくることであった。なぜなら，そこが彼女の**待望の地**であったからだ。

> The Man in the Saddle is a man who rides alone,
> Far away from the bunkhouse and his friends,
> And the horse he straddles is all he'll ever own,
> He's a traveler and his journey never ends,
> Get along, old pie, there's a buzzard in the sky,

Shake your tail, shake your tail, shake your tail,

For this desert sand surely ain't **the promised land**,

And I wouln't be found here dead. [Phrasefinder, *The Man in the Saddle*, 1950] 馬上の男はひとり馬を走らす，放牧場の場所と友達から離れて，乗っている馬は唯一の持ち物，彼は旅人で，旅は終わりを知らず，進め老いぼれまだら馬よ，禿鷹が空を飛びまわっているぞ，急げ急げ急げ，この砂漠は決して**待望の地**ではない，ここを死に場所にしたくない。

[**他の英訳聖書**] この聖書語句は他のところでも多く使われているので，特定の慣用句ではなく，聖書の中で含蓄された意味を持ち，それが比喩的に使われている。

Israel, do you want to go into **the land the LORD promised**（主が約束された土地）your ancestors? Do you want to capture it, live there, and become a powerful nation? Then be sure to obey every command I am giving you. <CEV>／ Be careful to obey all the commands I am giving you today. Then you will live and multiply, and you will enter and occupy **the land the LORD swore**（主が誓われた土地）to give your ancestors. <NLT>

[laugh]

laugh (one) to scorn　笑ってあざける →あざける

KJV All they that see Me **laugh Me to scorn**; they shoot out their lip, they shake their head. [詩篇 2:7] 私を見る者はみな，**私をあざけります**。彼らは口をとがらせ，頭を振ります。

用例 This was too much, and we **laughed him to scorn**. [Howells, *Venetian Life*] これにはたまらなくなって，私たちは彼をあざけった。

[**他の英訳聖書**] KJV の慣用句を現代語にあわせるつもりか，CEV も NLT も現代風に意訳している。

Everyone who sees me **makes fun and sneers**.（おもしろがってあざける）They shake their heads. <CEV>／ Everyone who sees me **mocks me**.（私をばかにする）They sneer and shake their heads, saying <NLT>

[law]

a law unto oneself 自分自身に対する律法 →自分勝手

KJV For when the Gentiles, who have not the law, do by nature the things contained in the law, they, not having the law, are **a law unto themselves**.［ローマ人への手紙 2:14］たとえ律法を持たない異邦人も，律法の命じるところを自然に行えば，律法を持たなくとも，**自分自身が律法**なのです。

[用例] The old lady was **a law unto herself**. She never gave her attention to warnings by other people.［¶］その老婆は**自分勝手な人**であった。他の人々の忠告に決して耳を傾けなかった。

[他の英訳聖書] NLT は，他の英訳聖書と違って具体的で説明的である。

Those who are not Jews do not have the law, but when they freely do what the law commands, they are **the law for themselves**.（自分自身で律法）This is true even though they do not have the law. <CEV>／Even Gentiles, who do not have God's written law, show that **they know his law when they instinctively obey it**（自分の律法を知って本能的に従っている），even without having heard it. <NLT>

[leopard]

A leopard can't change its spots ヒョウはその斑点を変えられない →人は性格を変えられない

KJV **Can** the Ethiopian **change** his skin, or **the leopard his spots**? Then may ye also do good, that are accustomed to do evil.［エレミヤ書 13:23］クシュ人がその皮膚を，ひょうがその斑点を，変えることができようか。もしできたら，悪に慣れたあなたがたでも，善を行うことができるだろう。

[用例] You could change your hair from black to brown, but you can't change your character, as the Bible says: **A leopard can't change its spots**.［¶］髪の毛は黒からブラウンに変えようと思えば変えられるけど，聖書にあるように，**人はその性格を変えられない**よ。

Despite Kraken's impeccable performance, Dredd's unappealable decision was to fail him, believing that "**a leopard can't change its**

spots. Not this one, anyway." At the moment of announcing his verdict, Dredd tendered his resignation and requested permission to take the long walk, leaving the city forever. ［Wikipedia, *Democracy (Judge Dredd Storyline)*］クラーケンの申し分ない行為にもかかわらず，ドレッド判事は「**人は性格を変えられない**。こいつも結局同じだ」と思い，控訴不可能の判決をして彼を有罪にしてしまった。判決をしたすぐ後で，ドレッド判事は辞表を提出し，長い留守の許可を願って町を永遠に去ってしまった。

［他の英訳聖書］ パターンは KJV の踏襲であるが，change という動詞では「斑点を変える」のであって，「消す」のではないので，CEV は remove を，NLT では take away を使って，その意を明確にしている。

Can you ever change and do what's right? Can people change the color of their skin, or **can a leopard remove its spots**? (ヒョウは斑点を取り除くことができるか) If so, then maybe you can change and learn to do right. <CEV>／ Can an Ethiopian change the color of his skin? **Can a leopard take away its spots**? Neither can you start doing good, for you have always done evil. <NLT>

【 light 】

hide／put one's light under a bushel　枡ます の下に隠す →自分の能力を誇示しない

KJV Neither do men light a candle and **put it under a bushel**, but on a candlestick, and it giveth light unto all that are in the house. ［マタイの福音書5：15］また，あかりをつけて，**それを枡の下に置く者は**ありません。燭台の上に置きます。そうすれば，家にいる人々全部を照らします。

［用例］ I didn't know he could sing to his own guitar accompaniment. He's been **hiding his light under a bushel** all these years. ［¶］彼がギターの弾き語りができるなんて知らなかった。ずっと**その能力を隠していた**な。

  "Deanna's genius had to be unfolded, but it was hers and hers alone, always has been, always will be, and no one can take credit for discovering her. You **can't hide that kind of light under a bushel**. You just can't, no matter how hard you try!" [Joe Pasternak, *Deanna Durbin*, 1936]「デアナの天才ぶりは隠せなかった。しかし，それはあくまでも彼女自身に備わったのもので，いつもそうであったし，これからもそうであろう。だれも彼女の才能を見出したことで手柄にすることはできない。だれでも**あの才能は誇示せざるをえない**。いくらそうしないように心がけても誇示してしまうのだ。」

[他の英訳聖書] いずれも「不必要なことをする」の意味で使われている。「謙遜」の意味合いは，英訳聖書には表れていない。

And no one would light a lamp and **put it under a clay pot**.（それをつぼの下に置く）A lamp is placed on a lampstand, where it can give light to everyone in the house. <CEV>／ No one lights a lamp and then **puts it under a basket**.（それをバスケットの下に置く）Instead, a lamp is placed on a stand, where it gives light to everyone in the house. <NLT>

[loin]

souls out of one's loins　自分から生まれた者 →子孫

KJV And all **the souls that came out of the loins** of Jacob were seventy souls: for Joseph was in Egypt already.［出エジプト記 1:5］ヤコブから**生まれた者**の総数は七十人であった。ヨセフはすでにエジプトにいた。

[用例] The prince was a lawless shameless youth;

　From his father's loins he sprang without ruth. [D. G. Rossetti, *The White Ship*]

　王子は手に負えない，恥知らずな青年だった。

　父の子として自責の念なしに**生まれた**。

[他の英訳聖書] 多くは KJV を踏襲せず，descendants としている。さらに砕けた語である families も CEV に見かける。

When Jacob went to Egypt, his son Joseph was already there. So Jacob took **his eleven other sons and their families**.（ほかの 11 人の息子とその家族）<CEV>／ In all, Jacob had seventy **descendants**（子孫）in Egypt, including Joseph, who was already there. <NLT>

[ヘブル語慣用語句の意味] seed と同じように，これもヘブル語に

起因する意味で，loins = descendants <WL> としている。

gird up one's loins　腰に帯を締める →ふんどしを締めてかかる

KJV **Gird up now thy loins** like a man; for I will demand of thee, and answer thou Me. ［ヨブ記 38:3］さあ，あなたは勇士のように**腰に帯を締めよ**。わたしはあなたに尋ねる。わたしに示せ。

[用例] He had an interview for a job. He felt nervous before it, as he had no idea of what the president would ask him. But he **girded up his loins** and entered the room. ［¶］彼は就職の面接試験を受けた。社長が何を聞いてくるか分からないので不安になった。しかし，**意を決して**部屋に入った。

The term "**gird your loins**" was used in the Roman Era meaning to pull up and tie your lower garments between your legs to increase your mobility in battle. In the modern age, it has become an idiom meaning to prepare yourself for the worst. ［Wikipedia, *Loin*］「ふんどしを締めてかかれ」という語句はローマ時代に下腹部の衣装を引っ張って締めるの意で用いられ，戦場での動きをよくするためのものであった。現代では，最悪の事態に備えて準備するの意の慣用句語句になっている。《［注］上記の文はこの慣用句語句の過去と現代の意味の対比を示したものである。》

[他の英訳聖書]　KJV は用語が古いので，CEV も NLT もともに大胆に意訳している。

Now **get ready to face me**!（用意して私にむかい合え）Can you answer the questions I ask? <CEV>／**Brace yourself**（身構えよ）like a man, because I have some questions for you, and you must answer them. <NLT>

[ヘブル語慣用語句の意味]　WL によれば，この語句が get ready（用意する）の比喩的表現であるとのことである。すると，この比喩はヘブル語から始まったことになる。

[long]

go to one's long home　永遠の家へと行く →死ぬ

KJV Also when they shall be afraid of that which is high, and fears shall be in the way, and the almond tree shall flourish, and the grasshopper shall be a burden, and desire shall fail: because man **goeth to his long home**, and the mourners go about the streets［伝道者 12:5］彼らはまた高い所を恐れ，道でおびえる。アーモンドの花は咲き，いなごはのろのろ歩き，ふうちょうぼくは花を開く。だが，人は**永遠の家へと歩いて行き**，嘆く者たちが通りを歩き回る。

[用例] This is the grave-digger, this will **send** many of them **to their long homes**; I haven't done with them yet!［Hazlitt, *The Fight*］こいつは墓掘り人だ。多くの連中を**死に送る**が，わしはまだこの連中に用があるのだ。

[**他の英訳聖書**] 下記の3つの英訳聖書に共通しているのは home である。そして，その前に来る動詞句はみな異なっている。home の前に来る形容詞は everlasting か eternal である。このような傾向は他の英訳聖書にも言えて，KJV の long は現れない。

You will be afraid to climb up a hill or walk down a road .Your hair will turn as white as almond blossoms. You will feel lifeless and drag along like an old grasshopper. We each **go to our eternal home**（永遠の家路につく），and the streets are filled with those who mourn. <CEV>／Remember him before you become fearful of falling and worry about danger in the streets; before your hair turns white like an almond tree in bloom, and you drag along without energy like a dying grasshopper, and the caperberry no longer inspires sexual desire. Remember him before you **near the grave, your everlasting home**（永遠の家である墓に近くなる），when the mourners will weep at your funeral. <NLT>／Also, they are afraid of heights and dangers on the road; the almond tree blossoms, the grasshopper loses its spring, and the caper berry has no effect; for man **is headed to his eternal home**（永遠の住処(すみか)に向かっている），and mourners will walk around in the street. <HCS>

[lot]

cast in one's lot among／with　一緒にくじを引く →仲間になる

KJV **Cast in thy lot among** us, let us all have one purse.［箴言 1:14］おまえも，われわれの**間でくじを引き**，われわれみなで一つの財布を持とう。

[用例] Yonder woman, Sir, you must know, was the wife of a certain learned man, English by birth, but who had long dwelt in Amsterdam, whence some good time agone he was minded to cross over and **cast in his lot with** us of the Massachusetts. [Hawthorne, *The Scarlet Letter*] 旦那様, 覚えて置いてください。向こうの女性はある学識ある方の奥さんです。その方は生まれは英国で, ながくアムステルダムに住んでいましたが, かなり前に海を渡る気になって, マサチューセッツ州のわれわれの**仲間になった**のです。

[**他の英訳聖書**] KJVの踏襲が圧倒的な中にあって, CEVのみ現代的な用法を用い, join our gangとしている点が際立つ。

If you **join our gang**（われわれの仲間に入る）, you'll get your share. <CEV>／ Come, **throw in your lot with**（一緒にくじを引く）us; we'll all share the loot. <NLT>

M

[make]

made before the hills ⇒ **old**

[man]

the inner man 内なる人 →隠れた品性，(ユーモラスに) 胃腸

KJV He would grant you, according to the riches of His glory, to be strengthened with might by His Spirit in **the inner man**. ［エペソ人への手紙 3:16］どうか父が，その栄光の豊かさに従い，御霊により，力をもって，あなたがたの**内なる人**を強くしてくださいますように。

［用例］Let's discuss the matter in hand and get it over with before we warm **the inner man**. ［¶］腹ごしらえする前に，当面の問題を討論して片付けてしまおう。

The magical power is in the inward or **inner man**. A certain proportion of **the inner man** longs for the external in all things. When the person is in the appropriate disposition an appropriate connection between man and object can be attained. ［Francis Barrett (occultist), 2009］魔術は人の**隠れた品性**に存在する。ある程度の**品性**はすべての事柄の外界現象になりたがる。それで，人が適切な心理状態にあると，人間と対象物の適切なつながりが達成される。

［他の英訳聖書］ CEV はかなりの意訳で，KJV の比喩性を無くしている。また，NLT では抽象名詞を訳出して意訳を試みている。しかし，いずれも，ユーモラスな訳は現代英語の意訳で，英訳聖書には現れていない。

I pray that his Spirit will make you become **strong followers**. (力強い僕(しもべ)) <CEV> ／ I pray that from his glorious, unlimited resources he will empower you **with inner strength** (内にある品性で) through his Spirit. <NLT>

[manna]

manna from heaven　天からの食物 →困ったときの助け

KJV And when the children of Israel saw it, they said one to another, It is **manna**: For they knew not what it was. And Moses said unto them, "This is **the bread which the LORD hath given you to eat**.［出エジプト記 16:15］イスラエル人はこれを見て,「**これは何だろう**」と互いに言った。彼らはそれが何か知らなかったからである。モーセは彼らに言った。「これは**主があなたがたに食物として与えてくださったパン**です。《［注］1611 年の欽定訳聖書オリジナルには It is Manna. が記されているが, 21KJV では "What is this?" と直訳されている。これは Manna がヘブル語に由来しているからで, 翻訳が難しいからであると思われる。》

[用例] The magazines were **manna from heaven**, killing my time while I was waiting for him.［¶］雑誌は**天の恵み**で, 彼を待っている間の暇つぶしになった。

［他の英訳聖書］　Manna が未知のものを意味するということから, 現代英訳聖書は皆 What is this? としている。これは慣用句になりえないから, Manna from heaven が文脈から推察されて生まれたものと思われる。The bread / the food 以下はやさしい語句を使っているので, KJV をほとんど継承している。

The people had never seen anything like this, and they started asking each other, "**What is it?**"（これは何だろう）Moses answered, "This is **the bread that the LORD has given you to eat**（主があなたがたに食物として与えてくださったパン）<CEV>／ The Israelites were puzzled when they saw it. "**What is it?**"（これは何だろう）they asked each other. They had no idea what it was. And Moses told them, "It is **the food the LORD has given you to eat**（主があなたがたに食べるよう与えてくださった食物）<NLT>

［アラム語慣用語句の意味］　オリジナルと同じ What is this? である。

[master]

serve two masters　二人の主人に仕える　→相反する主義・主張に忠実である

KJV　No man can **serve two masters**; for either he will hate the one and love the other, or else he will hold to the one and despise the other. Ye cannot serve God and mammon.［マタイの福音書 6:24］だれも，ふたりの主人に仕えることはできません。一方を憎んで他方を愛したり，一方を重んじて他方を軽んじたりするからです。あなたがたは，神にも仕え，また富にも仕えるということはできません。

[用例] If you want to be successful in life, you cannot **serve two masters**: becoming a millionaire and getting an honorable achievement. ［¶］人生に成功したければ，**相反することはできる**はずがない。百万長者になり，同時に名誉ある業績をあげることはできない。

After the battle, Zhang Ren was captured and offered a position in Liu Bei's army. He refused, saying "A loyal officer cannot **serve two masters**. I decline". He was then executed by Liu Bei. Later, Liu Bei buried him respectfully due to his loyalty to his master.［Wikipedia, *Zhang Ren*（張任）］戦いのあと，張任は劉の軍に捕らえられ，その軍で働くように地位を勧められたが，彼は断って，「忠臣は**二君に事(つか)えず**。断る」と言った。それで劉将軍によって処刑されたが，後に，劉将軍は彼がおのれの主人に忠節だったとの理由で，丁重に葬った。

[他の英訳聖書]　いずれの英訳聖書も「二人の主人」という人間を対称にしていて，比喩的表現を残している。

You cannot **be the slave of two masters**!（二人の主人の奴隷になる）You will like one more than the other or be more loyal to one than the other. You cannot serve both God and money. <CEV>／No one can **serve two masters**.（二人の主人に仕える）For you will hate one and love the other; you will be devoted to one and despise the other. You cannot serve both God and money. <NLT>

[measure]

fill up the measure 目盛りの不足分を満たす → (非道な行為の)不足分を加える, (悪事の)仕上げをする

KJV Fill ye up then **the measure** of your fathers. [マタイの福音書 23:32] おまえたちも父祖たちの罪の**目盛りの不足分を満たし**なさい。《[注] 預言者たちを殺した罪はその後にキリストを十字架につけることで仕上げをする。》

[用例] There comes an end to all things; the most capacious **measure is filled** at last. [Stevenson, *Dr. Jekyll and Mr. Hyde*] すべてに終わりがやってくる。**最大の不足が埋められる**。

[他の英訳聖書] KJV の measure を使うのは伝統的な英訳聖書にある。しかし, HCS にように, 何の不足分かを明示して, sins (罪) を補っているものもある。

But you prove that you really are the relatives of the ones who killed the prophets. So keep on **doing everything they did**. (犯したことをすべてやる) <CEV> / But in saying that, you testify against yourselves that you are indeed the descendants of those who murdered the prophets. Go ahead and **finish what your ancestors started**. (祖先がし始めたことを終わらせる) <NLT> / You therefore testify against yourselves that you are sons of those who murdered the prophets. Fill up, then, **the measure of your fathers' sins**! (父祖の罪の目盛り不足分) <HCS>

[ギリシャ語慣用語句の意味] HL は finish what your ancestors began (祖先が始めたことを終わらせる) としている。しかし, これだと, 何を始めたのかが分からない。文脈依存の文である。

[mercy]

leave to someone's/something's tender mercies/mercy だれかの (何かの) 優しい寛大さにすがる → だれかの (何かの) 非道に任せる

KJV A righteous man hath regard for the life of his beast, but **the tender mercies of the wicked are cruel**. [箴言 12:10] 正しい者は, 自分の家畜のいのちに気を配る。**悪者のあわれみは, 残忍である**。

[用例] Aborigines on the island were left to **the tender mercies of**

people involved in its development. [¶] 島の原住民は島の開発に携わる**人々の非道**に任せられていた。

[他の英訳聖書] 多くの英訳聖書は tender mercy の持つ比喩的アイロニーを消して，具体的な表現に代えている。その中で，HCS は even を使って merciful acts のアイロニーを残している。

Good people are kind to their animals, but **a mean person is cruel**. (意地悪な人は残酷だ) <CEV>／ The godly care for their animals, but **the wicked are always cruel**. (邪悪な人はいつも残酷だ) <NLT>／ A righteous man cares about his animal's health, but (**even**) **the merciful acts of the wicked are cruel**. (邪悪な人というものは，哀れみの振る舞いですら残酷である) <HCS>

[mess]

mess of pottage 一椀のあつもの →犠牲の大きすぎる小利

KJV Then Jacob **gave Esau bread and pottage of lentiles**; and he did eat and drink, and rose up, and went his way: thus Esau **despised his birthright**. [創世記 25:34] ヤコブはエサウにパンとレンズ豆の**煮物を与えた**ので，エサウは食べたり，飲んだりして，立ち去った。こうしてエサウは**長子の権利を軽蔑した**のである。

[用例] We have been selling our human birthright to the things of the mind and of the spirit for **the mess of pottage** of material achievements and mechanical accomplishments. [*Recent Giants in American Civilization*] 我々はこころや精神に関する事柄への**相続権**を売って，物質的な業績や機械的な成果の**小利**を得ようとしている。

[他の英訳聖書] CEV と NLT はまったく同じ語句を使い，HCS になると，豆の種類と使用動詞で KJV に忠実である。しかし，英訳聖書全体については基本的パラダイムは大同小異である。

Jacob then gave Esau **some bread and some of the bean stew** (いくらかのパンと豆の煮物), and when Esau had finished eating and drinking, he just got up and left, showing how little he thought of **his rights as the first-born**. (長子の権利) <CEV>／ Then Jacob gave **bread and lentil stew** (パンとレンズ豆の煮物) to Esau; he ate, drank, got up, and went away. So Esau despised **his birthright**. (相続権) <HCS>

[mind]

be of one mind 一つ心になる →同意する

KJV Finally, brethren, farewell. Be perfect, be of good comfort, **be of one mind**, live in peace; and the God of love and peace shall be with you.［II コリント人への手紙 13:11］終わりに，兄弟たち。喜びなさい。完全な者になりなさい。慰めを受けなさい。**一つ心になりなさい**。平和を保ちなさい。そうすれば，愛と平和の神はあなたがたとともにいてくださいます。

[用例] A young German Durchlaucht deigned to explain to his aide de camp how very handsome he thought Miss Newcome. All our acquaintances **were of one mind**.［Thackeray, *The Newcomes*］若いドイツ将校のドゥルヒラウフトは新しく来られた婦人はたいへんな美人だともったいぶった調子で副官に説明した。我々の知人はみな**同意した**。

Homonoia is the concept of order and unity, **being of one mind** together or union of hearts. It was used by the Greeks to create unity in the politics of classical Greece. It saw widespread use when Alexander the Great adopted its principles to govern his vast Empire.［Wikipedia, *Homonoia*］ギリシャ語のホモノイアは秩序と統一の概念で，心が一つであること，心の統一を意味する。古代ギリシャ政治で統一を図るためにギリシャ人によって使われた。アレクサンダー大王が自分の広大な帝国を支配するためにこの原則を採ったときに，広まった用語である。

[他の英訳聖書] CEV も NLT も KJV の慣用句をかなり意訳している。現代語では be of one mind with 〜の形で使われるが，be of one mind だけで使われるのはあまりないからであろう。その点 one = the same とし，with 以下なしで使っている HCS は KJV に忠実である。
Good-by, my friends. Do better and pay attention to what I have said. Try to get along and **live peacefully with each other**.（お互いに仲よく生きる）<CEV>／Dear brothers and sisters, I close my letter with these last words: Be joyful. Grow to maturity. Encourage each other. **Live in harmony and peace**.（一致して平和に生きる）Then the God

of love and peace will be with you. <NLT>／ Finally, brothers, rejoice. Be restored, be encouraged, **be of the same mind** (同じ心で), be at peace, and the God of love and peace will be with you. <HCS>

[mite]

widow's mite　やもめの小銭 →少額の献金，貧者の一灯

　KJV And there came a certain poor widow, and she threw in **two mites**, which make a farthing. And he called unto him his disciples, and saith unto them, Verily I say unto you, That this poor widow hath cast more in, than all they which have cast into the treasury. ［マルコの福音書 12:42f］そこへひとりの貧しいやもめが来て，**レプタ銅貨を二つ**投げ入れた。それは一コドラントに当たる。すると，イエスは弟子たちを呼び寄せて，こう言われた。「まことに，あなたがたに告げます。この貧しいやもめは，献金箱に投げ入れていたどの人よりもたくさん投げ入れました。」

　［用例］I had always cordially approved of missionary efforts, and had at times contributed **my mite** towards their support and extension. ［Butler, *Erewhon*］私はいつも宣教師の努力にこころからの賛意を表し，時々**わずかなお金**を彼らの支援と拡充のために捧げました。

［他の英訳聖書］　KJV の慣用語句は現代英語の coin に代えられてほとんどの英訳聖書に現れるが，ASV だけ mite に固執しているところから見ると，保守性が強いという伝統があるのであろう。

Finally, a poor widow came up and put in **two coins** (2 枚の硬貨) that were worth only a few pennies. Jesus told his disciples to gather around him. Then he said: I tell you that this poor widow has put in more than all the others. <CEV>／ Then a poor widow came and dropped in **two small coins**. (2 枚の小さな硬貨) Jesus called his disciples to him and said, "I tell you the truth, this poor widow has given more than all the others who are making contributions. <NLT>／ And there came a poor widow, and she cast in **two mites**, which make a farthing. And he called unto him his disciples, and said unto them, Verily I say unto you, This poor widow cast in more than all they that are casting into the treasury. <ASV>

mountain

[money]

Love of money is the root of all evil　金銭愛があらゆる悪の根 →金銭欲は諸悪の根源

KJV For **the love of money is the root of all evil**: which while some coveted after, they have erred from the faith, and pierced themselves through with many sorrows.［Ⅰテモテへの手紙 6:10］**金銭を愛することが，あらゆる悪の根**だからです。ある人たちは，金を追い求めたために，信仰から迷い出て，非常な苦痛をもって自分を刺し通しました。

[用例] Money may well be **the root of all evil**, but we cannot live without it. The question is how to use it.［¶］金は**諸悪の根源**だけど，なしではすまされない。問題はどう使うかだ。

"**The love of money is the root of all kinds of evil**" is rather more subtle than misquoted "money is the root of all evil" — money is in itself morally neutral, but the attitude to it, including love of it, is what is important.［Phrase Finder, *It is Easier for a Camel to Go through the Eye of a Needle*, 2003］「**金銭欲は諸悪の根源**」は間違って引用されている「金は諸悪の根源」とはかなり微妙な違いがある。金は本来道徳的に中立であるが，金を愛することも含めて金に対する態度が重要である。

[**他の英訳聖書**]　ほとんどの英訳聖書は KJV を踏襲しているが，CEV のように root の代わりに動詞の cause を使ったり，evil の代わりに trouble を使ったりして平易化しているものもある。

The love of money causes all kinds of trouble.（金銭愛はすべての問題の元になる）Some people want money so much that they have given up their faith and caused themselves a lot of pain. <CEV>

[mote]

mote in one's own eye　⇒ **beam**

[mountain]

move mountains　信仰は山を動かす →不可能を可能にする

KJV And though I have the gift of prophecy, and understand all mysteries, and all knowledge; and though I have all faith, so that I could **re-**

move mountains, and have not charity, I am nothing. [Ⅰコリント人への手紙 13:2] また，たとい私が預言の賜物を持っており，またあらゆる奥義とあらゆる知識とに通じ，また，**山を動かすほどの完全な信仰**を持っていても，愛がないなら，何の値うちもありません。

> [用例] I have faith in the power of love, especially true love, which can **move mountains** because it endures forever, never changing at any time. [¶] 私は愛の力，とくに**不可能を可能にする**真の愛の力を信じています。それはいつのときも変わることなく，永遠に続くのですから。

[他の英訳聖書] 定型化しているので，どの英訳聖書も KJV を踏襲している。

What if I could prophesy and understand all secrets and all knowledge? And what if I had faith that **moved mountains**? I would be nothing, unless I loved others. <CEV>／If I had the gift of prophecy, and if I understood all of God's secret plans and possessed all knowledge, and if I had such faith that I could **move mountains**, but didn't love others, I would be nothing. <NLT>

[multitude]

hide a multitude of sins　多くの罪を隠す →汚れをおおう

KJV Let him know, that he which converteth the sinner from the error of his way shall save a soul from death, and shall **hide a multitude of sins**. [ヤコブの手紙 5:20] 罪人を迷いの道から引き戻す者は，罪人のたましいを死から救い出し，また，**多くの罪をおおう**のだということを，あなたがたは知っていなさい。

> [用例] You can wear a patterned sweater for a long period, because it **hides a multitude of sins**. [¶] 模様のあるセーターは**汚れがうまく目立たない**ので，長く着られる。

[他の英訳聖書] HCS のように KJV の慣用語句を残しているものもあるが，多くは CEV や NLT のように multitude を many に簡易化して，forgive の動詞を使う CEV か，forgiveness の名詞を使う NLT の差があるのみである。

If you turn sinners from the wrong way, you will save them from death, and **many of their sins will be forgiven**.(彼らの多くの罪は赦される)<CEV>／You can be sure that whoever brings the sinner back will save that person from death and **bring about the forgiveness of many sins**.(多くの罪の赦しをもたらす)<NLT>／He should know that whoever turns a sinner from the error of his way will save his life from death and **cover a multitude of sins**.(多くの罪をおおう)<HCS>

N

[name]

My name is legion　私の名前はレギオンです →大勢です

KJV And Jesus asked him, "What is thy name?" And he answered, saying, "**My name is Legion**, for we are many." ［マルコの福音書 5:9］それで，「おまえの名は何か」とお尋ねになると，「**私の名はレギオンです。私たちは大勢ですから**」と言った。

[用例] Every year at Christmastime, donation cards for charity keep pouring in. It is really hard to decide to whom to give, for **their name is Legion**. ［¶］毎年クリスマスが来ると，寄付依頼の多くのカードが入ってくる。**大勢**なので慈善援助をだれにやるのかほんとうに難しい。

[他の英訳聖書]　ラテン語から来たレギオンはもともとローマ軍団の意味で，それが多数から構成されていたことから，「大勢」が比喩的に使われた。レギオンをそのまま使うか，「大勢」の代名詞として使うかの違いである。

Jesus asked, "What is your name?" The man answered, "**My name is Lots**（私の名前は「大勢」です）, because I have lots' of evil spirits." <CEV>／Then Jesus demanded, "What is your name?" And he replied, "**My name is Legion**（私の名前はレギオンです）, because there are many of us inside this man." <NLT>

[アラム語慣用語句の意味]　Lamsa（1985）は I have many wrong ideas; I am a hopeless case.（私は多くの間違った考えを持っている。私はどうしようもない奴だ）と訳している。このアラム語は「大勢」の意味が隠されて，「悪魔」の意味が前面に出ている。

[neighbour]

love thy neighbour as thyself　隣人を自分自身のように愛する →互いに愛し合う

KJV Thou shalt not avenge, nor bear any grudge against the children of thy people, but thou shalt **love thy neighbour as thyself**: I am the LORD.［レビ記 19:18］復讐してはならない。あなたの国の人々を恨んではならない。**あなたの隣人をあなた自身のように愛しなさい**。わたしは主である。

〔用例〕We don't care about what our neighbor will think of us, but we know our duty we owe to him, that is, **love your neighbor as yourself**.［¶］私たちの隣人が私たちをどう考えようと構わない。しかし，隣人に対する責務は知っている。すなわち，**隣人を自分のように愛せよ**ということである。《［注］your, our などの人称代名詞の所有格がつくと，聖書的なニュアンスが付き，総称的な「隣人」になるようである。》

[他の英訳聖書] CEV のように丁寧にパラフレーズしている英訳聖書もあるが，大多数は KJV を踏襲している。

Stop being angry and don't try to take revenge. I am the LORD, and I command you to **love others as much as you love yourself**.（自分を愛するように他人を愛する）<CEV>

[noise]

noise abroad　雑音が外に出る →広く言いふらす

KJV And fear came on all that dwelt round about them: and all these sayings were **noised abroad** throughout all the hill country of Judaea.［ルカの福音書 1:65］そして，近所の人々はみな恐れた。さらにこれらのことの一部始終が，ユダヤの山地全体にも**語り伝えられて行った**。

〔用例〕Though the family tried to keep it secret, the news of his suicide was **noised abroad** in the most extraordinary way; everyone seemed to be talking about it a few hours after it had actually happened.［Lyell, *Principles of Geology*］家族は秘密にしておこうとしたが，彼の自殺のニュースはとてつもなく異常に**広く広がった**。実

際に起こったあと数時間もみんなが話し合っているようだった。

The fame of his learning and sanctity was soon **noised abroad**, and scholars of all ages flocked from every side to his monastic retreat — young laymen and clerics, abbots, and bishops. [Wikipedia, *Finnian of Clonard*] 彼が学識があり神聖さを備えているという名声がすぐに**広まって**，あらゆる年齢の学者たちがあらゆるところから彼の隠遁の修道所に集まってきた。若い平信徒も聖職者も僧院長もそして司教もである。

[他の英訳聖書] KJV の慣用語句 noise abroad を使っているのは ASV のみで，類似の ESV さえも使っていない。ほとんどの英訳聖書は talk about という現代英語語句を使っている。

All the neighbors were frightened because of what had happened, and everywhere in the hill country people **kept talking about these things**. (これらのことを話し続けた) <CEV>／ Awe fell upon the whole neighborhood, and the news of what had happened **spread throughout** (広がった) the Judean hills. <NLT>／ Fear came on all those who lived around them, and all these things were being **talked about throughout** (全体に広く話された) the hill country of Judea. <HCS>／ And fear came on all that dwelt round about them: and all these sayings were **noised abroad** throughout all the hill country of Judaea. <ASV>

[number]

number days 日々を数える →長く生きられない

KJV So teach us to **number our days**, that we may apply our hearts unto wisdom. [詩篇 90：12] それゆえ，私たちに**自分の日を正しく数える**ことを教えてください。そうして私たちに知恵の心を得させてください。

[用例] I knew **my days of working for that firm were numbered**. After all, the final day came today. [¶] その会社で**長く働けない**ことは分かっていた。ついに，その日が今日来た。

[他の英訳聖書] 現代英語の慣用語句「長く生きられない」には，「残り時間を賢く使う」の意味がない。KJV 以外の他の英訳聖書，特に NLT と HCS には両方の意味がうまく表されている。

Teach us to **use wisely all the time we have**. (残りの時間を賢く使う) <CEV> ／ Teach us to **realize the brevity of life, so that we may grow in wisdom**. (命の短さを悟り，賢くなるように) <NLT> ／ Teach us to **number our days carefully so that we may develop wisdom in our hearts**. (自分の日々を注意深く数え，知恵を伸ばすように) <HCS>

[ヘブル語慣用語句の意味] WL は use time wisely（時を賢く使う）としていて，特に命の短さを表してはいない。

[old]

as old as the hills/made before the hills 丘と同じくらい古い/丘より先に造られた →とても古い

KJV Art thou the first man that was born? Or wast thou **made before the hills**? [ヨブ記 15:7] あなたは最初に生まれた人か。あなたは**丘より先に生み出された**のか。

[用例] But this Boy — the tale is **as old as the Hills** — came out, and took all things seriously. [Kipling, *Plain Tales from the Hills*] この話は**とても古い**話ですが，しかし，この子が出てきて，すべての事柄を深刻に受け取ったのです。

You can use "**as old as the hills**" for a person. But be sure you are familiar with the sense of humor of the person you're using it on, especially if that person is female. [Wikipedia, *As Old as the Hills*] この「**とても古い**」という慣用語句を人にあてはめることができるが，それを使う相手のユーモア感覚をよく知っていることが肝要。とくに相手が女性の場合は。

Another reference has an entry for the "same old seven and six." A retired colonel says that phrase is **old as the hills** — "I have heard this expression, which is very common in the military, all my life - practically since Robert E. Lee was a second lieutenant." It's a response to "How are things?" and means unlucky — seven + six = 13. [Wikipedia, *Same Old Same Old*] 別の参考書に「古い同類の7足す6 (same old seven and six)」という慣用句がある。退役大佐がこの語句は**とても古い**ものだとして，「私はこの表現をずっと聞いていた。軍隊ではごくありふれた表現だ。実際にはロバート・E・リー少尉以来だな」と言っていた。それは「ご機嫌いかが」に対する応答で，不幸だ (7+6 →13) という意味である。

[他の英訳聖書] 用語が平易なので,そのまま比喩的に使っている英訳聖書が多い。

Were you the first human? Are you **older than the hills**?(丘よりも古い)<CEV>／ Were you the first person ever born? Were you born **before the hills were made**?(丘ができる前に)<NLT>

[one]

as one man 一人の人間として →一斉に,こぞって

KJV And all the people arose **as one man**, saying, We will not any of us go to his tent, neither will we any of us turn into his house. [士師記 20:8] そこで,民はみな,こぞって立ち上がって言った。「私たちは,だれも自分の天幕に帰らない。だれも自分の家に戻らない。」

用例 When the pianist finished his performance, the audience rose **as one man** to applaud him. [¶] ピアニストが演奏を終えると,聴衆は一斉に立ち上がって彼に拍手した。

[他の英訳聖書] 伝統的な英訳聖書(例として,NIV など)は KJV の as one man を踏襲しているが,この慣用語句の意味はいろいろな連語で表せるので,変化のとんだ意訳(例として,in agreement, in unison, united)がされている。

The whole army was **in agreement**(同意して), and they said, "None of us will go home. <CEV>／ And all the people rose to their feet **in unison**(一斉に) and declared, "None of us will return home! No, not even one of us! <NLT>／ Then all the people stood **united**(結合して) and said, "None of us will go to his tent or return to his house. <HCS>／ All the people rose **as one man**, saying, "None of us will go home. No, not one of us will return to his house. <NIV>

P

[parable]

take up one's parable　ことわざを唱える →話す番になる

KJV And he **took up his parable** and said: "Balaam the son of Beor hath said, and the man whose eyes are open hath said, ... ［民数記 24：3］彼は**彼のことわざを唱えて**言った。「ベオルの子バラムの告げたことば。目のひらけた者の告げたことば…」

[用例] My Aunt Susan **took up the parable** with an affectionate glance at her husband. [H. G. Wells, *Tono-Bungay*] 叔母のスーザンは夫に優しいまなざしを向けて**語り始めた**。

[他の英訳聖書]　CEV も NLT も KJV の慣用句は完全に意訳されて，別の平易な動詞で置き換えられている。HCS は parable に代えて poem を使っているだけ古風を残している。

And Balaam **said**:（言った）"I am the son of Beor, and my words are true, so listen to my message!" <CEV>／ And this is the message he **delivered**:（伝えた）"This is the message of Balaam son of Beor, the message of the man whose eyes see clearly." <NLT>／ And he **proclaimed his poem**:（彼の詩を唱えた）The oracle of Balaam son of Beor, the oracle of the man whose eyes are opened <HCS>

[parting]

the parting of the ways　道の分かれ目 →道標，人・組織との別れ

KJV For the king of Babylon stood at **the parting of the way**, at the head of the two ways, to use divination: he made his arrows bright, he consulted with images, he looked in the liver. ［エゼキエル書 21:21］バビロンの王は，**道の分かれ目**，二つの道の辻に立って占いをしよう。彼は矢を振り混ぜて，テラフィムに伺いを立て，肝を調べる。

[用例] For him ... **the parting of the ways** was much less painful; from the age of eight he had, in effect, been wafted by gentle parents and far-sighted teachers in ballet-school, and had continued complacently enough from there. [*The Guardian*, 1975] 彼にとって**人生の分かれ目**は全然苦痛ではなかった。8歳のときから事実上やさしい両親と先見の明のあるバレー教室の教師によってゆったりと教育され，それからのんびりと過ごしてきたのである。

The Parting of the Ways is an historic site in Sweetwater County, Wyoming, USA, where the Oregon and California Trails fork from the original route to Fort Bridger to an alternative route. [Wikipedia, *Parting of the Ways*] その**道標**はアメリカ，ワイオミング州のスウィートウォーター郡にある歴史的場所で，オレゴンとカルフォルニア街道がフォート・ブリジャーへ行く本道から分かれて，別の道に通ずるところである。

[**他の英訳聖書**] KJV の古風な表現は生かされずに他の同意語に代えられている。CEV は signpost，NLT は fork，HCS は split に代えている。

When the Babylonian king stands at **that signpost** (その道標), he will decide which way to go by shaking his arrows, by asking his idols, and by carefully looking at the liver of a sacrificed animal. <CEV>／ The king of Babylon now stands at **the fork** (分岐点), uncertain whether to attack Jerusalem or Rabbah. He calls his magicians to look for omens. They cast lots by shaking arrows from the quiver. They inspect the livers of animal sacrifices. <NLT>／ For the king of Babylon stands at **the split** (分岐点) in the road, at the fork of the two roads, to practice divination: he shakes the arrows, consults the idols, and observes the liver. <HCS>

[pass]

pass all understanding すべての考えに勝る →人の考えを超越する

KJV And the peace of God, which **passeth all understanding**, shall keep your hearts and minds through Christ Jesus. [ピリピ人への手紙 4:7] そうすれば，**人のすべての考えにまさる**神の平安が，あなたがたの心と思いをキリスト・イエスにあって守ってくれます。

[用例] I was sure St. John Rivers — pure-lived, conscientious, zealous as he was — had not yet found that peace of God which **passeth all understanding**. [Brontë, *Jane Eyre*] 確かなことは，聖ジョン・リバースは心の清い，良心的で，熱情的な人でしたが，**人の考えを超越する神の平安**をまだ見つけていなかったのです。

[他の英訳聖書] KJVの慣用句をいずれも現代風に意訳している。HCSのみKJVに似たようなsurpassという動詞とthoughtという名詞を使っている。

Then, because you belong to Christ Jesus, God will bless you with peace that **no one can completely understand**. (だれも完全には理解できない) And this peace will control the way you think and feel. <CEV>／ Then you will experience God's peace, which **exceeds anything we can understand**. (私たちのどんな理解をも超える) His peace will guard your hearts and minds as you live in Christ Jesus. <NLT>／ And the peace of God, which **surpasses every thought** (すべての思いを凌駕する), will guard your hearts and your minds in Christ Jesus. <HCS>

[pearl]

cast pearls before swine 豚の前に真珠を投げる →高価なものを価値の知らない者に与えるようなもので無駄である

KJV Give not that which is holy unto the dogs, neither **cast ye your pearls before swine**, lest they trample them under their feet, and turn again and rend you. [マタイの福音書7:6] 聖なるものを犬に与えてはいけません。また**豚の前に，真珠を投げて**はなりません。それを足で踏みにじり，向き直ってあなたがたを引き裂くでしょうから。

[用例] The teacher tried to explain the story of Christmas to his students, but it was just **casting pearls before swine**, because they just thought of gifts from Santa Claus. [¶] 先生はクリスマスの話を生徒に聞かせようとしたが，それはただ**豚の前に真珠を投げるようなもので無駄**だった。なぜなら，彼らはただサンタクロースからの贈り物を考えていたからである。

[他の英訳聖書] この語句は広く伝わり，ことわざ化しているので，

意訳する必要がなく，そのまますべての英訳聖書に残されている。

Don't give to dogs what belongs to God. They will only turn and attack you. Don't **throw pearls down in front of pigs**. (豚の前に真珠を投げ出す) They will trample all over them. <CEV>／ Don't waste what is holy on people who are unholy. Don't **throw your pearls to pigs**! (豚に真珠を投げる) They will trample the pearls, then turn and attack you. <NLT>

[アラム語慣用語句の意味] Wise sayings before fools (ばか者の前の賢いことわざ) がアラム語の意味であるとLamsa (1985) はしているが，これさえも比喩的意味を持っていて，解説が必要である。

[place]

in high places 高き所で →偉い人々の中で

KJV How are the mighty fallen in the midst of the battle! O Jonathan, thou was slain **in thine high places**. [IIサムエル記1:25] ああ，勇士たちは戦いのさなかに倒れた。ヨナタンは**おまえの高き所で**殺された。

[用例] Often he would hint of his contacts **in high places**. [*Daily Mirror*, 1974] 彼はしばしば**お偉いかたがた**にコネがあるとほのめかしたものだった。

[他の英訳聖書] KJVの原義は具体的な場所であったのであろう。これを比喩的に解釈したのは文脈依存である。後の英訳聖書はすべて具体的な場所を表していて，その具体的な場所からは比喩的解釈は無理であろう。

How the mighty have fallen in battle! Jonathan is dead **on Gilboa's hills**. (ギルボア山で) <CEV>／ Oh, how the mighty heroes have fallen in battle! Jonathan lies dead **on the hills**. (丘で) <NLT>

[possess]

possess one's soul 自分の命を勝ち取る →沈着である

KJV In your patience **possess ye your souls**. [ルカの福音書21:19] あなたがたは，忍耐によって，**自分のいのちを勝ち取る**ことができます。

[用例] Every man worthy of the name of man should know how to **possess his soul**, bearing with patience those things which energy cannot change. [OED] 人間に値する人は**沈着**になる仕方を知り，忍耐を持って活力が変えられない物事を耐えるべきである。

[**他の英訳聖書**] NLT は KJV の動詞を代えただけである。他方，CEV では表現の意訳が著しい。NIRV と HCS はともに gain life（永らえる）を使って，「沈着さ」を表している。

You will **be saved**（救われる）by being faithful to me. <CEV>／By standing firm, you will **win your souls**.（自分の命を勝ち取る）<NLT>／If you stand firm, you will **gain life**.（永らえる）<NIRV>／By your endurance **gain your lives**.（永らえる）<HCS>

[potter]

potter's field　陶器師の畑 →貧者・外国人の墓

KJV And they took counsel and bought with them **the potter's field**, to bury strangers in. [マタイの福音書27:7] 彼らは相談して，その金で**陶器師の畑**を買い，旅人たちの墓地にした。

[用例] When I wrote a letter ... you did not put it in the respectable part of the magazine, but interred it in that '***potter's field***', the Editor's Drawer. [Mark Twain (OED)] 私が手紙を書いたとき，貴方は雑誌のれっきとした箇所に載せないで，**貧者の墓**である編集者の引き出しに埋めてしまった。

Before Forest Lawn Cemetery was founded, the northwest corner of the property was used as a **Potter's Field** for poor people and people whose identities were not known. It was used from at least the 1880s through the 1960s. [Wikipedia, *Forest Lawn Memorial Park*] フォレスト・ローン墓地が造られる前に，その土地の北西地帯は貧しい人々や身元不詳の人々のための**貧者の墓**として使われていた。少なくとも 1880 年代から 1960 年代まで使用されていた。

[**他の英訳聖書**] KJV の the potter's field を節を用いた表現にして説明的にしているか <CEV>，慣用句をそのまま使用している <NLT>。

Then they had a meeting and decided to buy **a field that belonged to someone who made clay pots**.（陶器を作る人の所有である畑）They wanted to use it as a graveyard for foreigners. <CEV>／After some discussion they finally decided to buy **the potter's field**（陶器師の畑），

and they made it into a cemetery for foreigners. <NLT>

[power]

the powers that be　存在している権威 →上位にいる権威者

KJV Let every soul be subject unto the higher powers. For there is no power but from God; **the powers that be** are ordained by God. ［ローマ人への手紙 13:1］人はみな，上に立つ権威に従うべきです。神によらない権威はなく，**存在している権威**はすべて，神によって立てられたものです。

[用例] Here, again, there was a feeble show of resistance, but ... Ernest ... recanted and submitted himself to **the powers that were**. ［Butler, *The Way of All Flesh*］またまたか細い抵抗の兆しが見えたが，アーネストは撤回して**当局**に服従した。

Angelus dedicates himself to "helping the helpless," and becomes a Champion of **The Powers That Be**, who send him psychic visions through his employees Doyle, and later Cordelia. ［Wikipedia, *Angel*］アンゲラスは無力の人々を助けることに身をささげ，**上にいる権威者（神）**の擁護者になる。神は彼に使用人ドイルとコルデリアを使って心霊洞察力を送る。

[他の英訳聖書]　KJV の抽象的な内容を CEV と WE と NLT は具体的な内容にしている。特に前者の 2 英訳聖書はより一般的な用語の rulers を好んで使っている。他の英訳聖書は be をそのままか，exist に代える程度で KJV の語法を踏襲している。

Obey the rulers who have authority over you. Only God can give authority to anyone, and he puts **these rulers** (これらの支配者) in their places of power. <CEV>／ Everyone must submit to governing authorities. For all authority comes from God, and **those in positions of authority** (権威ある地位にある者) have been placed there by God. <NLT>／ Every person must obey the rulers over him. Every ruler has his power from God. And **the rulers** (支配者) are put there by God. <WE>／ Everyone must submit to the governing authorities, for there is no authority except from God, and **those that exist** (存在する者) are instituted by God. <HCS>

Q

[quick]

quick and dead 生身と死体 →生きている者と死んだ者

KJV And he commanded us to preach unto the people, and to testify that it is he which was ordained of God to be the Judge of **quick and dead**. ［使徒の働き 10:42］イエスは私たちに命じて，このイエスこそ**生きている者と死んだ者**とのさばき主として，神によって定められた方であることを人々に宣べ伝え，そのあかしをするように，言われたのです。

[用例] Lo! as I looked back for seventy leagues through the mighty cathedral, I saw **the quick and the dead** that sang together to God, together that sang to the generations of man. [De Quincey, *The English Mail-Coach*] 巨大な大聖堂から 350 キロ先を振り返ってみると，見よ，そこには**生きている者と死んだ者**が共に神に賛美し，幾世代の人間に歌をささげていた。

[他の英訳聖書]　すべての英訳聖書は KJV の慣用語句のうち，quick を living に代えて現代風にしている。この用法は古風なので，避けたのであろう。

God told us to announce clearly to the people that Jesus is the one he has chosen to judge **the living and the dead**.（生きている者と死んだ者）<CEV>

R

[reap]

reap as one sows　種を蒔くように刈り取る →行為の結果を甘受する

KJV Be not deceived, God is not mocked; for **whatsoever a man soweth, that shall he also reap**. ［ガラテヤ人への手紙 6:7］思い違いをしてはいけません。神は侮られるような方ではありません。人は**種を蒔けば，その刈り取りもすることになります**。

用例　If we conform to the narrow limitations of a purely mechanical outlook, we shall never see the wood for the trees and we shall **reap as we sow**. ［*The Scientific Symposium*］狭い限界をもつ，純粋に機械的な展望に合わせていれば，木を見て森を見なくなり，**その結果を甘受する**ことになろう。

[他の英訳聖書]　KJV の慣用句をそのまま踏襲するものもあるが，CEV のパターンを取る英訳聖書が多い。

You cannot fool God, so don't make a fool of yourself! You will **harvest what you plant**. (植えたものを刈り取る) <CEV> ／ Do not be fooled about this. God cannot be fooled. A man **gets what he plants**. (植えたものをうる) <WE> ／ Don't be deceived: God is not mocked. For **whatever a man sows he will also reap**. (蒔くものをまた刈り取る) <HCS>

[redeem]

redeem the time　歳月を取り戻す →機会を最大限に利用する

KJV **Redeeming the time**, because the days are evil. ［エペソ人への手紙 5:16］機会を十分に生かして用いなさい。悪い時代だからです。

用例　He worked, not by faith, but by sight, with indefatigable energy, **redeeming the time**. ［OED］彼は目に見えない力でなく，目に見える力で，不屈のエネルギーで，**機会を最大限に利用して**，働いた。

[他の英訳聖書]　KJV の慣用句は完全に意訳されている。NLT のパターンは多くの英訳聖書が採用しているが，その中で CEV のスタイルは特異である。なお，日本語訳聖書はすでに意訳文を採用している。

These are evil times, so **make every minute count**. (あらゆる時を大切にせよ) <CEV> / **Make the most of every opportunity** (あらゆる機会を最大限に利用せよ) in these evil days. <NLT>

[reed]

reed shaken with the wind　風に揺れる葦 →はかない存在

KJV　And as they departed, Jesus began to say unto the multitudes concerning John, What went ye out into the wilderness to see? **A reed shaken with the wind**?［マタイの福音書 11:7］この人たちが行ってしまうと，イエスは，ヨハネについて群衆に話しだされた。「あなたがたは，何を見に荒野に出て行ったのですか。**風に揺れる葦ですか。**」

[用例]　With relation to this universe, man is, in extent, little more than a mathematical point; in duration but a fleeting shadow; he is a mere **reed shaken in the winds** of force.［Huxley, *Lectures on Evolution*］この宇宙に関しては，人間は空間的広がりの点では数学の点にすぎず，時間的広がりの点ではつかの間の影にすぎず，要するに，自然の力の前には**はかない存在**にすぎない。

[他の英訳聖書]　KJV を踏襲しているのは ASV のみで，他は shaken を blown about <CEV> や swayed <NLT> に代えたりしている。この慣用語句は定型化しているので，意訳している英訳聖書はない。

As John's followers were going away, Jesus spoke to the crowds about John: What sort of person did you go out into the desert to see? Was he like **tall grass blown about by the wind**? (風に揺れるひょろ長い草) <CEV> / As John's disciples were leaving, Jesus began talking about him to the crowds. "What kind of man did you go into the wilderness to see? Was he **a weak reed, swayed by every breath of wind**?" (風が吹くたびに揺れる弱い葦) <NLT> / And as these went their way, Jesus began to say unto the multitudes concerning John, What went ye out into the wilderness to behold? **a reed shaken with the wind**? <ASV>

broken reed　いたんだ葦の杖 →頼りにならない援助

KJV Lo, thou trustest in the staff of this **broken reed**, in Egypt, whereon if a man lean, it will go into his hand and pierce it. So is Pharaoh king of Egypt to all who trust in him. ［イザヤ書36:6］おまえは，あのいたんだ葦の杖，エジプトに拠り頼んでいるが，これは，それに寄りかかる者の手を刺し通すだけだ。エジプトの王，パロは，すべて彼に拠り頼む者たちにそうするのだ。

[用例] He promised to look after my interests when I was away, but I find I've been relying on **a broken reed**. He has done absolutely nothing, with the result that I've lost thousand of pounds. [Lyell, *Principles of Geology*] 彼は私の留守中に私の利害関係のことの面倒を見てくれると約束したが，それが**頼りにならない約束**だと分かった。彼はまったく何もしなかったのだ。結局私は数千ポンドを失ってしまった。

［他の英訳聖書］ KJV の比喩は残っているが，stick を使ったり <CEV>，体重で壊れるような弱さを強調したり <NLT> して，意訳の度合いを強めている。

Is he depending on Egypt and its king? That's the same as leaning on **a broken stick,**（折れた杖）and it will go right through his hand. <CEV> ／ On Egypt? If you lean on Egypt, it will be like **a reed that splinters beneath your weight**（あなたの重さで裂ける葦）and pierces your hand. <NLT>

[respecter]

no respecter of persons　人を差別待遇しない者 →社会的偏見に左右されない者

KJV Then Peter opened his mouth, and said, Of a truth I perceive that God is **no respecter of persons**. ［使徒の働き10:34］そこでペテロは，口を開いてこう言った。「これで私は，はっきりわかりました。神はかたよったことをなさらず。」

[用例] The very first condition of legal justice is that it shall be **no respecter of persons**; that it shall hold the balance impartially. [Shaw, *An Intelligent Woman's Guide to Socialism*] そもそも司法裁判の第一

条件は**社会的偏見に左右されない**ということで、はかりをかたよらないように保つことです。

　Francis was **no respecter of persons**, whatever their rank or position. He rebuked the King of Naples for his ill-doing and in consequence suffered persecution. [Wikipedia, Francis of Paola] フランシスは社会的身分や地位が何であれ，**社会的偏見に左右されない人**であった。ナポリの王様の悪行を叱りつけたので，その結果迫害を受けることになった。

[**他の英訳聖書**]　CEV と NLT は現代語法に書き換えて，それぞれ treat 〜 alike と show no favoritism を使っているが，伝統的な英訳聖書である ASV と ESV は興味ある対比を示す。ASV が KJV のパターンを保つのに反し，ESV は no partiality に代えて意訳している。

Peter then said: Now I am certain that God **treats all people alike**. (すべての人を公平に扱う) <CEV>／ Then Peter replied, "I see very clearly that God **shows no favoritism**." (えこひいきをしない) <NLT>／ And Peter opened his mouth and said, Of a truth I perceive that God is **no respecter of persons**. <ASV>／ So Peter opened his mouth and said: "Truly I understand that God shows **no partiality**." (一辺倒ではない) <ESV>

[rib]

smite under the fifth rib　五番目のあばら骨を打つ →こころを打つ

KJV Howbeit he refused to turn aside: wherefore Abner with the hinder end of the spear **smote him under the fifth rib**, that the spear came out behind him; and he fell down there, and died in the same place: and it came to pass, that as many as came to the place where Asahel fell down and died stood still. [II サムエル記 2:23] それでもアサエルは，ほかへ行こうとはしなかった。それでアブネルは，槍の石突きで**彼の下腹を突き刺した**。槍はアサエルを突き抜けた。アサエルはその場に倒れて，そこで死んだ。アサエルが倒れて死んだ場所に来た者はみな，立ち止まった。

　[用例] If ever this thing ended, he would come up here again and see what it was like without **an ache under his fifth rib**. (i.e. in his heart.) [Galsworthy, *Soames and the Flag*] このことが終わるようなことがあれば、彼はここに再び現れ、**こころの痛み**なしにそれがどんなものであったかを知るであろう。

[**他の英訳聖書**] KJV の慣用語句をそのまま使用している英訳聖書はない。すべてが意訳していて、打たれたからだの部分を stomach (腹) としているのが圧倒的に多い。

But Asahel would not turn back, so Abner **struck him in the stomach** (彼のお腹を打った) with the back end of his spear. The spear went all the way through and came out of his back. Asahel fell down and died. Everyone who saw Asahel lying dead just stopped and stood still. <CEV>／ But Asahel refused to turn back, so Abner **thrust the butt end of his spear through Asahel's stomach** (槍の取っ手部分をアサヘルの腹に刺した), and the spear came out through his back. He stumbled to the ground and died there. And everyone who came by that spot stopped and stood still when they saw Asahel lying there. <NLT>

[**root**]

root of the matter 事の原因 →真実/中心事

KJV But should ye say, 'Why persecute we him?' — seeing **the root of the matter** is found in me. [ヨブ記 19:28] もし、あなたがたが、**事の原因**を私のうちに見つけて、「彼をどのようにして追いつめようか」と言うなら。

用例 We are here to try a case of heresy; and no sooner do we come to **the root of the matter** than we are taken back by idiots who understand nothing but horses. [Shaw, *Saint Joan*] 我々はここに異端信仰事件の法廷を開くことになっている。その**真実**にいたればすぐに、馬のことしか分からぬ馬鹿どもに驚かされるのだ。

Brass-headed tacks were used in upholstering chairs, especially at the foundations of the chairs, and in taking a chair apart to reupholster it from the bottom up, craftsmen might have said they were getting down to business, to **the root of the matter**, getting down to the brass tacks. [Phrase Finder, *Brass Tacks*] 真鍮をつけた留め金は椅

子の覆いをつけるのに使われた。とくに椅子の基礎的な部分で使われた。椅子をばらばらにして覆いの張り替えをするにあたっては,職人はさあ本番だ,**本仕事**に取り掛かるぞと言って真鍮の留め金を手に取ったであろう。

[**他の英訳聖書**] KJV の慣用句を CEV も NLT も大胆に意訳している。単なる語句の意訳にとどまらず,句それ自体の節の形での意訳を試みている。それに反し,HCS は the root of the problem として,慣用句の形を残している。

My friends, you think up ways to blame and torment me, saying I **brought it on myself**. (自分自らもたらした) <CEV> ／ How dare you go on persecuting me, saying, 'It's **his own fault**'? (彼自身の過ち) <NLT> ／ If you say, "How will we pursue him, since **the root of the problem** (その問題の原因) lies with him?" <HCS>

[run]

he who runs may read 読む者が急使として走る →いとも簡単に分かる

KJV And the LORD answered me and said: "Write the vision and make it plain upon tablets, that **he may run that readeth it**. [ハバクク書 2:2] 主は私に答えて言われた。幻を書きしるせ。幻を板の上に書いて確認せよ。**これを読む者が急使として走る**ために。

[用例] But it is not a book which **he who runs may read**, and it may be better understood fifty years hence than it is at the present day. [Oscar Browning, *Sordello*] しかし,これは**容易に分かる**本ではない。現在よりも 50 年後により分かるものかもしれない。

[**他の英訳聖書**] KJV は文脈なしには理解が難しいから,CEV と HCS では一般的に適用できるように意訳し,NLT では原義の runner を生かしながら平易に意訳している。

Then the LORD told me: "I will give you my message in the form of a vision. Write it **clearly enough to be read at a glance**." (一目見て十分読めるようにはっきりと) <CEV> ／ The LORD answered me: Write down this vision; clearly inscribe it on tablets so **one may easily read it**. (容易に読めるように) <HCS> ／ Then the LORD said to me, "Write my answer plainly on tablets, so that **a runner can carry the correct message to others**. (急使が正しいメッセージを他人に持っていくことができるように) <NLT>

S

[sackcloth]

in/wearing sackcloth and ashes 荒布をまとい,灰をかぶって悔い改める →愚かなことをして悲しんでいる

KJV Woe unto thee, Chorazin! Woe unto thee, Bethsaida! For if the mighty works which were done in you had been done in Tyre and Sidon, they would have repented long ago **in sackcloth and ashes**. [マタイの福音書 11:21] ああコラジン。ああベツサイダ。おまえたちのうちで行なわれた力あるわざが,もしもツロとシドンで行なわれたのだったら,彼らはとうの昔に**荒布をまとい,灰をかぶって悔い改めて**いたことだろう。

[用例] A deplorable error and misfortune, for which humanity should mourn **in sackcloth and ashes**. [Mill, *Liberty*] 嘆かわしい過ちと不幸,それに対し人類は**悲しんで**嘆くべきである。

Four knights heard the King exclaim "Who shall rid me of this turbulent priest?" and then murdered Becket on the steps of the altar in Canterbury Cathedral. The King didn't mean for the knights to kill Becket and is supposed to have expressed remorse for this killing. He attended Canterbury **in sackcloth and ashes** as a sign of penance. [Wikipedia, *Church and State in Medieval Europe*] 4人の騎士は王様が「この不穏な司祭を俺の前から取り除いてくれる者はおらぬか」と叫ぶのを聞いて,ベケットをカンタベリー寺院の祭壇の階(きざはし)の上で殺してしまった。王様は騎士たちにベケットを殺させる意図はなかったので,この殺人に対して深い悔恨の念を表したに違いない。彼は**愚かなことをしたことを悲しんで**,ざんげのしるしとして**荒布をまとい灰をかぶって**,カンタベリーの礼拝に出た。

[他の英訳聖書] CEVのようにKJVの語句をほとんどそのまま使うタイプと,NLTのようにもとの語句に説明的語句を加えるタイプが

You people of Chorazin are in for trouble! You people of Bethsaida are in for trouble too! If the miracles that took place in your towns had happened in Tyre and Sidon, the people there would have turned to God long ago. They **have dressed in sackcloth and put ashes on their heads**.(荒布を着て灰を頭にかぶっていた)<CEV>／What sorrow awaits you, Korazin and Bethsaida! For if the miracles I did in you had been done in wicked Tyre and Sidon, their people would **have repented of their sins long ago, clothing themselves in burlap and throwing ashes on their heads to show their remorse**.(ずっと前に罪を悔い改め、バーラップを着て灰を頭にまき、悔恨の意を表した)<NLT>

[safe]

safe and sound　無事な姿で →元気で／無傷で

KJV And he said unto him, 'Thy brother is come, and thy father hath killed the fatted calf, because he hath received him **safe and sound**.' [ルカの福音書15:27] しもべは言った。「弟さんがお帰りになったのです。**無事な姿**をお迎えしたというので、お父さんが、肥えた子牛をほふらせなさったのです。」

[用例] Fortunately my husband came home **safe and sound** after traveling for a week in the Middle East.［¶］幸運なことに、夫は中東に1週間旅行して**無事**に帰宅しました。

Believing Guinefort to have devoured his son, the knight slew the dog. He then heard a child crying; he turned over the cot and found his son lying there, **safe and sound**, along with the body of a viper. Guinefort had killed the snake and saved the child. [Wikipedia, *Saint Guinefort*] ギネフォート（飼い犬）が息子を食べてしまったと思った騎士は即座にその犬を切り殺してしまった。そのあとで、彼は子供の泣き声を聞き、ベビーベッドをひっくり返すと、息子が**無傷**でそこに寝ていた。そのそばにはマムシの死体が横たわっていた。ギネフォートがその蛇を殺して息子を助けたのであった。

[他の英訳聖書]　KJV の safe and sound は現代でも流通する慣用句だ

と思ったが，NLT, WE, YLT など多くの英訳聖書で，他の平易な表現に意訳している。

The servant answered, "Your brother has come home **safe and sound**, (無事な姿で) and your father ordered us to kill the best calf." <CEV>／'Your brother is back,' he was told, 'and your father has killed the fattened calf. We are celebrating because of his **safe return**.' (無事の帰還) <NLT>／The servant said, "Your brother has come home. Your father has killed the fat young cow because your brother is **home and he is well**." (帰ってきて元気だ) <WE>／and he said to him — Thy brother is arrived, and thy father did kill the fatted calf, because **in health** (健康で) he did receive him back. <YLT>

[salt]

the salt of the earth　地の塩 →世に役立つ人

KJV Ye are **the salt of the earth**, but if the salt has lost his savor, wherewith shall it be salted? It is thenceforth good for nothing, but to be cast out and to be trodden under foot of men. [マタイの福音書5：13] あなたがたは，**地の塩**です。もし塩が塩けをなくしたら，何によって塩けをつけるのでしょう。もう何の役にも立たず，外に捨てられて，人々に踏みつけられるだけです。

[用例] I know that journalists have a bad reputation. A while back on television I was asked what I thought about them, and I said they are **the salt of the earth**. [*The Guardian*, 1975] ジャーナリストが評判が悪いのは知っています。少し前にテレビで彼らのことをどう思うかと聞かれ，**世に役立つ人**たちと答えました。

[他の英訳聖書] 「地の塩」という訳語はことわざ化しているので，英訳聖書全般に一般化している。例外的な CEV は冗長の感がする。
You are **like salt for everyone on earth**. (地上においてすべての人に役立つ塩のよう) But if salt no longer tastes like salt, how can it make food salty? All it is good for is to be thrown out and walked on. <CEV>／You are **the salt of the earth**. (地の塩) But what good is salt if it has lost its flavor? Can you make it salty again? It will be thrown out and trampled underfoot as worthless. <NLT>

[アラム語慣用語句の意味] Lamsa によれば，the flavor of this world; good conduct（この世の香り；善行）の意であるという。しかし，このアラム語の意味では，文脈にある深遠な意味が出てこない。

[Samaritan]

good Samaritan よきサマリア人 →困っている人に手を差し伸べる善良な人

KJV But a certain **Samaritan**, as he journeyed, came where he was: and when he saw him, he had compassion on him, and went to him, and bound up his wounds, pouring in oil and wine, and set him on his own beast, and brought him to an inn, and took care of him. ［ルカの福音書 10:33f］ところが，ある**サマリヤ人**が，旅の途中，そこに来合わせ，彼を見てかわいそうに思い，近寄って傷にオリーブ油とぶどう酒を注いで，ほうたいをし，自分の家畜に乗せて宿屋に連れて行き，介抱してやった。

［用例］Of whom (two noble young Americans) the one fell sick, whilst the other supported his penniless comrade, and out of sixpence a day absolutely kept but a penny for himself, and giving the rest to his sick companion. "I should like to have known that **good Samaritan**, sir," our colonel said. ［Thackeray, *The Newcomes*］2 人の若い貴公子のアメリカ人のうち，1 人が病気に倒れ，もうひとりがその文無しの友を助けた。一日 6 ペンスの中からまったく 1 ペニーしか自分自身に取っておかず，残りは病気の友に与えた。「**あのよきサマリア人のような親切な人**のことをもっと前に知っていたらと思います」と中佐は言った。

Good Samaritan laws are laws or acts protecting from liability those who choose to aid others who are injured or ill. They are intended to reduce bystanders' hesitation to assist, for fear of being sued or prosecuted for unintentional injury or wrongful death. ［Wikipedia, *Good Samaritan Laws*］**親切な世話人**規則（**よきサマリア人**規則）とはけが人や病人を助けようとする人々を，法律上の責務から守ろうとする規則や法令である。意図したわけではない傷害や不法行為で死亡したのだと訴えられたり訴追されたりすることを恐れ

て，見物人が他人を助けるのを躊躇してしまうことのないように作られたものである。

[他の英訳聖書] もともと good Samaritan（よきサマリア人）という語句はなく，33節以下に書いてある内容から，判断した名称である。したがって，他の英訳聖書はそのまま KJV を踏襲したり，CEV のようにサマリアという地名で表したりしている。NLT の記述はサマリア人がユダヤ人から嫌われていることが分かるようにしている。

A man from Samaria（サマリアからの人）then came traveling along that road. When he saw the man, he felt sorry for him and went over to him. He treated his wounds with olive oil and wine and bandaged them. Then he put him on his own donkey and took him to an inn, where he took care of him. <CEV>／ Then **a despised Samaritan**（嫌われているサマリア人）came along, and when he saw the man, he felt compassion for him. Going over to him, the Samaritan soothed his wounds with olive oil and wine and bandaged them. Then he put the man on his own donkey and took him to an inn, where he took care of him. <NLT>

[scale]

The scales fall from someone's eyes 目からうろこが落ちる →真実が分かる

KJV And immediately there **fell from his eyes something like scales**, and he received sight forthwith, and arose, and was baptized. [使徒の働き 9:18] するとただちに，サウロの**目からうろこのような物が落ちて**，目が見えるようになった。彼は立ち上がって，バプテスマを受けた。

[用例] The words were few and simple, but the manner with which they were uttered was ineffable: **the scales fell from my eyes**, and I felt that I had no right to try and induce her to infringe one of the most inviolable customs of her country, as she needs must do if she were to marry me. [Butler, *Erewhon*] ことばは少なく単純だったが，発せられた時の態度はことばで言い表せないものだった。**私は真実が分かった**。私には彼女に説き伏せて彼女の国の侵すべからざる慣習を破らせようとする権利なんかないと感じた。もし彼女が私と結

[他の英訳聖書] 2つの翻訳の流れが確認できる。一つは KJV のように there に始まる文形式ともう一つは CEV に代表されるような表題文の形式である。

Suddenly **something like fish scales fell from Saul's eyes**（うろこのようなものがサウルの目から落ちた）, and he could see. He got up and was baptized. <CEV>／ And straightway there **fell from his eyes as it were scales**（うろこのように彼の目から落ちた）, and he received his sight; and he arose and was baptized. <ASV>

[score]

three score and ten　70歳　→平均寿命

KJV The days of our years are **threescore years and ten**; and if by reason of strength they be fourscore years, yet is their strength labour and sorrow; for it is soon cut off, and we fly away.［詩篇90：10］私たちの齢は**七十年**。健やかであっても八十年。しかも，その誇りとするところは労苦とわざわいです。それは早く過ぎ去り，私たちも飛び去るのです。

[用例] Now, past his **threescore and ten years**, Bradley was showing no impairment of his mental faculties. [*Collected Papers of Henry Bradley*] ブラドレーは**平均寿命**を過ぎても，精神機能はなんら損なっていなかった。

[他の英訳聖書] 平均寿命というのは時代によって，また国によって変わるから，70歳は旧約時代のパレスチナ地方の基準である。しかし，当時の平均年齢感覚を現代に当てはめるかどうかは聖書の知識とも関係してくる。無難なのは70という数字をそのまま書き表すことであるから，ほとんどの英訳聖書は seventy years としている。やや古い用法である threescore and ten は標準的な英訳聖書の ASV や ESV を除いては避けている。

We can expect **seventy years**（70歳）, or maybe eighty, if we are healthy, but even our best years bring trouble and sorrow. Suddenly our time is up, and we disappear. <CEV>／ **Seventy years** are given to us! Some even live to eighty. But even the best years are filled with pain and trouble; soon they disappear, and we fly away. <NLT>／ The days of our years are **threescore years and ten**, Or even by reason of strength fourscore years; Yet is their pride but labor and sorrow; For it is soon gone, and we fly away. <ASV>

[season]

in season and out of season 旬でも旬でなくても →時期を選ばず

KJV Preach the word; be earnest **in season, out of season**, convict, rebuke, exhort, in all long-suffering and teaching.［Ⅱテモテへの手紙 4:2］みことばを宣べ伝えなさい。**時が良くても悪くてもしっかりや りなさい。**寛容を尽くし，絶えず教えながら，責め，戒め，また勧め なさい。

[用例] I quite understand any fellow being worried at not having work in these difficult times, but he never leaves me in peace. Every day, **in season and out of season**, he's round at my office at all hours, begging me to get him a job. [Lyell, *Principles of Geology*] この困難 な時代に仕事を持たないで不安でいる人のことは分かるが，彼は私 をいらいらさせる。なぜなら，毎日，**時期を選ばず**，いつも事務所 をうろうろしていて，仕事を見つけてくれと頼むのだ。

[他の英訳聖書]　KJV の season は物理的にも精神的にも意味の適用 が普遍的に可能であるが，各英訳聖書はより具体的な語句を添えて分 かりやすく意訳している。

I command you to preach God's message. Do it willingly, **even if it isn't the popular thing to do**. (やることに評判がよくなくても) You must correct people and point out their sins. But also cheer them up, and when you instruct them, always be patient. <CEV>／ Preach the word of God. Be prepared, **whether the time is favorable or not**. (時が良 くても悪くても) Patiently correct, rebuke, and encourage your people with good teaching. <NLT>／ Tell people the word of God. Be ready to do it **at any time**. (いつでも) Show people they are wrong and talk to them about it. Tell them what they should do. Be very patient with them and teach them in many ways. <WE>／ Proclaim the message; persist in it **whether convenient or not**; (都合が良くても良くなくても) rebuke, correct, and encourage with great patience and teaching. <HCS>

[seed]

thy seed　汝の種 →子孫

KJV That in blessing I will bless thee, and in multiplying I will multiply **thy seed** as the stars of the heaven, and as the sand which is upon the sea shore; and thy seed shall possess the gate of his enemies. ［創世記 22:17］わたしは確かにあなたを大いに祝福し，**あなたの子孫**を，空の星，海辺の砂のように数多く増し加えよう。そしてあなたの子孫は，その敵の門を勝ち取るであろう。

[用例] The Bible tells us that we are all **the seed** of Adam, from which bad people as well as good people have descended. So we cannot be proud of it. ［¶］聖書によれば，私たちはみんなアダムの**子孫**だが，よい人々も悪い人々も出てきている。だから，それを誇りにすることはできない。

[他の英訳聖書]　seed は民族を形成する父方の代表者がいて，それに続く人々を指すが，日本語の「子孫」は一般の人々の後継者も指す。descendant はまさに前者を意味するが，offspring よりも期間が長い。英訳聖書は圧倒的に descendant と訳しているが，HCS など若干の英訳聖書は offspring を使っている。

I will bless you and give you such a large family, that someday **your descendants** (子孫) will be more numerous than the stars in the sky or the grains of sand along the beach. They will defeat their enemies and take over the cities where their enemies live. <CEV>／ I will indeed bless you and make **your offspring** (子孫) as numerous as the stars in the sky and the sand on the seashore. Your offspring will possess the gates of their enemies. <HCS>

[ヘブル語慣用語句の意味]　seed を descendant <WL> として比喩的に使うのはヘブル語に始まる。

[seethe]

seethe a kid in its mother's milk　母親のミルクで子ヤギを煮る →愛情過多で子を駄目にする

　KJV The first of the firstfruits of thy land thou shalt bring into the house of the LORD thy God. Thou shalt not **seethe a kid in his mother's milk**. ［出エジプト記 23：19］あなたの土地の初穂の最上のものを，あなたの神，主の家に持って来なければならない。**子やぎを，その母親の乳で煮てはならない。**

　［用例］Thou hast destroyed her by means of her best affections ― It is a **seething of the kid in the mother's milk**! ［Scott, *Kenilworth*］お前は彼女の最高の愛情を引き出して彼女を駄目にしてしまった。**愛情過多で子を駄目にしたケースだ。**

　［他の英訳聖書］いずれも，使う動詞は違っていても，KJV のパターンを採っていて，意訳してない。この慣用語句の理由は分からないらしい。ユダヤ教の教師は後に肉とミルクを同時に食卓に出すのを禁じた規則を作ったとのことである。

Each year bring the best part of your first harvest to the place of worship. Don't **boil a young goat in its mother's milk**. <CEV>／As you harvest your crops, bring the very best of the first harvest to the house of the LORD your God. You must not **cook a young goat in its mother's milk**. (子ヤギをその母親のミルクで料理する) <NLT>

[sepulcher]

whited sepulcher　白く塗った墓 →偽善者

　KJV Woe unto you, scribes and Pharisees, hypocrites! For ye are like unto **whited sepulchers**, which indeed appear beautiful outwardly, but are within full of dead men's bones and of all uncleanness. ［マタイの福音書 23：27］わざわいだ。偽善の律法学者，パリサイ人。おまえたちは**白く塗った墓**のようなものです。墓はその外側は美しく見えても，内側は，死人の骨や，あらゆる汚れたものがいっぱいです。

　［用例］How much among us might be likened to **a whited sepulcher**; outwardly all pomp and strength; but inwardly full of horror and despair and dead-men's bones! ［Carlyle, *Characteristics*］我々の

うちどれほどのものが**偽善者**にたとえられるか分からない。外面は華麗と力でいっぱいだが，内面は恐怖と失望と，それに死人の骨で満ちている。

The apocalyptic beast let loose has become a reality to our generation, and nobody knows what is still ahead of us. It is understandable therefore that books on the devil have been on the increase lately. ... If the attempts of this school have not yet borne much fruit, it is because we fear the devil's sight more than his activity, and because of a very understandable reticence to force open our **whited sepulchers**. [R. J. Zwi Werblowsky, *Lucifer and Prometheus*, 1952] 解き放たれた黙示録の獣は我々の世代に現実となり，だれもこれからどうなっていくのか分からない。したがって，悪魔についての本が最近増えてきている。もし，この研究の試みがまだ実を結んでいないなら，それは我々が悪魔の働きよりもその姿を恐れ，我々の**偽善者**ぶりを白日にさらすことを明らかに抑えているからだ。

[**他の英訳聖書**] KJV の sepulcher を使うものか，或いは CEV や NLT のような tomb や grave <WE> を使うものに大別できる。しかし，いずれも意訳せず，もとの比喩表現を残している。

You Pharisees and teachers are in for trouble! You're nothing but show-offs. You're like **tombs that have been whitewashed**. (白く塗った墓) <CEV>／ What sorrow awaits you teachers of religious law and you Pharisees. Hypocrites! For you are like **whitewashed tombs** (白く塗った墓) — beautiful on the outside but filled on the inside with dead people's bones and all sorts of impurity. <NLT>／ You scribes and Pharisees will have trouble. You who are not true to yourselves! You are like **graves that have been painted white**. (白く塗った墓) Outside they look very nice. But inside they are full of dead men's bones and all kinds of dirt. <WE>

[**sheep**]

separate/tell the sheep from the goats　羊と山羊を分ける → 善人と悪人を区別する

KJV And before Him shall be gathered all nations, and He shall separate them one from another as a shepherd **divideth his sheep from the goats**. [マタイの福音書 25:32] そして,すべての国々の民が,その御前に集められます。彼は,羊飼いが**羊と山羊とを分ける**ように,彼らをより分けます。

[用例] We should **separate the sheep and goats**, but the really interesting question. ... why some people are goats, and others sheep ... that question would be left unsolved. [Herbert Read, *Essays*] **善人と悪人を区別**しなければならない。しかし,ほんとうに興味ある問題は,なぜある人々は悪人で,別の人々は善人なのかということである。その問題は未解決のままであろう。

[**他の英訳聖書**] すべての英訳聖書が KJV を踏襲している。この慣用句がそれ自体典型的なことわざを構成していて,変えようがないからであろう。

lost/stray sheep 失われた/迷える羊 →道に迷った人間

KJV But He answered and said, "I am not sent but unto the **lost sheep** of the house of Israel." [マタイの福音書 15:24] しかし,イエスは答えて,「わたしは,イスラエルの家の**失われた羊**以外のところには遣わされていません」と言われた。

[用例] I entered, and beheld my **stray lamb** seated on the hearth, rocking herself in a little chair that had been her mother's when a child. [E. Brontë, *Wuthering Heights*] 部屋に入って見てみると,私の**いなくなっていた子**が暖炉の前に座って,彼女の母親が子供のころ座っていた小さな椅子を揺らしていた。

[**他の英訳聖書**] lost sheep は隠喩として確立していて,どの英訳聖書にも使われているが,若干のもの(CEV や WE など)では直喩になっている点が異なる。

Jesus said, "I was sent only to the people of Israel! They are like a flock of **lost sheep**." (失われた羊) <CEV>／ Then Jesus said to the woman, "I was sent only to help God's **lost sheep** (失われた羊) — the people of Israel." <NLT>／ He said, 'I was sent only to the people of Israel. They are like **lost sheep**.' (失われた羊) <WE>

[side]

pass by on the other side 反対側を通り過ぎる →知らない振りして助けない

KJV And by chance there came down a certain priest that way. And when he saw him, he **passed by on the other side**. [ルカの福音書 10:31] たまたま，祭司がひとり，その道を下って来たが，彼を見ると，**反対側を通り過ぎて行った**。

[用例] Lord Herringbone may dress himself in a snuff-brown suit, with snuff-brown shirt and shoes: it skills not; the undiscerning public, occupied with grosser wants, **passes by** regardless **on the other side**. [Carlyle, *Sartor Resartus*] ヘリングボーン卿は暗黄褐色の背広に同色のシャツを着，同色の靴を履いているかもしれないが，特に目立つ存在ではなく，洞察力の欠ける大衆はもっと大きな貧困にとらわれていて，無頓着に**知らない振りして反応しない**。

[他の英訳聖書] 他の動詞を使って，多少の変化をしているが，大きな変化はない。その中で，NLT はかなり具体的な描写をして，比喩性を減じている。

A priest happened to be going down the same road. But when he saw the man, he **walked by on the other side**. (反対側を歩き去った) <CEV>／By chance a priest came along. But when he saw the man lying there, he **crossed to the other side of the road and passed him by**. (道の反対側に渡って，通り過ぎた) <NLT>

[sin]

The sins of the fathers are visited upon children 父の咎(とが)を子に報いる →先人の過ちで罰を受ける

KJV Thou shalt not bow down thyself to them, nor serve them; for I, the LORD thy God, am a jealous God, **visiting the iniquity of the fathers upon the children** unto the third and fourth generation of them that hate Me. [出エジプト記 20:5] それらを拝んではならない。それらに仕えてはならない。あなたの神，主であるわたしは，ねたむ神，わたしを憎む者には，**父の咎を子に報い**，三代，四代にまで及ぼす。

[用例] We all have Irish friends. We must not **visit the sins of a few**

fanatics on another lovely Celtic nation ... [BBC radio, *Any Questions*, 1974 (Clive Jenkins addressing a Welsh audience)] 私たちにはアイルランドの友達がいる。2, 3の狂信者の咎を他の愛すべきケルトの人々に負わせてはならない。

[他の英訳聖書] KJVのvisitの比喩的意味をCEVではpunishに（HCSも同様），NLTではlayに平易・具体化していて，理解しやすい。

Don't bow down and worship idols. I am the LORD your God, and I demand all your love. If you reject me, I will **punish your families for three or four generations**. (3, 4世代にわたって家族を罰する) <CEV>／ You must not bow down to them or worship them, for I, the LORD your God, am a jealous God who will not tolerate your affection for any other gods. I **lay the sins of the parents upon their children**; (親の咎を子に課する) the entire family is affected — even children in the third and fourth generations of those who reject me. <NLT>

[skin]

by the skin of one's teeth　歯の皮だけで →かろうじて

KJV My bone cleaveth to my skin and to my flesh, and I have escaped **with the skin of my teeth**. [ヨブ記 19:20] 私の骨は皮と肉にくっついてしまい，私は**ただ歯の皮だけでのがれた**。

用例 We asked the driver to drive to the airport at full speed and caught the plane **by the skin of our teeth**. [¶] 運転手に全速力で空港に走らせるよう頼んで，**かろうじて**飛行機に乗れた。

　The arrow scratched the camera, ricocheted off the wall and hit the dartboard. The cameraman survived **by the skin of his teeth** because he was crouching down. [Wikipedia, *Codex Atanicus*] 矢はカメラをかすって，壁に跳ね返りダーツ盤に当たった。カメラマンは腰をかがめていたので，**かろうじて**避けることができた。

[他の英訳聖書] 多くがKJVを踏襲している中で，CEVの意訳振りは突出している。

I am skin and bones — **just barely alive**. (命からがら生きている) <CEV>／ I have been reduced to skin and bones and have escaped death **by the skin of my teeth**.（歯の皮だけで）<NLT>

[smoking]

quench smoking flax　くすぶる灯心を消す →才能を妨げる

KJV A bruised reed shall He not break, and **the smoking flax shall He not quench**; He shall bring forth judgment unto truth.［イザヤ書 42:3］彼はいたんだ葦を折ることもなく，**くすぶる燈心を消す**こともなく，まことをもって公義をもたらす。

［用例］A: "I've spoken to several artists about the boy, and they all tell me that he has really astonishing talent; yet his father sneers at everything he paints, and insists on his being a clerk in the City; it's really treating the lad shamefully."

B: "Yes, but how many parents, d'you suppose, **quench the smoking flax**?"［Lyell, *Principles of Geology*］

A:「あの子について数人の芸術家に話してみたが，みんな彼は驚くべき才能の持ち主だと言っている。ところが，彼の父親は彼が描くものをことごとく嘲笑し，彼は町で店員になるんだといって聞かないのだ」。

B:「知っている。どんなに多くの世の親たちは子の**才能を妨げて**いることか」。

[他の英訳聖書]　KJV の比喩表現は生かしたまま，CEV も NLT も HCS も動詞を平易な put out に代えて，それぞれ目的語を平易な dying flame, flickering candle, smoldering wick にしている。KJV の flax が古い亜麻布を意味しているからである。

He won't break off a bent reed or **put out a dying flame**（くすぶる灯心を消す）, but he will make sure that justice is done. <CEV>／He will not crush the weakest reed or **put out a flickering candle**.（くすぶるろうそくの火を消す）He will bring justice to all who have been wronged. <NLT>／He will not break a bruised reed, and He will not **put out a smoldering wick**;（くすぶる芯を消す）He will faithfully bring justice. <HCS>

[son]

son of man 人の子 →他の人々

KJV Thy wickedness may hurt a man as thou art; and thy righteousness may profit the **son of man**. [ヨブ記 35:8] あなたの悪は，ただ，あなたのような人間に，あなたの正しさは，ただ，**人の子**に，かかわりを持つだけだ。《[注] son of man を大文字ではじめるときは，「救世主キリスト」を表しているが，標記のように小文字ではじめているときは，「アダムの子孫」など一般に人間を表す。下記の例文は「救世主キリスト」の例。》

[用例] Mr. Grobe believes that this **Son of Man**, who hated all base and mean things, still lives in any heart that will open to him. [T. F. Powys, *Mr. Weston's Good Wine*] グローブ氏は，**救世主キリスト**はすべての利己的な，卑しい事柄を憎んでいたので，キリストにすべてを捧げる人の心には現在も住んでいると信じている。

[他の英訳聖書] KJV の踏襲を避けて，すべてヘブル語慣用語句に従っている。

The evil or good you do only affects **other humans**.（他の人々に）<CEV>／ No, your sins affect only people like yourself, and your good deeds also affect only **humans**.（人々に）<NLT>

[ヘブル語慣用語句] WL は son of man = other humans（他の人々）としている。したがって，ヘブル語起源の英語慣用語句ということになる。

[soul]

soul 魂 →者，人

KJV The **soul** which hath touched any such shall be unclean until even, and shall not eat of the holy things, unless he wash his flesh with water. [レビ記 22:6] このようなものに触れる**者**は，夕方まで汚れる。その者は，からだに水を浴びずに，聖なるものを食べてはならない。

[用例] 現代英語は次のような慣用語句として使われている。

(1) happy/sensitive/brave/simple, etc **soul** E.g. He is really quite a spiritual **soul**.（彼はほんとうに霊的な**人**だ）

(2) Not a (living) **soul** (= no one) E.g. Nobody will tell a **soul** about

it.（だれにもそのことは言わないでしょう）

(3) Not a **soul** in sight/not a soul to be seen E.g. The night was dark and still, and there was not a **soul** in sight.（夜は暗く静かで，**だれ**も見かけなかった）

(4) Poor (old) **soul** (= used to show pity for someone) E.g. The poor old **soul** had fallen and broke his leg.（かわいそうに，その**老人**は倒れて足の骨を折ってしまった）

[他の英訳聖書] いずれも KJV を踏襲せず，一般的な人称に代えている。

if **you**（あなた）have touched an unclean creature of any sort, including an unclean person. Once you are unclean, you must take a bath, but you still cannot eat any of the sacred food until evening. <CEV>／The **man**（人）who is defiled in any of these ways will remain unclean until evening. He may not eat from the sacred offerings until he has bathed himself in water. <NLT>

[ヘブル語慣用語句の意味] soul = person <WL> としていて，ヘブル語ではありふれた用法である。

[sour]

sour grapes 酸っぱいぶどう →負け惜しみ

KJV In those days they shall say no more, the fathers have eaten **a sour grape**, and the children's teeth are set on edge.［エレミヤ書 31:29］その日には，彼らはもう，「父が**酸いぶどう**を食べたので，子どもの歯が浮く」とは言わない。

用例 It may sound like **sour grapes** but I tell you I have no other feeling than congratulations on his success in the exam.［¶］**負け惜しみ**に聞こえるかもしれないが，彼が試験に合格したことをお祝いしている気持ちだけです。

For many graduate students, the ambivalence about being in school (Am I good enough? Smart enough? Creative enough? Does my adviser respect me? Can I make a contribution?) manifests in a **sour-grapes** scenario that can get in the way of learning.［Rachei Toor, *Reading like a Graduate Student*, 2009］多くの大学院生にとっ

て，学ぶことの相反する感情（たとえば，私はよい学生か，私はとても賢いか，私はとても創造的か，指導教官は私を尊敬しているか，私は貢献できるか等）は学問の邪魔になる**負け惜しみ**という筋書きに現れる。

[**他の英訳聖書**] sour grapes の文中の位置は違っているが，この慣用語句はどの英訳聖書でも堅く守られている。

No longer will anyone go around saying, "**Sour grapes** eaten by parents leave a sour taste in the mouths of their children." <CEV>／ The people will no longer quote this proverb: 'The parents have eaten **sour grapes**, but their children's mouths pucker at the taste.'<NLT>

[spare]

spare the rod and hate the child　むちを控える者はその子を憎む →愛のむちは子供を育てる

KJV He that **spareth his rod hateth his son**, but he that loveth him chasteneth him in good season.［箴言 13:24］**むちを控える者はその子を憎む**者である。子を愛する者はつとめてこれを懲らしめる。《[注] この意を汲んで一般化したことわざは Spare the rod and spoil the child（むちを控えれば子供を駄目にする）である。》

[用例] The discipline of the family in those days was of a far more rigid kind than now. The frown, the harsh rebuke, the **frequent application of the rod**, enjoined by Scriptural authority, were used, not merely in the way of punishment for actual offences, but as a wholesome regimen for the growth and promotion of all childish virtues.［Hawthorne, *The Scarlet Letter*］当時の家庭のしつけは今よりはるかに厳しいものだった。眉を寄せて厳しく叱ったり，聖書で課せられているような愛の**むちを時々使ったり**したものだ。それは実際の道徳違反の罰則としてばかりでなく，こどもの徳全体の成長と促進のための健全な枠組みとしても行われたものであった。

[**他の英訳聖書**] KJV の格言の裏側から言っているのが CEV で，文字通りに言い表しているのが NLT である。

If you love your children, you will correct them; **if you don't love them, you won't correct them**.（彼らを愛していなければ正すこと

はしない）<CEV>／**Those who spare the rod of discipline hate their children**.（しつけのむちを控える者はその子を憎む）Those who love their children care enough to discipline them. <NLT>

[spirit]

The spirit is willing but the flesh is weak　心は燃えていても肉体は弱い →やる気があっても体が利かない

KJV Watch and pray, that ye enter not into temptation: **the spirit indeed is willing, but the flesh is weak**."［マタイの福音書26：41］誘惑に陥らないように，目をさまして，祈っていなさい。**心は燃えていても，肉体は弱いのです**。

[用例] Meantime, watch and pray that you enter not into temptation: **the spirit**, I trust, **is willing, but the flesh**, I see, **is weak**.［C. Brontë, *Jane Eyre*］その間，誘惑に陥らないように，目を覚まして祈っていなさい。思うに，**やる気があっても体がついていかない**ものさ。

While use of the Utica crib was widely criticized and infamous among patients, some found it to have important therapeutic value. A patient who slept in the Utica crib for several days commented that he had rested better and found it useful for "all crazy fellows as I, **whose spirit is willing, but whose flesh is weak**."［*Journal of Insanity*, 1864］ユーティカベッド（ニューヨーク州ユーティカ市精神病センターで使われていた格子の檻(おり)のようなベッド）の使用は広く批判され，患者間で悪名高きものだったが，それには重要な治療上の価値があると認めている人もいた。ユーティカベッドで数日寝た患者はよく休めたし，自分みたいに頭のおかしな人間は**やる気があっても体が利かない**から，このベッドは役に立つとコメントしていた。

［他の英訳聖書］　多くの英訳聖書は KJV の踏襲であるが，CEV のみ現代風に変えて分かりよくしている。

Stay awake and pray that you won't be tested. **You want to do what is right, but you are weak**.（よいことをやろうとするが，体が弱い）<CEV>

[still]

a still small voice　かすかな細い声 →良心

KJV And after the earthquake a fire, but the LORD was not in the fire; and after the fire **a still small voice**. [I 列王記 19:12] 地震のあとに火があったが，火の中にも主はおられなかった。火のあとに，**かすかな細い声**があった。

[用例] Strong wind, earthquake shock, and fire may pass away; but I shall follow the guiding of that **still small voice** which interprets the dictates of conscience. [C. Brontë, *Jane Eyre*] 強い風，地震の衝撃，そして火事は過ぎ去ってしまうだろう。けれども，私は良心の指図を伝える，あの**かすかな細い声**の導きに従っていこう。

The high calling of ELI teachers is to help their students and clients respond to **a still, small voice** in their heart beckoning them to connect with those who are cut off from them by language — to reach out, not only to Americans, but to the students of 90 different countries who grace our campus at the University of Delaware each year. [Dr. Scott G. Stevens, *From the Director's Desk*, 2001] 英語教育研究所の教師たちの高い職業意識によって助けられて，学生たちや利用者たちは自分の心の**良心**に応えて働いている。その良心によって彼らは言語によって切り離された人々とつながりを持つよう促され，アメリカ人ばかりでなく，毎年デラウェア大学のキャンパスを豊かにしている 90 の異国の学生たちにも手を差し伸べているのである。

[他の英訳聖書]「静けさ」を強調する gentle が CEV と NLT で使われ，同様に soft が HCS で使われている。ともに KJV の「かすかな，細い」という small の持つ比喩性が弱められている。さらに，KJV の voice を比喩化して，CEV は breeze と自然現象を使い，NLT は人の声ではあるが，やわらかい whisper に代えている。HCS にいたっては voice と whisper を並立させている。

Then there was a fire, but the LORD was not in the fire. Finally, there was **a gentle breeze**.（そよ風）<CEV>／ And after the earthquake there was a fire, but the LORD was not in the fire. And after the fire there was

the sound of a gentle whisper. (静かなささやきの音) <NLT>／After the earthquake there was a fire, but the LORD was not in the fire. And after the fire there was **a voice, a soft whisper**. (穏やかなささやき) <HCS>

[stone]

cast the first stone at ～　～に最初の石を投げる　→～をまっさきに非難攻撃する

KJV So when they continued asking him, he lifted up himself, and said unto them, He that is without sin among you, let him **first cast a stone at her**. ［ヨハネの福音書8:7］けれども，彼らが問い続けてやめなかったので，イエスは身を起こして言われた。「あなたがたのうちで罪のない者が，**最初に彼女に石を投げなさい。**」

[用例] Unmarried! I do not deny that is a serious blow. But after all, who has the right to **cast a stone against** one who has suffered? Cannot repentance wipe out an act of folly? Why should there be one law for men, and another for women? ［Wilde, *Importance of Being Earnest*］未婚だって！　それが重大な一撃であるとは思うが，結局だれが苦しんでいる人を**攻撃する**権利があるのか。悔い改めて愚かな行為を消し去ることはできないのか。いったいなぜ男性と女性に別々の法律があるのか。

[他の英訳聖書]　throw a stone（石を投げる）の部分は各英訳聖書は変化がない。その前後に CEV や NLT，HCS のように変化が出る。

They kept on asking Jesus about the woman. Finally, he stood up and said, "If any of you have never sinned, then **go ahead and throw the first stone at her!**"（行って最初に彼女に石を投げなさい）<CEV>／They kept demanding an answer, so he stood up again and said, "All right, but let the one who has never sinned **throw the first stone!**" <NLT>／When they persisted in questioning Him, He stood up and said to them, "The one without sin among you should be **the first to throw a stone at her.**"（まず最初に彼女に石を投げる）<HCS>

[straight]

keep to the straight and narrow 小さな門を通り,狭い道を行く →真正直な生活をする

KJV Because **strait is the gate, and narrow is the way** which leadeth unto life, and few there be that find it. [マタイの福音書 7:14] いのちに至る**門は小さく,その道は狭く**,それを見いだす者はまれです。

[用例] Nobody knew that such an honest man, who had **kept to the straight and narrow** all his life, was deceiving a lot of people in the bank where he worked. [¶] あのようにずっと**真正直な生活を**していた正直者が職場の銀行の多くの人々をだましていたなんてだれも分からなかった。

... lashing out at a new wife isn't ideal behaviour for **keeping her on the straight and narrow**. [*Woman*, 1974] 新妻に厳しく叱責することは彼女に**まともな生活をさせる**理想的な仕打ちではない。

[他の英訳聖書] CEV も NLT も gate (gateway) to life として,KJV の後置修飾節を前置修飾に変えている。どんな gate かという点で明確になっている。他の英訳聖書は HCS のように後置修飾のままである。

But **the gate to life is very narrow. The road that leads there is so hard to follow** (命に至る門はとても狭く,そこへ行く道は辿り難い) that only a few people find it. <CEV> / But **the gateway to life is very narrow and the road is difficult** (命に至る通路はとても狭く,その道は困難である), and only a few ever find it. <NLT> / **How narrow is the gate and difficult the road that leads to life** (命に至る門はなんと狭く,その道はなんと険しいか), and few find it. <HCS>

[strain]

strain at/out a gnat and swallow a camel ぶよは漉して除くが,らくだは飲み込む →小さいことに拘るが,大きなことを見逃す

KJV Ye blind guides, who **strain out a gnat and swallow a camel**! [マタイの福音書 23:24] 目の見えぬ手引きども。ぶよは,漉して除くが,らくだは飲み込んでいます。

[用例] Bland ignorance of the ways of God and the meaning of the universe gives free scope for magnificent conjecture; and we **swallow the poetical sublime without straining at the gnat of mysticism**. [Rylands, *Words and Poetry*] 神のやり方や宇宙の意味を漫然と無視すると，壮大な推測を好き勝手に広げることになる。そして私たちは**神秘主義に注意することなく，詩的崇高さを見逃してしまう**。

[他の英訳聖書] ぶよとらくだの対比はよく知られていて，その比喩表現は他の英訳聖書にも引き継がれている。

You blind leaders! You **strain out a small fly but swallow a camel**. (小さなハエは濾して除くが，らくだは飲み込む) <CEV> ／ Blind guides! You strain your water so you won't accidentally **swallow a gnat, but you swallow a camel**! (ぶよは間違っても飲み込まないが，らくだは飲み込む) <NLT>

[strength]

on the strength of　力を得て →励まされて

KJV And he arose, and ate and drank, and went **in the strength of** that meat forty days and forty nights unto Horeb the mount of God. [Ⅰ列王記 19:8] そこで，彼は起きて，食べ，そして飲み，この食べ物に**力を得て**，四十日四十夜，歩いて神の山ホレブに着いた。

[用例] "Heathcliff frequently visits at the Grange," answered I, "though more **on the strength of** the mistress having known him when a boy, than because the master likes his company ...." [E. Brontë, *Wuthering Heights*]「ヒスクリフはしばしば農場を訪ねます」と私は答えた。「けれども，旦那さんが彼と一緒にいるのを好んでいるからではなくて，奥様が少年のころの彼を知っていた**からなんです**けれどね」。

[他の英訳聖書] KJV の名詞を中心とした表現を CEV と NLT では動詞を中心とした表現に代えている。

So Elijah sat up and ate and drank. The food and water **made him strong enough** (十分力づけてくれた) to walk forty more days. At last, he reached Mount Sinai, the mountain of God. <CEV> ／ So he got up and ate and drank, and the food **gave him enough strength** (十分に力を与えた) to travel forty days and forty nights to Mount Sinai, the mountain of God. <NLT>

go from strength to strength　力から力に進む →さらに成功する

KJV They **go from strength to strength**, every one of them in Zion appeareth before God.［詩篇 84:7］彼らは，**力から力へと進み**，シオンにおいて，神の御前に現れます。

> ［用例］Can we doubt that presently our race will more than realize our boldest imaginations, that it will achieve unity and peace, ……, **going on from strength to strength** in a ever-widening circle of adventure and achievement?［H. G. Wells, *A Short History of the World*］やがて人類はとてつもない大胆な想像をかき立て，統合と平和を達成し，冒険と達成の拡大していく輪の中で**さらに成功を加速させて行く**ことは間違いない。
>
> Old Buckenham Hall School is described by the Good Schools Guide as being: "A virtually perfect country prep **going from strength to strength**".［Wikipedia, *Old Buckenham Hall School*］オールド・バッケナム・ホール・スクールは事実上完璧な地方の私立初等教育学校で**ますます成功している**と優秀学校ガイドに記載されている。

［他の英訳聖書］ほとんどが KJV を踏襲する中で，CEV は現代口語的英語を使って grow stronger としている。

Your people **grow stronger**（より強くなる）, and you, the God of gods, will be seen in Zion. <CEV>／ They **go from strength to strength**; each appears before God in Zion. <HCS>

[stricken]

stricken in years　年を重ねて →年とって

KJV Now Abraham and Sarah were old and well **stricken in age**, and it ceased to be with Sarah after the manner of women.［創世記 18:11］アブラハムとサラは**年を重ねて**老人になっており，サラには普通の女にあることがすでに止まっていた。

> ［用例］There she (=Hester) beheld another countenance, of a man well **stricken in years**, a pale, thin, scholar-like visage, with eyes dim and bleared by the lamp-light that had served them to pore over

many ponderous books. [Hawthorne, *The Scarlet Letter*] そこで彼女, ヘスターは別の表情を見た。相当の**年**をとった男の表情だった。青ざめた, 細面の学者風の顔つきで, ランプの明かりでぼやけた, かすんだ目をしていた。そのランプの明かりで, 彼は大きな書物を熟読していた。

The matter was referred to Queen Victoria, whose approval cleared the way for the marriage on December 16, 1839. Palmerston was 55 at the time, and Lady Cowper was 52.They set up their home at Broadlands and the union was, by all accounts, a decidedly happy one. Of it, Lord Shaftesbury said, "His attentions to Lady Palmerston, when they both of them were well **stricken in years**, were those of a perpetual courtship." [Wikipedia, Emily Lamb, Lady Cowper] その事柄はヴィクトリア女王に諮問され, 女王が承認したので, 1839年12月16日に結婚への道が開けた。パーマーストンが55歳, クーパー婦人が52歳であった。彼らはブロードランドに居を構え, その結婚はだれに聞いても断然幸福そのものであった。これについて, シャフツベリー卿は「彼の夫人への心遣いは, 二人ともかなり**年配**であったので, 絶えず礼儀正しいものであった」と述べた。

[**他の英訳聖書**] KJV のこの慣用句は冗漫のように思われる。その点, HCS も同類である。CEV と NLT はともに very old と簡略化している。

Abraham and Sarah were **very old** (たいへん年をとって), and Sarah was well past the age for having children. <CEV>／Abraham and Sarah were both **very old** (たいへん年をとって) by this time, and Sarah was long past the age of having children. <NLT>／Abraham and Sarah were **old and getting on in years**. (高齢で年をとってきていた) Sarah had passed the age of childbearing. <HCS>

[sufficient]

Sufficient for/unto the day is the evil thereof 労苦はその日その日に十分ある →心配ごとはその日だけでも十分ある

KJV Take therefore no thought for the morrow, for the morrow shall take thought for the things of itself. **Sufficient unto the day is the**

evil thereof. [マタイの福音書 6:34] だから，あすのための心配は無用です。あすのことはあすが心配します。**労苦はその日その日に，十分あります。**

[用例] Puddle abruptly controlled her thoughts; this was no way to be helpful to Stephen. **Sufficient unto the day was the evil thereof.** Getting up she went into her bedroom where she bathed her face and tidied her hair. [Radclyffe Hall, *The Well of Loneliness*] パドルは急に自分の思いを抑えた。このことをしても決してスティーブンには役に立たない。**心配ごとはこの日だけでもいっぱいあるのだ。**彼女は起き上がって，寝室に行った。そこで顔を洗い，髪をとかした。

[他の英訳聖書] KJV の evil を「不幸なこと・心配ごと」ととらえれば，この意味での evil は現代英語では多く用いられない。したがって，CEV では worry を，NLT と HCS では trouble に代えている。

Don't worry about tomorrow. It will take care of itself. **You have enough to worry about today**. (今日心配することはいっぱいあるのだ) <CEV>／ So don't worry about tomorrow, for tomorrow will bring its own worries. **Today's trouble is enough for today**. (今日の苦労は今日で十分) <NLT>／ Therefore don't worry about tomorrow, because tomorrow will worry about itself. **Each day has enough trouble of its own**. (毎日独自の面倒なことがたくさんあるのだ) <HCS>

[sun]

Let not the sun go down upon your wrath 日が暮れるまで憤ったままでいてはいけない →怒りを翌日に持ち越すな

KJV Be ye angry, and sin not: **let not the sun go down on your wrath**. [エペソ人への手紙 4:26] 怒っても，罪を犯してはなりません。**日が暮れるまで憤ったままでいてはいけません。**

[用例] How calm are the heavens and the earth! ... The sun is ready to set: **let it never set**, O Leofric, **on your anger**. [W. S. Landor, *Leofric and Godiva*] 天地はなんと静かなのだろう。太陽はまさに沈もうとしているが，レオフリックよ，**お前の怒りを翌日に持ち越してはならない。**

[他の英訳聖書] KJV はいわば遠まわしの言い方で怒りを持続しては

いけないと言っているわけで，これを直截的に言い表しているのがCEVである。他方，NLTはKJVの名詞wrathを含む句を節にした点を除いては，KJVの表現を踏襲している。

Don't get so angry that you sin. **Don't go to bed angry**. (怒ってベッドに入ってはいけない) <CEV>／And don't sin by letting anger control you. **Don't let the sun go down while you are still angry**. (怒ったままで日が暮れてはならない) <NLT>

[sweat]

by/in the sweat of one's brow/face 額に汗して →労働によって

KJV **In the sweat of thy face** shalt thou eat bread, till thou return unto the ground; for out of it wast thou taken: for dust thou art, and unto dust shalt thou return. [創世記3:19] あなたは，**顔に汗を流して**糧を得，ついに，あなたは土に帰る。あなたはそこから取られたのだから。あなたはちりだから，ちりに帰らなければならない。

[用例] None of these ... will ever tell you, that they have found the law of heaven an unkind one ― that **in the sweat of their face** they should eat bread, till they return to the ground. [J. Ruskin, *The Mystery of Life and Its Arts*] これらのどれをとってもあなたに教えまい。それは天国の規則は冷酷なものだということで，地に戻るまで**労働してパンを食べろ**ということです。

He and the other leaders saw no need to go back to Africa since Africans had aided in the building of America by "**the sweat of their brow**." They had as much right to stay in America as other immigrants. [James E. Newton & Harman R. Carey, *Diamonds of Delaware and Maryland's Eastern Shore: Seven Black Men of Distinction*, 1997] 彼とそのほかの指導者たちはアフリカに帰る必要はないと思った。なぜなら，アフリカ人が自らの**労働によって**アメリカの建設を助けてきたからである。彼らには他の移住者と同様にアメリカに留まる権利があった。

[他の英訳聖書] ほとんどがKJVの慣用語句を踏襲している。それほど定型化しているといえるが，わずかに，CEVのように，動詞

sweat の一語で簡潔に処理しているものもある。

You will have to **sweat**(汗して)to earn a living; you were made out of soil, and you will once again turn into soil. <CEV>／**By the sweat of your brow** will you have food to eat until you return to the ground from which you were made. For you were made from dust, and to dust you will return. <NLT>

[sword]

beat swords into ploughshares　剣を鋤(すき)に打ち直す →平和な生活に変える

KJV And he shall judge among many people, and rebuke strong nations afar off; and they shall **beat their swords into plowshares**, and their spears into pruninghooks: nation shall not lift up a sword against nation, neither shall they learn war any more.［ミカ書4:3］主は多くの国々の民の間をさばき，遠く離れた強い国々に，判決を下す。彼らは**その剣を鋤に**，その槍をかまに**打ち直し**，国は国に向かって剣を上げず，二度と戦いのことを習わない。

用例 His (Wells's) book is a book of salvation and damnation ... of warnings to flee from the wrath to come, of prophesies of **swords turned into ploughshares** and spears into pruning-hooks.［Robert Lynd, *Essays*］ウェルズの本は救済と天罰に関する本で，来るべき神の怒りから逃れよとの警告と**剣を鋤に**，槍を枝打ち用鎌にして**平和な生活に変われ**との予言の本である。

The term "**Ploughshares**" is a reference to the biblical prophesy of Isaiah Ch. 2 and Micah Ch. 4. "They shall **beat their swords into ploughshares**, and their spears into pruning-hooks; nation shall not lift up sword against nation, neither shall they learn war any more".［Wikipedia, *The Ploughshares Movement*］「すきの刃」という名称は聖書の預言書イザヤ書2章とミカ書4章に言及したものである。「彼らは**その剣を鋤に**，その槍をかまに**打ち直し**，国は国に向かって剣を上げず，二度と戦いのことを習わない」。《［注］「すきの刃」運動という反戦運動の名称がどこから来たのかを説明したもの。》

[他の英訳聖書]　CEV のように現代英語に変えるのは少数派で，多

くは NLT のように，動詞を変えることはあっても，KJV のパターンを踏襲している。

He will settle arguments between distant and powerful nations. They will **pound their swords** and their spears **into rakes** and shovels;（剣と槍を鍬(くわ)とシャベルに打ち直す）they will never again make war or attack one another. Everyone will find rest beneath their own fig trees or grape vines, and they will live in peace. This is a solemn promise of the LORD All-Powerful. <CEV>／The LORD will mediate between peoples and will settle disputes between strong nations far away. They will **hammer their swords into plowshares**（金槌(かなづち)で剣を鋤に打ち直す）and their spears into pruning hooks. Nation will no longer fight against nation, nor train for war anymore. <NLT>

T

[tale]

tale that is told　ひと息 →ありふれたこと

KJV For all our days are passed away in Thy wrath; we spend our years as **a tale that is told**.［詩篇 90：9］まことに，私たちのすべての日はあなたの激しい怒りの中に沈み行き，私たちは自分の齢を**ひと息**のように終わらせます。

[用例] It is because every dawn breaks as full of wonder as the first day of creation that life preserves the enchantment of **a tale that is never told**.［Gardiner, *On Living Again*］すべての夜明けは神の創造の日のように驚異に満ちているからこそ，生命は決して**ありふれたことではない**魅惑を持っているのである。

[他の英訳聖書]　CEV や NLT では「息」の出し方に特色があるが，KJV の慣用句は普通の「息」で，興味ある差がある。

Your anger is a burden each day we live, then life ends like **a sigh**.（ため息）<CEV>／We live our lives beneath your wrath, ending our years with **a groan**.（うめき声）<NLT>

[tare]

sow tares among someone's wheat　麦の中に毒麦を蒔く →善人をだまして害を及ぼす

KJV But while men slept, his enemy came and **sowed tares among the wheat**, and went his way.［マタイの福音書 13：25］ところが，人々の眠っている間に，彼の敵が来て**麦の中に毒麦を蒔いて**行った。

[用例] Marcus Aurelius saw it with its future yet unshown, and with **the tares among its professed progeny** not less conspicuous than the wheat.［M. Arnold, *Essays in Criticism*］マルクス・アウレリウスはまだ見ぬ未来と合わせてそれを見た。善人とまでは言えないが，宗門に入った子どもたちの中に害を及ぼすものが存在するのを

[他の英訳聖書] KJV の tares（毒麦）が分かりにくいのか，他の英訳聖書は weed（雑草）に代えている。また，wheat（麦）を field（畑）に代える CEV は原義の比喩を損ねる心配がある。

But while everyone was sleeping, an enemy came and **scattered weed seeds in the field**（畑に雑草の種を蒔いた）and then left. <CEV>／But that night as the workers slept, his enemy came and **planted weeds among the wheat**（麦の中に雑草を植えた），then slipped away. <NLT>

[アラム語慣用語句の意味] wheat を field に代えると具合が悪くなる点がアラム語慣用句で示される。それは，wheat and tares が good people and bad people と意訳されているからである。

[Thomas]

a doubting Thomas 疑い深いトマス →疑い深い人

KJV The other disciples therefore said unto him, "We have seen the Lord." But he said unto them, "**Unless I shall see in His hands the print of the nails, and put my finger into the print of the nails, and thrust my hand into His side, I will not believe.**"［ヨハネの福音書 20:25］それで，ほかの弟子たちが彼に「私たちは主を見た」と言った。しかし，トマスは彼らに「**私は，その手に釘の跡を見，私の指を釘のところに差し入れ，また私の手をそのわきに差し入れてみなければ，決して信じません**」と言った。

用例 "I wonder if it will be any good!" "You are **a Doubting Thomas**. Yes, it will be of good."［W. Stead, *After Death*］「それは少しでもよいであろうか。」「お前は**疑い深い人**だな。確かにそれはよいことだよ。」

[他の英訳聖書] 慣用句 a doubting Thomas は特定の語句から来たのではなく，文脈全体から含意されたものである。したがって，大枠において KJV の踏襲である。

So they told him, "We have seen the Lord!" But Thomas said, "First, I must see the nail scars in his hands and touch them with my finger. I must put my hand where the spear went into his side. **I won't believe** unless I do this!"(このことをしなければ信じません)<CEV>／They told him, "We have seen the Lord!" But he replied, "**I won't believe it unless I see**(…を見なければ信じません) the nail wounds in his hands, put my fingers into them, and place my hand into the wound in his side." <NLT>

[thorn]

a thorn in someone's flesh／side　肉体に一つのとげ →耐えざる苦痛の種

KJV And lest I should be exalted above measure through the abundance of the revelations, there was given to me **a thorn in the flesh**, the messenger of Satan to buffet me, lest I should be exalted above measure.［IIコリント人への手紙 12:7］また，その啓示があまりにもすばらしいからです。そのために私は，高ぶることのないようにと，**肉体に一つのとげ**を与えられました。それは私が高ぶることのないように，私を打つための，サタンの使いです。

[用例] These auctions ... are **a thorn in our flesh**. Once they were selling wine at exorbitant prices.... Now prices are ridiculously low...［*Daily Mail*, 1974］このオークションにはいつも**苦痛の種**がある。ワインが途方もない高値で売られたかと思うと，今度は馬鹿げた安値で売られる。

In one exchange with Campbell, she retorted "Don't be addled man. Don't talk stupid!" Nevertheless, she had her supporters. Fellow councillor, Bill Kilbourn spoke fondly of her. "Decent, fearless, independent. True was **a thorn in the flesh of the smooth men** at Metro (council)."［Wikipedia, *True Davidson*］キャンベルとのやり取りで，彼女は「頭の混乱した馬鹿なことを言うな」と言い返したが，彼女には支援者がいた。議員仲間であるビル・キルボーンは彼女のことを愛情をこめて「トルーは礼儀正しくて，恐れを知らず，独立心が強い人だが，行政府のお世辞のうまい男連中には**耐えられない苦痛の種**だった」と語った。

［他の英訳聖書］　CEVはKJVのthornを意訳しているが，他の英訳聖書は何らかの形でthornを生かしている。

Of course, I am now referring to the wonderful things I saw. One of Satan's angels was sent to **make me suffer terribly**（私にとてつもない苦しみを与える）, so that I would not feel too proud. <CEV>／even though I have received such wonderful revelations from God. So to keep me from becoming proud, I was given **a thorn in my flesh**（肉体に一つのとげ）, a messenger from Satan to torment me and keep me from becoming proud. <NLT>

[アラム語慣用語句の意味] Lamsa (1985) はその意味として, grievance; annoyance（苦痛, 苦悩）を挙げているが, 英語の意訳とほとんど変わらない。

[tooth]

gnash one's teeth at/over 歯ぎしりをする →怒りを表す

KJV But the children of the kingdom shall be cast out into outer darkness: there shall be weeping and **gnashing of teeth**.〔マタイの福音書 8:12〕しかし, 御国の子らは外の暗やみに放り出され, そこで泣いて**歯ぎしりする**のです。

[用例] Can you fancy a moonlight conclave, and ghouls feasting on the fresh corpse of a reputation: ... the jibes and sarcasms, the laughing and **the gnashing of teeth**?〔Thackeray, *The Newcomes*〕月が出ている夜のローマ教皇選挙秘密会議を想像できますか。悪霊が評判という新鮮な死体をむさぼり, 嘲笑と皮肉に満ちて, あざ笑いし, **怒りを表す**のです。

And it came to pass.
Early in the morning, toward the last day of the semester.
There arose a great multitude, smiting the books and wailing,
And there was much weeping and **gnashing of teeth**,
For the day of judgement was at hand.〔University of Delaware, *From Buddy*, 1995〕ついに来た。朝早く学期の終わりの日に近づく。大勢の者が本をたたきつけ, うめく。そして泣き喚き, **歯ぎしりして怒る**。なぜって審判の日が近いからだ。

[他の英訳聖書] KJV の gnashing of teeth（歯ぎしりする）はそれ自体「怒っている」のかそれとも「悔しがっている」のか分かりづら

い。それで，CEV のように，in pain（苦痛で）を補足する英訳聖書も出てくる。

But the ones who should have been in the kingdom will be thrown out into the dark. They will cry and **grit their teeth in pain**. (苦痛で歯をぎしぎしさせる) <CEV> ／ But many Israelites — those for whom the Kingdom was prepared — will be thrown into outer darkness, where there will be weeping and **gnashing of teeth**. (歯ぎしりする) <NLT>

set/put one's teeth on edge　歯が浮く　→不快にする

KJV In those days they shall say no more: "The fathers have eaten a sour grape, and **the children's teeth are set on edge**." ［エレミヤ書 31:29］その日には，彼らはもう，「父が酸いぶどうを食べたので，**子どもの歯が浮く。**」とは言わない。

［用例］ And certainly few can hear any modern version read as a substitute for the Authorised Version in public worship without feeling **their teeth set on edge**. [Baikie, *The English Bible*] 確かに公の礼拝で，欽定訳聖書の代わりの近代訳聖書を聞く者は必ず癪(しゃく)に障って**不快な思いをする**。

In his review in the New York Times, Vincent Canby called it "a movie guaranteed to **put all teeth on edge**. ... a movie of such unrelieved genteelness that it makes one long to head for Schrafft's for a double-gin martini, straight up, and a stack of cinnamon toast from which the crusts have been removed." [Wikipedia, *84 Charing Cross Road* (film)] ニューヨーク・タイムズの批評欄でヴィンセント・キャンビーは「この映画「チャリングクロス街84番地」は必ず人を**不快にする**映画である。どうしようもない上品ぶった映画で，シュラフトの店に行ってダブルジンのマティーニをストレートで飲み，パンの耳を切ったシナモンのトーストを食べたくなるほどである」と評した。

［他の英訳聖書］　KJV の慣用句をそのままの形で使うのはまれで，種々の変化にとんだ意訳をしている。いずれも現代語法になっている。

No longer will anyone go around saying, "Sour grapes eaten by parents leave a sour taste in the mouths of their children." (子供たちの口に酸っぱさを残す) <CEV>／The people will no longer quote this proverb: 'The parents have eaten sour grapes, but **their children's mouths pucker at the taste**.'(子供たちはその味に口をすぼめる) <NLT>

cast in one's teeth　ののしる →非難する

KJV The thieves also, who were crucified with Him, **cast the same in His teeth**. [マタイの福音書 27:44] イエスといっしょに十字架につけられた強盗どもも，**同じようにイエスをののしった**。

[用例] Neither can foreigners **throw the carnival in our teeth** with any effect: those who have seen it (at Florence, for example), will say that it is duller than anything in England. [Hazlitt, *Merry England*] 外国人は英国のカーニバルを引き合いに出して**我々を非難しても**何の効果もない。(例えばフィレンツェの) カーニバルを見た人は英国のどんな見世物よりも面白くないと言うでしょう。

[他の英訳聖書] この慣用句は「何をだれに」の観点が把握しにくいから，その点を CEV や NLT は明確にしている。

The two criminals also **said cruel things to Jesus**. (イエスに残酷なことを言った) <CEV>／Even the revolutionaries who were crucified with him **ridiculed him in the same way**. (同様に彼をからかった) <NLT>／In the same way even the criminals who were crucified with Him **kept taunting Him**. (彼をあざけり続けた) <HCS>

[twinkling]

in the twinkling of an eye　目の瞬きのうちに →一瞬にして

KJV In a moment, **in the twinkling of an eye**, at the last trumpet. For the trumpet shall sound, and the dead shall be raised incorruptible, and we shall be changed. [I コリント人への手紙 15:52] 終わりのラッパとともに，たちまち，**一瞬のうちに**です。ラッパが鳴ると，死者は朽ちないものによみがえり，私たちは変えられるのです。

[用例] Thick darkness came on; and, **in the twinkling of an eye**, I was far away from mountains. [De Quincey, *Confessions of an English Opium-Eater*] 暗黒がやって来て，**一瞬のうちに**私は山々から遠く離れてしまった。

The company — then hardly more than **a twinkle in the eyes** of its founders — immediately saw a fit, brought Marlow on board for a six-month position that drew on her dietetic and marketing know-how and then kept her on as the company's chief nutrition adviser. [*UD Messenger*, Vol. 17, No. 1. 2008] 会社の創設者たちは**一瞬にして**その案が会社の企画と適合しているとみて，マーロウを6か月間役員会に入れ，彼女の栄養士としてのマーケティングのノウハウを生かした。ついで，彼女は会社の栄養最高顧問として残ることになった。

[他の英訳聖書]　日本語訳聖書の方が意訳に徹底しているが，英語訳聖書の方はすべて eye の比喩を生かしている。日本語では「瞬」がもともと目の動作を表しているからである。

It will happen suddenly, **quicker than the blink of an eye**. (目の瞬きより早く) At the sound of the last trumpet the dead will be raised. We will all be changed, so that we will never die again. <CEV>／It will happen in a moment, **in the blink of an eye** (一瞬にして), when the last trumpet is blown. For when the trumpet sounds, those who have died will be raised to live forever. And we who are living will also be transformed. <NLT>

V

[vessel]

the weaker vessel　弱い器 →女性

KJV Likewise, ye husbands, dwell with your wives with understanding, giving honor unto the wife as unto **the weaker vessel**, and as being heirs together of the grace of life, that your prayers be not hindered. [Ⅰペテロの手紙3:7] 同じように，夫たちよ。妻が女性であって，自分よりも**弱い器**だということをわきまえて妻とともに生活し，いのちの恵みをともに受け継ぐ者として尊敬しなさい。それは，あなたがたの祈りが妨げられないためです。

[用例] Men should be more careful; this very celibacy leads **weaker vessels** astray. [Wilde, *The Importance of Being Earnest*] 男性はもっと気をつけなければならない。この禁欲主義そのものが**女性**を迷わすからだ。

　From her conclusions about the capacity of the female intellect, Drake suggests that maybe women were created **the weaker vessel** because they are meant to think, while stronger men are meant for action. [Wikipedia, Judith Drake] 女性の知性能力に関して，彼女は結論として「たぶん女性は思考に向いているから**弱い器，すなわち女性**として創造され，男性は行動に向いているから力強い男性として創造されていると示唆している」。

[他の英訳聖書]　KJVと比べると，CEVとNLTはごく平凡な意訳になっている。その点，HCSは意味の上ではKJVと並んでいる。

If you are a husband, you should be thoughtful of your wife. Treat her with honor, because she **isn't as strong as you are**（あなたより強くない），and she shares with you in the gift of life. Then nothing will stand in the way of your prayers. <CEV>／ In the same way, you husbands must give honor to your wives. Treat your wife with understanding as you live together. She may be **weaker than you are** (あなたより弱い), but she is your equal partner in God's gift of new life. Treat her as you should so your prayers will not be hindered. <NLT>／ Husbands, in the same way, live with your wives **with understanding of their weaker nature** (彼女らの弱い性質を理解して), yet showing them honor as co-heirs of the grace of life, so that your prayers will not be hindered. <HCS>

vessel of wrath　怒りの器 →死すべき人間

KJV What if God, choosing to show His wrath and to make His power known, endured with much longsuffering the **vessels of wrath** fitted for destruction. [ローマ人への手紙 9:22] ですが，もし神が，怒りを示してご自分の力を知らせようと望んでおられるのに，その滅ぼされるべき**怒りの器**を，豊かな寛容をもって忍耐してくださったとしたら，どうでしょうか。

[用例] Each eye wept that looked upon her, and the most hardened bigot regretted the fate that had converted a creature so goodly into a **vessel of wrath**, and a waged slave of the devil. [Scott, *Ivanhoe*] 彼女を見た人はすべて涙を流し，頑迷な人でさえもそんなに優しい人が**死すべき人**に変えられ，悪魔に買われた奴隷にされる運命を嘆いた。

[他の英訳聖書]　KJV の慣用句は若干の標準的な英訳聖書を除いて，すべて意訳されて，分かりよくなっている。文学的見地からはそれがよいかどうかは別問題である。

God wanted to show his anger and reveal his power against **everyone who deserved to be destroyed**. (当然滅ぼされる運命にある人すべてに) But instead, he patiently put up with them. <CEV>／ In the same way, even though God has the right to show his anger and his power, he is very patient with those on whom his anger falls, **who are destined for destruction**. (滅ぼされる運命にある) <NLT>／ What if God, desiring to show his wrath and to make known his power, has endured with much patience **vessels of wrath** (怒りの器) prepared for destruction. <ESV>

[voice]

a voice (crying) in the wilderness　荒野で叫ぶ者の声 →だれも気に留めない声

KJV For this is he that was spoken of by the prophet Isaiah, saying, "**The voice of one crying in the wilderness**: 'Prepare ye the way of the Lord, make His paths straight.'"［マタイの福音書3:3］この人は預言者イザヤによって，「**荒野で叫ぶ者の声**がする。『主の道を用意し，主の通られる道をまっすぐにせよ』」と言われたその人である。

[用例] Against this the present writer, even if **a voice crying in the wilderness**, utters his serious protest. [B. W. A. Massey (in *M. L. N.* 1934)] これに抗して筆者は，**だれにも気に留められない声**だが，真剣な抗議を唱える。

[**他の英訳聖書**]　「叫ぶ者」を明示的に扱う英訳聖書 NLT と非明示的に扱うもの CEV とに分かれる。後者は KJV の伝統に従っている。

John was the one the prophet Isaiah was talking about, when he said, "**In the desert someone is shouting**（荒野で叫ぶ者がいる）, 'Get the road ready for the Lord! Make a straight path for him.'" <CEV>／ The prophet Isaiah was speaking about John when he said, "He is **a voice shouting in the wilderness**（荒野で叫ぶ声）, 'Prepare the way for the LORD's coming! Clear the road for him!'" <NLT>

lift up one's voice　声を上げる →悲しんで（喜んで）叫ぶ

KJV And it came to pass, when the angel of the LORD spoke these words unto all the children of Israel, that the people **lifted up their voice** and wept.［士師記2:4］主の使いがこれらのことばをイスラエル人全体に語ったとき，民は**声をあげて**泣いた。

They shall **lift up their voice**, they shall sing; for the majesty of the LORD, they shall cry aloud from the sea.［イザヤ書24:14］彼らは，**声を張り上げて**喜び歌い，海の向こうから主の威光をたたえて叫ぶ。

[用例] And **a few voices are lifted up** in favour of the doctrine that the masses should be educated. [T. H. Huxley, *A Liberal Education*] 大衆は教育を受けるべきだという理論に**賛成の人**が2，3いた。

He **lifted up his voice** in thanksgiving for the world had warriors so wise. [Kipling, *Stalky & Co.*] 世の中にはとても賢い武人がいることに彼は**大きな声**で感謝した。

Aggie Fight Song! **Lift up your voices**, now's the time to sing. This is the day the Victory Bell will ring. Loyal Aggies, all for one. Never stopping 'til we've won. Because the Mustang will show our team the way to fight. Charging the enemy with all his might. Let's go. Let's win. Today's the day the Aggies will fight! Fight! Fight! [University of California at Davis, *Aggie Pack*, 2009 (カリフォルニア大学デーヴィス分校応援歌)] **叫べ**，大きな声で歌う時だ。勝利のベルが今日こそ鳴り響く。忠実なデーヴィス学生よ，一つになれ。勝利するまでやめるな。ムスタングがチームに戦い方を示してくれる。力の限り敵を攻撃せよ。さあ進め。勝利を得よう。今日こそデーヴィス学生が戦う日だ。戦え戦え。

[他の英訳聖書] KJV の lift up one's voice はそれ自体は中立的な意味合いで，悲しんで叫ぶのか，喜んで叫ぶのかが分からない。二つの聖書の箇所はその点，対照的な状況を示している。その状況を決定するのは，その後に来る語句に依存している。CEV と NLT はイザヤ書についてはそのパターンを踏襲しているが，士師記については双方とも KJV 慣用句を意訳して明示的にしている。

The Israelites started **crying loudly**. (大声で泣く) [士師記2:4] <CEV> / People in the west **shout** (叫ぶ); they joyfully praise the majesty of the Lord. [イザヤ書 24:14] <CEV> / When the angel of the LORD finished speaking to all the Israelites, the people **wept loudly**. (大声で泣いた) [士師記 2:4] <NLT> / But all who are left **shout** (叫ぶ) and sing for joy. Those in the west praise the LORD's majesty. [イザヤ書 24:14] <NLT>

W

[wage]

The wages of sin is death 罪の値は死である →罪を犯せば死に至る

KJV For **the wages of sin is death**; but the gift of God is eternal life through Jesus Christ our Lord. ［ローマ人への手紙 6:23］**罪から来る報酬は死です**。しかし，神の下さる賜物(たまもの)は，私たちの主キリスト・イエスにある永遠のいのちです。

[用例] And so far as you do not resist the fiend of disorder, you work disorder, and you yourself do the work of Death, which is **sin, and has for its wages, Death himself**. [J. Ruskin, *Work (Eng. Prose 19th. C.)*] 無秩序という悪魔に抵抗しなければ，無秩序を行っていることになり，あなた自身死の働きをすることになる。**それは罪であり，その結果は死そのものに至る**。

[他の英訳聖書] 定型化していて，NLT のように KJV のまま踏襲されているものが多い。その中で，CEV は動詞句 pay off with (～と清算する) を使ってユニークに言い換えている。

Sin pays off with death. (罪は死で清算される) But God's gift is eternal life given by Jesus Christ our Lord. <CEV>／ For **the wages of sin is death**, but the free gift of God is eternal life through Christ Jesus our Lord. <NLT>

[watch]

watch and pray 目を覚まして祈る →油断をしない

KJV **Watch and pray**, that ye enter not into temptation. The spirit indeed is willing, but the flesh is weak. ［マタイの福音書 26:41］誘惑に陥らないように，**目をさまして，祈っていなさい**。心は燃えていても，肉体は弱いのです。

[用例] "Dearest," rejoined her lover, "we have ever hitherto endeavoured to be all of these things; we have not been worldly people; let us **watch and pray** that we may so continue to the end." [Butler, *The Way of All Flesh*]「最愛の人よ」と彼女の愛人は応えた。「私たちは今までこういうふうになろうと努めてきた。**油断しないで**, 最後までそのようでありたいね」。

[**他の英訳聖書**] CEV と NLT は KJV の行為そのもの (watch and pray) に時間の長さを与えて, stay <CEV> と keep <NLT> を付加している。しかし, 基本的な表現枠組みの変化はない。WE では pray を talk with God に代えているが, その必要はないと思われる。

Stay awake and pray (目を覚まして祈っていなさい) that you won't be tested. You want to do what is right, but you are weak. <CEV>／**Keep watch and pray** (目を覚まして祈り続けなさい) so that you will not give in to temptation. For the spirit is willing, but the body is weak! <NLT>／**Watch and talk with God** (目を覚まして神と語りなさい), so that you will not do wrong. A person's heart can want to do it, but his body is weak. <WE>

[water]

in deep waters　大水の底にいる　→困難な状態にある

KJV I sink in deep mire where there is no standing; I am come **into deep waters** where the floods overflow me. [詩篇 69:2] 私は深い泥沼に沈み, 足がかりもありません。私は**大水の底に陥り**奔流が私を押し流しています。

[用例] "Poor Harry Jekyll," he thought, "my mind misgives me he is **in deep waters**!" [Stevenson, *Dr. Jekyll and Mr. Hyde*]「かわいそうなハリー・ジェキル, 彼は**困難な状態にある**のではないか」と彼は思った。

[**他の英訳聖書**] KJV にある「困難な状態」の比喩表現は CEV では訳出不要となっている。同じ詩篇でも 14 節では deep water が現れるが, 状態描写ではない。他方, NLT では in deep water の比喩的表現が踏襲されている。

I am sinking deep in the mud, and my feet are slipping. I am about to be swept under by a mighty flood. [詩篇 69:2] Cf. Don't let me sink in the mud, but save me from my enemies and **from the deep water**. (大水から) [詩篇 69:14] <CEV>／Deeper and deeper I sink into the mire; I can't find a foothold. I am **in deep water** (大水の底にある), and the floods overwhelm me. <NLT>

【wax】

wax fat and kick 肥え太って足でける →繁栄しすぎて手に負えない

KJV But Jeshurun **waxed fat and kicked**; thou hast waxed fat, thou art grown thick, thou art covered with fatness. Then he forsook God who made him, and lightly esteemed the Rock of his salvation. [申命記 32:15] エシュルンは**肥え太ったとき，足でけった**。あなたはむさぼり食って，肥え太った。自分を造った神を捨て，自分の救いの岩を軽んじた。

[用例] It is the interest of the king or aristocracy to keep them at a low level of intelligence ..., and even prevent them from being too well off, lest they should "**wax fat and kick**." [J. S. Mill, *Representative Government*] 王様や貴族の関心は彼らを低い知的水準に置いておくことにある。そして，**繁栄しすぎて手に負えなくならないように**あまり裕福にならないようにすることさえも考えている。

[**他の英訳聖書**] KJV の慣用句は CEV と NLT では完全に意訳され，それぞれ現代語句に代わっている。

Israel, you **grew fat and rebelled** (肥え太って反抗した) against God, your Creator; you rejected the Mighty Rock, your only place of safety. <CEV>／But Israel soon **became fat and unruly** (肥え太って手に負えなくなった); the people grew heavy, plump, and stuffed! Then they abandoned the God who had made them; they made light of the Rock of their salvation. <NLT>

【way】

in the way one should go 行く道にふさわしく →礼儀正しく／正当な方法で

KJV Train up a child **in the way he should go**, and when he is old he will not depart from it. [箴言 22:6] 若者を**その行く道にふさわし**

[用例] If ever I have a boy to bring up **in the way he should go**, I intend to make Sunday a cheerful day to him. [Aldrich, *Story of a Bad Boy*] もし一人の少年を**礼儀正しく**育て上げるとしたら，彼に日曜日を楽しい日にしてあげるつもりだ。

Bharata Muni's Natya Shastra (literally "Scripture of Dance," though it sometimes translated as "Science of Theatre'") is a keystone work in Sanskrit literature on the subject of stagecraft. The Natya Shastra dates to between the second century BC and the second century AD. The text specifically describes the proper **way one should go** about staging a Sanskrit drama. [Wikipedia, *Sanskrit Drama*] バラータ・ムニの「ナーチャ・シャストラ」（字句通りには「ダンス教書」を意味し，時には「演劇学」とも訳される）はサンスクリット文学で演出法の基本的教本である。ナーチャ・シャストラは紀元前2世紀と紀元2世紀の間に遡(さかのぼ)る。そのテキストは特にサンスクリット劇を演じる際に**正当な**演出**方法**を記述したものである。

[**他の英訳聖書**] KJV の慣用句は完全に意訳されている。CEV と HCS では現代的な表現になっており，NLT はやや硬いながら，正確な語句で代用している。

Teach your children **right from wrong** (善悪を), and when they are grown they will still do right. <CEV>／ Direct your children **onto the right path** (正しい道に), and when they are older, they will not leave it. <NLT>／ Teach a youth about **the way he should go** (進むべき道を); even when he is old he will not depart from it. <HCS>

[wayside]

fall by the wayside　道端に落ちる →望みなしとあきらめる

KJV A sower went out to sow his seed. And as he sowed, some **fell by the wayside**, and it was trodden down, and the fowls of the air devoured it. [ルカの福音書 8:5] 種を蒔(ま)く人が種蒔きに出かけた。蒔いているとき，**道ばたに落ちた**種があった。すると，人に踏みつけられ，空の鳥がそれを食べてしまった。

[用例] The priest began the service with a prayer for all those who had **fallen by the wayside**. [¶] 司祭は**自分から望みないとあきらめた**人々のための祈りで礼拝を始めた。

"Although Dean Howells is associated with a certain kind of realism, if you look at whom he supported, you see that his own definition of realism really changed with the times," Susan Goodman said. "Howells also published Henry James, and, without his support, James would have **fallen by the wayside**." [University of Delaware, *Daily: Post-Civil War Culture Clash Focus of English Prof's Book*, 2004]「デーン・ハウエルズはある種の写実主義に共鳴していたが,もし彼がだれを支援していたかを見れば,彼自身の写実主義が時代とともに実際に変化していることが分かる。ハウエルズはまたヘンリー・ジェームズを世に出した人で,彼の支援がなかったら,ジェームズは**望みないと途中であきらめてしまった**ことであろう」とスーザン・グッドマンは述べている。

[他の英訳聖書] KJV の wayside を別の具体的な単語で置き換えた英訳聖書が多いが,比喩性は継承している。

A farmer went out to scatter seed in a field. While the farmer was doing it, some of the seeds **fell along the road**(道路わきに落ちた)and were stepped on or eaten by birds. <CEV>／A farmer went out to plant his seed. As he scattered it across his field, some seed **fell on a footpath**(歩道に落ちた), where it was stepped on, and the birds ate it. <NLT>

[weak]

weak as water 震える →ぐらつく,不安定な

KJV All hands shall be feeble, and all knees shall be **weak as water**. [エゼキエル書 7:17] 彼らはみな気力を失い,彼らのひざもみな**震える**。

[用例] Here, then, we lay for an hour or two, aching from head to foot, as **weak as water**, and lying quite naked to the eye of any soldier should have strolled that way. [Stevenson, *Kidnapped*] そのとき,私たちはここで 1,2 時間横になり,頭のてっぺんから足の先まで痛みを覚え,**がたがたして**,もし兵士がその方向に歩いてきていた

[他の英訳聖書] CEV は KJV の完全な意訳であるが，NLT は他の多くの英訳聖書と同様に，KJV を踏襲している。HCS は直喩ではなく，隠喩の turn to water になっている。興味あるのは NAS の表現である。普通は like water は spend like water のように「浪費する」となってしまうが，ここでは become like water として原義を保っている。

Your hands will tremble, and your knees will **go limp**. (よろめく) <CEV> / Their hands will hang limp, their knees will be **weak as water**. (震える) <NLT> / All their hands will become weak, and all [their] knees will **turn to water**. (弱くなる) <HCS> / All hands will hang limp and all knees will **become like water**. (水のようになる) <NAS>

[wheel]

wheels within wheels　輪中の輪 →錯綜，こみ入った事情

KJV The appearance of the wheels and their work was like unto the color of beryl, and all four had the same likeness; and their appearance and their work was, as it were, **a wheel in the middle of a wheel**. [エゼキエル書 1:16] それらの輪の形と作りは，緑柱石の輝きのようで，四つともよく似ていて，それらの形と作りは，ちょうど，**一つの輪が他の輪の中にある**ようであった。

[用例] Truth is a very complex thing, and politics is a very complex business. They are **wheels within wheels**. [Wilde, *Ideal Husband*] 真理はとても複雑なもので，政治もとても複雑なビジネスだ。いろんなことが**複雑に絡み合っている**のだ。

Rhys Hughes's main project consists of authoring a 1,000-story cycle of both tightly and loosely interconnected tales. Hughes calls this cycle a "wheel", which in turn is formed by smaller "**wheels within wheels**". [Wikipedia, Rhys Hughes] ライス・ヒューズ [ウェールズの作家・随筆家] の主要プロジェクトは相互にしっかりと結び合いながら，しかし緩やかに関連している話を 1000 のサイクルでコンピュータプログラムにすることである。ヒューズはこのサイクルを「輪」と呼んでいるが，この輪は，これはこれでさらに**複雑な**小さな「**輪中の輪**」で形成されているのである。

[他の英訳聖書] CEV と NLT は KJV の wheels within wheels を動きの説明で具体化している。

Shining like chrysolite. each wheel was exactly the same and had **a second wheel that cut through the middle of it**. (2番目の輪が別の輪に食い込んでいる) <CEV>／The wheels sparkled as if made of beryl. All four wheels looked alike and were made the same; **each wheel had a second wheel turning crosswise within it**. (それぞれの輪は別の輪をその中に交差させていた) <NLT>

[wife]

old wives' tale/fable/story 年寄り女の空想話 →昔のばかげた話

KJV But reject profane and **old wives' fables**, and exercise thyself rather unto godliness. [I テモテへの手紙 4:7] 俗悪な，**年寄り女がするような空想話**を避けなさい。むしろ，敬虔のために自分を鍛練しなさい。

[用例] Give a woman **an old wife's tale** and a weaver-bird a leaf and a thread ... All holy men dream dreams, and by following holy men their disciples attain that power. [Kipling, *Kim*] 女性には**昔のばかげた話**をし，ハタオリドリには一枚の葉と糸を与えなさい。聖なる人はみな夢を見，それに従うことでその弟子たちはその力を獲得するのだから。

It's **an old wives' tale** that if you see a robin fall from its nest and return it, the mother will abandon the chick because she can "smell" the human's touch. [*UD Messenger* vol.5, No. 4. 1996: *Feathered and furry Friends*] もしコマドリが巣から落ちて，それを巣に戻すと，母鳥は人間の手が触れた匂いを知って，その子鳥を見捨ててしまうという**昔のばかげた話**がある。

[他の英訳聖書] KJV の比喩表現は現代英語では理解しにくいところから，CEV と HCS は現代風に直している。しかし，それで文学的価値を保てるかは別問題である。

Don't have anything to do with **worthless, senseless stories**. (価値のない，意味のない話) Work hard to be truly religious. <CEV>／Do not waste time arguing over godless ideas and **old wives' tales**. (年寄り女

の空想話）Instead, train yourself to be godly. <NLT>／ But have nothing to do with **irreverent and silly myths**.（関係ないばかばかしい神話）Rather, train yourself in godliness. <HCS>

[wind]

the four winds　四方 →いたるところ

KJV And He shall send His angels with a great sound of a trumpet, and they shall gather together His elect from **the four winds**, from one end of heaven to the other.［マタイの福音書 24:31］人の子は大きなラッパの響きとともに，御使いたちを遣わします。すると御使いたちは，天の果てから果てまで，**四方**からその選びの民を集めます。

[用例] Here, assembling from all **the four winds**, came the elements of an unspeakable hurly-burly.［Carlyle, *Sartor Resartus*］ここに**いたるところ**から集まって来たのはたいへんひどい騒がしい一団だった。

[他の英訳聖書]　KJV の慣用句は ASV など若干の英訳聖書に残っているが，the four winds の現代語訳とも言うべき，all over the world（earth）に代えられているものが多い。

And he shall send forth his angels with a great sound of a trumpet, and they shall gather together his elect from **the four winds**（四方），from one end of heaven to the other. <ASV>／ At the sound of a loud trumpet, he will send his angels to bring his chosen ones together from **all over the earth**.（地球中）<CEV>／ And he will send out his angels with the mighty blast of a trumpet, and they will gather his chosen ones from **all over the world**（世界中）— from the farthest ends of the earth and heaven. <NLT>

sow the wind and reap the whirlwind　風を蒔いてつむじ風を刈り取る →結果を悪くする行為をする

KJV For they have **sown the wind, and they shall reap the whirlwind**. It hath no stalk; the bud shall yield no meal; if so be it yield, the strangers shall swallow it up.［ホセア書 8:7］彼らは**風を蒔いて，つむじ風を刈り取る**。麦には穂が出ない。麦粉も作れない。たといできても，他国人がこれを食い尽くす。

[用例] If the IRA (Irish Republican Army) believe their cause is helped by massacres they are deluding themselves. They have plunged into a bloodbath of which they will be the ultimate victims. They have **sown the wind and they shall reap the whirlwind**. [*Daily Mirror*, 1974] もし IRA——アイルランド共和軍——が自分たちの大義名分を大量虐殺で主張できると思うなら，自己欺瞞に陥っていることになる。彼らは大量殺人に身を投じて，結果は自分たちが犠牲者になるのだ。**結果を悪くする行為をしていることになる**。

[他の英訳聖書] KJV の文体に似せて，動詞語句だけ代えている英訳聖書が多い中で，CEV のみ条件節を含む複文形式にして，理解しやすくしている。

If you scatter wind instead of wheat, you will harvest a whirlwind（麦の代わりに風を蒔くなら，つむじ風を収穫することになる）and have no wheat. Even if you harvest grain, enemies will steal it all. <CEV>／ They have **planted the wind and will harvest the whirlwind**.（風を植えて，つむじ風を収穫する）The stalks of grain wither and produce nothing to eat. And even if there is any grain, foreigners will eat it. <NLT>

[wine]

put new wine in/into old bottles/wineskins 新しいぶどう酒を古い皮袋に入れる →新しい考えを古い形式で述べる

KJV Neither do men **put new wine into old wineskins**, else the wineskins burst and the wine runneth out and the skins perish. But they put new wine into new wineskins, and both are preserved.［マタイの福音書 9:17］また，人は**新しいぶどう酒を古い皮袋に入れる**ようなことはしません。そんなことをすれば，皮袋は裂けて，ぶどう酒が流れ出てしまい，皮袋もだめになってしまいます。新しいぶどう酒を新しい皮袋に入れれば，両方とも保ちます。

[用例] Was Schoenberg merely **putting new wine into old bottles**? [*The Listener*, 1974] シェーンベルクはただ単に**新しい考えを古い形式で述べている**のか。

"Yes — I suppose so; but I feel like **new wine in an old bottle** here. My notion is that sash-windows should be put throughout, and these old wainscoted walls brightened up a bit. [Hardy, *Far from the Madding Crowd*] はい,そう思いますが,ここでは**古い形式のままで新しい考えを当てはめている**ような気がします。私の意見は全体を上げ下げ窓にし,羽目板をすこし明るいものにすべきだと思います。

[他の英訳聖書] この慣用句は確立して定型化しているので,CEVやNLTのように動詞を代える以外は他はKJVを踏襲している。

No one **pours new wine into old wineskins**. (新しいぶどう酒を古い皮袋に注ぐ) The wine would swell and burst the old skins. Then the wine would be lost, and the skins would be ruined. New wine must be put into new wineskins. Both the skins and the wine will then be safe. <CEV>／ No one **pours new wine into old wineskins**. The wine would swell and burst the old skins. Then the wine would be lost, and the skins would be ruined. New wine must be put into new wineskins. Both the skins and the wine will then be safe. <NLT>

[アラム語慣用語句の意味] Lamsa (1985) は New teaching mixed with the old teaching (古い教えと混交した新しい教え) としているが,これだと「古い形に新しい内容」という比喩が出てこないで,同じ内容の問題になってしまう。

[wing]

under one's wings　翼の下に →保護して

KJV O Jerusalem, Jerusalem, thou that killest the prophets and stonest them that are sent unto thee, how often would I have gathered thy children together, even as a hen gathereth her chickens **under her wings**, and ye would not! [マタイの福音書 23:37] ああ,エルサレム,エルサレム。預言者たちを殺し,自分に遣わされた人たちを石で打つ者。わたしは,めんどりがひなを**翼の下**に集めるように,あなたの子らを幾たび集めようとしたことか。それなのに,あなたがたはそれを好まなかった。

[用例] And the mother, with her child once more **under her wing**, happier than she had been for seven years past, during which her young prodigal had been running the thoughtless career of which he himself was weary. ... [Thackeray, *The Newcomes*] 自分の子がもう一度自分の保護のもとに戻った母親はその子がいなかった7年間よりも幸せであった。その7年の間,放蕩した息子は考えのないままに生活を送ってきて,それに自分で倦み疲れていたのであった。

[他の英訳聖書] under と beneath の違いこそあれ,wings は共有していて,KJV を踏襲している。この慣用句は定型化されたものであろう。

Jerusalem, Jerusalem! Your people have killed the prophets and have stoned the messengers who were sent to you. I have often wanted to gather your people, as a hen gathers her chicks **under her wings.** (翼の下に) But you wouldn't let me. <CEV>／O Jerusalem, Jerusalem, the city that kills the prophets and stones God's messengers! How often I have wanted to gather your children together as a hen protects her chicks **beneath her wings** (翼の下に), but you wouldn't let me. <NLT>

[wise]

wiser in one's generation 抜け目がない →世慣れた

KJV And the lord commended the unjust steward, because he had done wisely; for the children of this world are **in their generation wiser** than the children of light. [ルカの福音書 16:8] この世の子らは,自分たちの世のことについては,光の子らよりも**抜けめがない**ものなので,主人は,不正な管理人がこうも抜けめなくやったのをほめた。

[用例] Such songs certainly foster a patriotic and military spirit, and the government is **wise in its generation** to encourage them. [Letters of B. H. Chamberlain to L. Hearn] そのような歌は確かに愛国主義的な,軍国的な精神を鼓舞する。政府は彼らを励ますのに**世慣れた**ものだ。

[他の英訳聖書] ASV など2,3の英訳聖書は KJV の generation を使っているが,その連語形態は違っている。CEV や NLT はそれを現代用語に切り替えて,語法の変化を図っている。

And his lord commended the unrighteous steward because he had done wisely: for **the sons of this world are for their own generation wiser** (この世の人々は同世代より賢い) than the sons of the light. <ASV>／ And [his] master praised the dishonest (unjust) manager for acting shrewdly and prudently; for **the sons of this age are shrewder and more prudent and wiser in relation to their own generation [to their own age and kind]** (この時代の人々はこの世について, 同じ年齢や同じ仲間より抜け目なく, 用心深く賢い) than are the sons of light. <AB>／ The master praised his dishonest manager for looking out for himself so well. That's how it is! **The people of this world look out for themselves better** (この世の人々は自分の面倒を見るのがうまい) than the people who belong to the light. <CEV>／ The rich man had to admire the dishonest rascal for being so shrewd. And it is true that **the children of this world are more shrewd in dealing with the world around them** (この世の人々は自分の周りの世の中のことを扱うのがうまい) than are the children of the light. <NLT>

【 wit 】

at one's wit's end　分別が乱れる →途方に暮れて

KJV They reel to and fro and stagger like a drunken man, and are **at their wits' end**. [詩篇 107:27] 彼らは酔った人のようによろめき, ふらついて**分別が乱れた**。

[用例] It appears they were **at their wit's end** what to do. [Stevenson, *Treasure Island*] 彼らは何をすべきか**途方に暮れていた**ように思える。

I was **at my wit's end** where to get the money, but a sudden idea came to me. [Conan Doyle, *Adventures of Sherlock Holmes*] どこでお金を手に入れるか**途方に暮れた**が, 突然アイデアが浮かんだ。

The doctors discover that no one can free Tommy from his catatonic state but himself. On the street a group of local louts surround Tommy and carry him home. The parents, **at their wit's end** and considering having Tommy institutionalized, compassionately confront one another. [Wikipedia, *The Who's Tommy*, ミュージカル] 医者たちにはトミーは自分でしか彼の強硬症が治せないと分かってい

た。通りで無骨者たちがトミーを取り囲み家へ連れて行った。両親は**途方に暮れて**施設に収容してもらうことを考えたが，同情的になり互いに対立した。

[他の英訳聖書] よく使われる現代語法として LDOCE にも収録されているが，CEV では敢えて gave up all hope として平易化しているし，HCS は全体を主語を変えて平易な節にしている。

You staggered like drunkards and **gave up all hope**. (まったく落胆した) <CEV>／ They reeled and staggered like drunkards and were **at their wits' end**. (分別が乱れた) <NLT>／ They reeled and staggered like drunken men, and **all their skill was useless**. (彼らのやり方はまったく役に立たなかった) <HCS>

[woe]

Woe is me　ああ悲しいかな →もうだめだ，台無しだ

KJV Then said I, **Woe is me**! for I am undone; because I am a man of unclean lips, and I dwell in the midst of a people of unclean lips: for mine eyes have seen the King, the LORD of hosts. ［イザヤ書 6:5］そこで，私は言った。「ああ。**私は，もうだめだ**。私はくちびるの汚れた者で，くちびるの汚れた民の間に住んでいる。しかも万軍の主である王を，この目で見たのだから。」

[用例] Our only possible response before such a tremendous debt can be: **Woe is me**! ［¶］そのような途轍もない借金を前にして，私たちの可能な唯一の応答は「**もうだめだ**」です。

[他の英訳聖書] やや古い用法であるので，現代の一般向けの英訳聖書はそろって I'm doomed (だめだ) を使っている。Woe is me の me はもともと被害の与格であるから，NIV などは Woe to me を使っている。現在ではユーモアを込めた使い方が多い。

Then I cried out, "**I'm doomed**! (もうだめだ) Everything I say is sinful, and so are the words of everyone around me. Yet I have seen the King, the LORD All-Powerful." <CEV>／ Then I said, "**It's all over! I am doomed** (もう終わった。だめだ), for I am a sinful man. I have filthy lips, and I live among a people with filthy lips. Yet I have seen the King, the LORD of Heaven's Armies." <NLT>／ Then I said: **Woe is** me, for I am ruined(悲しいかな。もうだめだ), because I am a man of unclean lips and live among a people of unclean lips, [and] because my eyes have seen the King, the LORD of Hosts. <HCS>／ "**Woe to me**!" I cried. "**I am ruined**! For I am a man of unclean lips, and I live among a people of unclean lips, and my eyes have seen the King, the LORD Almighty." <NIV>

[wolf]

a wolf in sheep's clothing　羊のなりをした狼 →悪意のない振りをする人

KJV Beware of **false prophets**, who come to you **in sheep's clothing**, but inwardly they are ravening wolves.［マタイの福音書 7:15］にせ預言者たちに気をつけなさい。彼らは羊のなりをしてやって来るが，うちは貪欲な狼です。

[用例] When you purchase stock in companies like General Motors, you will usually have some fear about their future bankruptcy. But stock traders are often **wolves in sheep's clothing** and persuade customers to believe in their absolute stability, which is by no means true.［¶］ゼネラル・モーターズのような会社に投資をする場合，普通は将来破産するのではないかと心配する。しかし，トレーダーはしばしば**悪意のない振りをする人々**で，お客に絶対安全だと信じ込ませる。しかし，それは決してほんとうではない。

[他の英訳聖書]　CEV のように KJV の慣用句を現代的な用語を使ったり，NLT のように補足的説明を加えたりするものがある。

Watch out for false prophets! **They dress up like sheep**((にせ預言者は) 羊のようななりをしている), but inside they are wolves who have come to attack you. <CEV>／ Beware of false prophets who come **disguised as harmless sheep**(無害な羊のようななりをして) but are really vicious wolves. <NLT>

[word]

a word in season　励ましの言葉 →必要なときの忠告

KJV The Lord GOD hath given Me the tongue of the learned, that I should know how to speak **a word in season** to him that is weary. He wakeneth morning by morning; He wakeneth Mine ear to hear as the learned. ［イザヤ書50:4］神である主は，私に弟子の舌を与え，疲れた者をことばで**励ますことを教え**，朝ごとに，私を呼びさまし，私の耳を開かせて，私が弟子のように聞くようにされる。

[用例] **A word in season** from his teacher would have encouraged him to study further for entering higher education, but unfortunately he had no good teacher in his school days. ［¶］先生が**時宜を得た言葉**をかけてくれていたら上級学校進学のため勉強するようにとの励ましになったでしょうけれど，残念ながら，学校時代に彼にはよき先生がいなかった。

[他の英訳聖書] KJV の比喩的意味を CEV では噛み砕いて述べ，NLT ではさらに敷衍させて his words of wisdom としている。HCS にいたっては，長い節を用いてどのような知恵であるかを説明している。

The LORD God gives me **the right words to encourage**（励ましの正しい言葉）the weary. Each morning he awakens me eager to learn his teaching. <CEV>／ The Sovereign LORD has given me **his words of wisdom**（主の知恵の言葉），so that I know how to comfort the weary. Morning by morning he wakens me and opens my understanding to his will. <NLT>／ The Lord GOD has given Me **the tongue of those who are instructed to know how to sustain the weary with a word**.（疲れた者を言葉で支える仕方を教えられた者の舌）He awakens [Me] each morning; He awakens My ear to listen like those being instructed. <HCS>

put words into another's mouth　他人の口に言葉を授ける →本人が言いもしないことを言ったことにする

[KJV] And come to the king, and speak on this manner unto him. So Joab **put the words in her mouth**. ［Ⅱサムエル記14:3］王のもとに行き，王にこのように話してくれまいか。」こうしてヨアブは**彼女の口にことばを授けた**。

[用例] Stop **putting words into my mouth** — I never said I disliked the job. I rather preferred it to the one I was doing. ［¶］私がそう

言ったなんて言うのはやめてくれ。その仕事が嫌いだなんて言ったことないよ。むしろ,そのときやっていた仕事よりそのほうが好きだったのだ。

The youngsters have maintained ... that they are innocent. They claim that they were frightened, and **words were put into their mouths**. [*Daily Mirror*, 1974] その若者たちは自分たちは無罪だと主張した。脅迫されて**自分たちが言ったことにされた**のだと言い張っている。

[他の英訳聖書]　KJV を踏襲しているのは伝統的な英訳聖書の ESV, NKJV などで,他は CEV や NLT のように平易な tell her what to say(言うべきことを告げる)に代えている。ただし,例文にあげてあるように,現代英語の慣用語句としては,相手を非難するような意味合いをこめた表現になっている。

Joab told her, "Put on funeral clothes and don't use any makeup. Go to the king and pretend you have spent a long time mourning the death of a loved one." Then he **told her what to say**. (言うべきことを告げた) <CEV>／ Then go to the king and tell him the story I am about to tell you." Then Joab **told her what to say**. <NLT>／ Go to the king and speak thus to him." So Joab **put the words in her mouth**. <ESV>

[worm]

worm　虫けら同様 →苦痛で

KJV But I am **a worm** and no man, a reproach of men and despised by the people. [詩篇 22:6] しかし,私は**虫けら**です。人間ではありません。人のそしり,民のさげすみです。

[用例] The writhing **worm** and no man ... groaned hideously. [Doughty, *Arabia Deserta*] 苦痛に身もだえする**虫けら**で人間ではないその男はぞっとするうめき声を出した。

[他の英訳聖書]　現代語法に直しがちな CEV でさえも KJV を踏襲して worm を使っているが,no man のところはもっと分かりやすい形にしている。worm は英和辞典にも載っているように現代英語に歴然と残っている。

But I am merely **a worm** (虫けら同様), far less than human, and I am hated and rejected by people everywhere. <CEV>／ But I am **a worm and not a man. I am scorned and despised by all!** <NLT>

[wrestle]

wrestle with (an angel) （神と）戦う →（神に）祈りで抗争する

KJV And Jacob was left alone, and there **wrestled a man with him** until the breaking of the day.［創世記32:24］ヤコブはひとりだけ，あとに残った。すると，ある人が夜明けまで**彼と格闘した**。

[用例] Starbuck seemed **wrestling with an angel**, but turning from the door, he placed the death-tube in its rack, and left the place.［H. Melville, *Moby Dick*］スターバックは**心の中で神と争っている**ようであったが，ドアから身を引き，ショットガンをラックにかけ，その場所を離れた。

[他の英訳聖書] 例文に出てくるような比喩的な意味は英訳聖書には現れない。旧約聖書の時代では実際に戦った状況として描かれているからであろう。

Afterwards, Jacob went back and spent the rest of the night alone. A man came and **fought with Jacob**（ヤコブと争った）until just before daybreak. <CEV>／ This left Jacob all alone in the camp, and a man came and **wrestled with him**（彼と争った）until the dawn began to break. <NLT>

[writing]

the writing on the wall 壁に書かれた文字 →不吉・不幸の前兆

KJV In the same hour came forth fingers of a man's hand, and **wrote opposite the candlestick upon the plaster of the wall of the king's palace**; and the king saw the part of the hand that wrote.［ダニエル書5:5］すると突然，人間の手の指が現われ，**王の宮殿の塗り壁の，燭台の向こう側の所に物を書いた**。王が物を書くその手の先を見た。

[用例] The new increase in gasoline prices is **the writing on the wall** for a lot of individual drivers.［¶］ガソリン価格の値上がりは多くの個人運転者には**不幸の前兆**だ。

I once worked for a German born man, named Bernie. Bernie moved to Australia just before the 2nd world war because he could see **the writing on the wall**. [Phrasefinder, *From Hull, Hell and Halifax, God Lord Delivers Us!* 2003] 私はかつてドイツ生まれのバーニーという人のところで働いていました。彼は**不吉の前兆**を見てとっていたので，第2次大戦のちょうど前にオーストラリアに移住しました。

[**他の英訳聖書**] CEV に代表されるように，すべての英訳聖書は KJV を踏襲している。その意味するところがイザヤ書5章全体で示されるので，この語句の比喩的意味がそのまま慣用句として残された。

Suddenly a human hand was seen **writing on the plaster wall of the palace**. (宮殿の塗り壁に書きもの) The hand was just behind the lampstand, and the king could see it writing. <CEV>

Y

[yea]

yea and nay しかりと否 →優柔不断

KJV But as God is true, our word toward you was not "**yea**" and "**nay**." [Ⅱコリント人への手紙1:18] しかし，神の真実にかけて言いますが，あなたがたに対する私たちのことばは，「しかり」と言って，同時に「否」と言うようなものではありません。

[用例] There had been a good deal of dealers' **yea and nay** about it. [Ruskin, *Praeterit*] それについてはたくさんの業者は**優柔不断**でなかなか決められなかった。

Each House shall keep a journal of its proceedings, and from time to time publish the same, excepting such parts as may in their judgment require secrecy; and the **yeas and nays** of the members of either House on any question shall, at the desire of one fifth of those present, be entered on the journal. [*Constitution of the United States, Section 5*] それぞれの議会は議事録を保管し，ときどき，秘密を必要とすると判断される部分を除いて，同じものを出版する。どの事柄についても，両議会の議員の**賛否の意見**は出席の五分の一が望めば，議事録に記載される。《[注] 上例のように，yea and nay が複数で表わされると，文字通り「賛成と反対」の意で取られ，「優柔不断」の意とならない。しばしば比喩性を持たせるためには単数形でないといけない一つの例となるであろう。》

[他の英訳聖書] KJVのように，be動詞後に直接 yea and nay を付加しているのは HCS で，NLT はその前の動詞主要部に変化をつけ，前置詞 between を挿入して意味を明確にしている。CEV は否定語を No の前に置いたために「優柔不断」の意が出てこない。全英訳聖書を通して，Yea and nay は当然，現代語の yes and no に代えている。

As God is faithful, our message to you is not "**Yes and no**."(しかりと

否）<HCS>／As surely as God is faithful, my word to you does not waver **between "Yes" and "No."**（しかりと否の間で）<NLT>／God can be trusted, and so can I, when I say that our answer to you has always been **"Yes" and never "No."**（しかりであって決して否でない）<CEV>

[編者略歴]
小野経男（おの　つねお）

1931年生まれ。1960年東京都立大学大学院修了。1971〜1973年，1975年，2000年，ハーバード大学留学（変形生成文法統語論専攻）。名古屋大学言語文化部教授（同大学院文学研究科で「英語学特殊研究」，「応用言語学」を担当）。同大学定年後，名古屋学院大学教授，同大学院外国語学研究科長，同大学外国語センター長，同大学図書館長を歴任。現在，名古屋大学名誉教授，岐阜済美学院（中部学院大学・短大・大学院・済美高校・幼稚園）学院長。著書に，『現代の英文法第9巻「助動詞」』（研究社），『意外性の英文法』（大修館書店），『誤文心理と文法指導』（大修館書店），『アメリカの文明と言葉』（泰文堂），『英語教育ノウハウ講座 No.4「指導に役立つ英文法の知識」』（開隆堂），『新英文法』（数研出版），『5つの動詞で話せる役立ち英会話』（K.K. ベストセラーズ），『ハーバードで通じる英会話』（講談社），『英語類義動詞の構文事典』（大修館書店），『遠くて近い道』（新教出版），ほか。

聖書に由来する英語慣用句の辞典
ⓒ Ono Tsuneo, 2011　　　　　　　　　　　　　　NDC 834／xvi, 202p, 4／20 cm

初版第1刷 ——— 2011年6月25日

編　者	小野経男
発行者	鈴木一行
発行所	株式会社 **大修館書店** 〒113-8541 東京都文京区湯島2-1-1 電話 03-3868-2651（販売部）03-3868-2292（編集部） 振替 00190-7-40504 [出版情報] http://www.taishukan.co.jp
装丁者	井之上聖子
印刷所	壮光舎印刷
製本所	牧製本

ISBN 978-4-469-24561-5　　　　　　　　　　　　　　Printed in Japan

®本書のコピー，スキャン，デジタル化等の無断複製は著作権法上での例外を除き禁じられています。本書を代行業者等の第三者に依頼してスキャンやデジタル化することは，たとえ個人や家庭内の利用であっても著作権法上認められておりません。

英語名句事典

外山滋比古、新井明、岡本靖正、栗原裕ほか 編

名句は生きている。小説に、映画に、テーブルスピーチに。英文学の二大源泉、聖書とシェイクスピア、歴史に残る「名演説」、そして「マザーグース」「ことわざ」から「現代詩」にいたるまで…。英語文化のエッセンスを伝える名句中の名句を厳選し、日本語訳と分かりやすい解説を加えた待望の引用句事典。各句を題材とする図版多数収録。索引付。

●菊判・函入・668ページ　定価5,775円

定価＝本体＋税5％（2011年5月現在）

聖書の動物事典

ピーター・ミルワード 著　中山理 訳

聖書には多くの動物が登場する。本書の第1部はエッセイ「聖書の動物入門」で、第2部は登場する動物を網羅した「聖書の動物事典」である。100種の動物をとりあげ、聖書の中でのイメージや記載に関して解説し、典拠とした章節を、和文・英文対応させて示す。また、訳注では、種の特定に関する諸説を紹介し、19世紀イギリスの書籍からとった美しい銅版画70典を収めた。

●四六判・386ページ　定価2,625円

定価＝本体＋税5％（2011年5月現在）

ヨーロッパ人名語源事典

梅田修 著

ヨーロッパの人名の、起源、意味、イメージ、愛称や通称などを読み物としてまとめた。歴史上の人物、政治家、俳優などが、カタカナからは思いもよらないつながりを見せる。図版多数、詳細な索引付き。民族を超え、時代を超え、変化しながら今に生きる名前の数々をたどる、読み物ふう事典。
【付録】男女各100名称10か国対照表／各国命名事情／各種日本語訳聖書の人名表記　ほか
●菊判・418ページ　定価5,670円

定価＝本体＋税5％（2011年5月現在）

シップリー
英語語源辞典
Dictionary of Word Origins

ジョーゼフ T. シップリー 著
梅田修、眞方忠道、穴吹章子 訳

波瀾万丈の言葉の放浪記

ギリシア・ローマから、中近東から、アジアから、いろいろな経路でブリテン島にやってきた英語の単語の歴史を、時に脱線しながら、時にさりげないユーモアを交えて語る名著の完訳。知的好奇心を刺激し、言葉のおもしろさを実感させる「読む辞典」。

●Ａ５判・函入・778ページ　定価6,300円

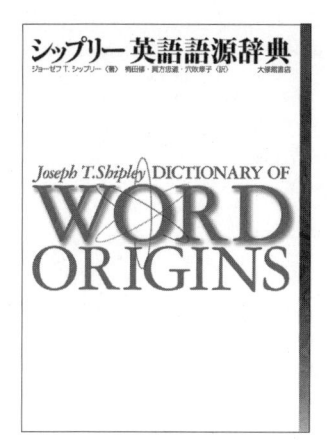

定価＝本体＋税5%（2011年5月現在）